OLD TESTAMENT MESSAGE

A Biblical-Theological Commentary

Carroll Stuhlmueller, C.P. and Martin McNamara, M.S.C.

EDITORS

Old Testament Message, Volume 3

EXODUS, LEVITICUS NUMBERS

with
Excursuses on
Feasts/Ritual and Typology

Rita J. Burns

Michael Glazier, Inc.
Wilmington, Delaware

First published in 1983 by: MICHAEL GLAZIER, INC., 1723 Delaware Avenue, Wilmington, Delaware 19806
Distributed outside U.S., Canada & Philippines by: GILL & MACMILLAN, LTD., Goldenbridge, Inchicore, Dublin 8 Ireland

Library of Congress Catalog Card Number: 83-81651
International Standard Book Number
  Old Testament Message series: 0-89453-235-9
  EXODUS, LEVITICUS, NUMBERS
    0-89453-238-3 (Michael Glazier, Inc.)
    7171-1167-9 (Gill & Macmillan, Ltd.)

The Bible text in this publication is from the Revised Standard Version of the Bible, copyrighted 1946, 1952, ©1971, 1973 by the Division of Christian Education of the National Council of the Churches of Christ in the U.S.A., and used by permission.

Cover design by Lillian Brulc
Typography by Susan Pickett
Cartography by Lucille Dragovan
Printed in the United States of America

TABLE OF CONTENTS

The Book of Exodus

6   *Contents*

The Book of Leviticus

The Book of Numbers

Editors' Preface

Old Testament Message brings into our life and religion today the ancient word of God to Israel. This word, according to the book of the prophet Isaiah, had soaked the earth like "rain and snow coming gently down from heaven" and had returned to God fruitfully in all forms of human life (Isa 55:10). The authors of this series remain true to this ancient Israelite heritage and draw us into the home, the temple and the market place of God's chosen people. Although they rely upon the tools of modern scholarship to uncover the distant places and culture of the biblical world, yet they also refocus these insights in a language clear and understandable for any interested reader today. They enable us, even if this be our first acquaintance with the Old Testament, to become sister and brother, or at least good neighbor, to our religious ancestors. In this way we begin to hear God's word ever more forcefully in our own times and across our world, within our prayer and worship, in our secular needs and perplexing problems.

Because life is complex and our world includes, at times in a single large city, vastly different styles of living, we have much to learn from the Israelite Scriptures. The Old Testament spans forty-six biblical books and almost nineteen hundred years of life. It extends through desert, agricultural and urban ways of human existence. The literary style embraces a world of literature and human emotions. Its history began with Moses and the birth-pangs of a new people, it came of an age politically and economically under David and Solomon, it reeled under the fiery threats of prophets like Amos and Jeremiah. The people despaired and yet were re-created with new hope during the Babylonian exile. Later reconstruction in the homeland and then the trauma of apocalyptic movements prepared for the revelation of "the mystery hidden for ages in God who created all things" (Eph 3:9).

While the Old Testament telescopes twelve to nineteen hundred years of human existence within the small country of Israel, any single moment of time today witnesses to the reenactment of this entire history across the wide expanse of planet earth. Each verse of the Old Testament is being relived somewhere in our world today. We need, therefore, the *entire* Old Testament and all twenty-three volumes of this new set, in order to be totally a "Bible person" within today's widely diverse society.

The subtitle of this series—"A Biblical-Theological Commentary"—clarifies what these twenty-three volumes intend to do.

Their *purpose* is theological: to feel the pulse of God's word for its *religious* impact and direction.

Their *method* is biblical: to establish the scriptural word firmly within the life and culture of ancient Israel.

Their *style* is commentary: not to explain verse by verse but to follow a presentation of the message that is easily understandable to any serious reader, even if this person is untrained in ancient history and biblical languages.

Old Testament Message—like its predecessor, *New Testament Message*—is aimed at the entire English-speaking world and so is a collaborative effort of an international team. The twenty-one contributors are women and men drawn from North America, Ireland, Britain and Australia. They are scholars who have published in scientific journals, but they have been chosen equally as well for their proven ability to communicate on a popular level. This twenty-three book set comes from Roman Catholic writers, yet, like the Bible itself, it reaches beyond interpretations restricted to an individual church and so enables men and women rooted in biblical faith to unite and so to appreciate their own traditions more fully and more adequately.

Most of all, through the word of God, we seek the blessedness and joy of those

who walk in the law of the Lord!...

who seek God with their whole heart (Ps. 119:1-2).

Carroll Stuhlmueller, C.P.   Martin McNamara, M.S.C.

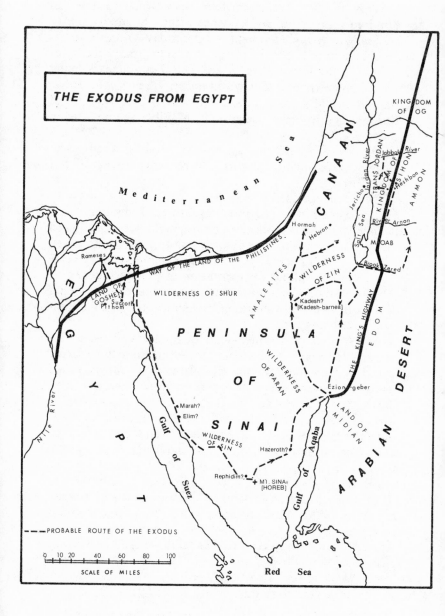

GENERAL INTRODUCTION

In recent years much has been written about the notion of passage. It has been pointed out that passage is a constant in our lives as individuals and as groups, that it is common to all human experience. Something of who we are continuously passes away even as something of who we are becoming struggles to be born.

The story which we review in the pages of this volume comes from ancient Israel. It is a story about passage. It begins in bondage and ends in blessing. The contours of the passage are the coming out of Egypt and the coming into the Promised Land. The journey encompasses call and struggle, trust and commitment. In the Books of Exodus, Leviticus and Numbers our ancestors in faith point to their own human passage and they call its mystery Sacred. They tell us that in their passage they encountered the Holy and learned to call God by name.

We open the pages of these biblical books to tell once again a story told by generations of believers over the course of some three thousand years. In so doing we turn to our own roots and to our own story.

THE BOOK OF EXODUS

INTRODUCTION TO THE BOOK OF EXODUS

Contents

The Book of Exodus contains an account of Israel's great deliverance from bondage to Pharaoh (Exod 1:1—15:21), a brief narrative about life in the wilderness along Israel's journey from the sea to Sinai (Exod 15:22—18:27), and an account of a profound encounter with God at Sinai, a meeting wherein Israel received the law and formalized a covenantal relationship with its redeemer, Yahweh (Exod 19-40). In the overall text of Exodus the wilderness traditions constitute a relatively short link between the two huge complexes of material treating redemption and covenant. These great complexes are best viewed according to the gradual unfolding movements with which they are presented in the texts.

The exodus story begins with Israel's bondage (Exod 1-2). The biblical writers carefully delineate the struggle between two claims made on Israel— Pharaoh's claim and Yahweh's claim as articulated by Moses, Yahweh's spokesperson and mediator (Exod 3:1—7:7). The struggle intensifies through the course of the plagues (Exod 7:8—11:10) in such a way that the death-dealing at the beginning of the struggle finally turns back upon Pharaoh through the deaths of the first-born of all Egyptian households. Yahweh then delivers Israel from death-ridden Egypt. The biblical account of this exodus is heavily laden with cultic regulations for a religious observance which would carry the power of this singular event to future generations (Exod 12-13). A final confrontation between Yahweh and the Egyptians takes place at the sea (Exod 14). There Yahweh dramatically rescues the freed slaves and the conflict is definitively resolved. Finally, Moses and Miriam lead in celebrating the community's proclamations about the religious dimension of the deliverance (Exod 15:1-21).

The second great complex of tradition, the Sinai material of Exod 19-40, can also be viewed in smaller sections. Chapters 19, 20, and 24 constitute the core narrative about the formalization of the covenant at Mount Sinai. The event includes theophany, the gift of the law, and rituals intended to symbolize the meaning of Yahweh's covenant with Israel. The only other narrative portion of the Sinai materials appears in chapters 32-34, the account of the sin around the golden calf and the renewal of the covenant. The remainder of the Sinai materials are legal traditions: the so-called Covenant Code (Exod 20:22—23:33) and the beginning of the great corpus of Priestly law (Exod 25-31 and 35-40) which extends through the entirety of the Book of Leviticus and into the Book of Numbers (Num 1:1—10:10).

Literary Forms

The preceding survey of the contents of the Book of Exodus indicates that the biblical text represents divergent literary forms which were at home in different arenas of life in ancient Israel. Narrative predominates in the first half of the book, although even there we encounter poetry (Exod 15:1-18, 21) and liturgical legislation (Exod 12-13). Laws predominate in the second half of the book, different kinds of law representing a broad expanse of lived observance in ancient Israel's religious life. Thus, the Book of Exodus is a complex fabric of tradition in which the contributions of storytellers and poets have been woven together with those of cultic officials and lawyers.

History and the Book of Exodus

A proper understanding of the Book of Exodus requires that readers be aware of the distance which lay between the events referred to and the narration about those events. The Book of Exodus was not intended as an eyewitness account of events as they actually happened in history. Rather, the biblical text gathers up and speaks the faith of generations of believers who, separated from the events by several hundred years, offered their interpretation of what the experience of their ancestors revealed about God and about their relationship with God. The Book of Exodus, then, must be read as religious creed and not as historical chronicle.

This is not to say that the accounts which appear in the Book of Exodus have no relationship to actual events. Certainly the exodus story has its roots in ancient historical memory. When the witness of the biblical text is viewed alongside extra-biblical records from the ancient Near Eastern world it is possible to posit a broad outline of historical events underlying the biblical account. For example, according to Egyptian records Pharaohs Seti I (c. 1305-1290 B.C.) and Rameses II (c. 1290-1224 B.C.) moved Egypt's capital from Thebes to the Delta region and undertook significant building campaigns there using as slave labour the services of marginated peoples who were referred to as Habiru (or 'Apiru). Biblical scholarship has seen parallels between the Habiru and the Hebrews and between the above-mentioned building campaigns and the witness of Exod 1:11 which says that the Hebrews were forced to work on the construction of store-cities in the Delta region. Moreover, one of the store-cities is said to have borne the name of the Pharaoh Rameses. These correspondences have led to the commonly-held view that there really was an exodus event in which some Hebrews were freed of their bondage to Pharaoh. Scholars date this event at approximately 1290 B.C.

The foregoing is a brief summary of the probable historical situation which formed the starting point of the exodus story. The biblical writers have supplied many details, of course, but readers must be aware that these belong to tradition and not necessarily to history. Moreover, one must be cautious about envisioning a single massive escape of slaves who subsequently spent exactly forty years in the desert before their children came into the land of Canaan. It is possible that the exodus was a gradual process, a series of escapes by oppressed peoples, and that a nucleus of these groups belonged to those who later took control (perhaps gradually) of the land of Canaan. Whatever the case, readers should keep in mind that the actual exodus event was too insignificant to be recorded in Egyptian or other ancient Near Eastern documents.

Theology and the Book of Exodus

If the biblical writers did not record exact eyewitness historical events as they occurred, we must ask what they did intend by their accounts. As stated above, the biblical texts are separated from the events they narrate by several hundred years. The writers sought to witness to the *mysterious dimension* of events in Israel's past. The texts rest on firm faith convictions that the people of Israel did not come to be as a result of their own initiative. Rather, the biblical writers record the conviction that the good fortunes of an insignificant powerless "mixed multitude" stemmed from the gracious involvement of a powerful and merciful Mystery who worked within Israel's history, bringing it out of bondage and shaping it into a people for the Divine Self. Thus, the biblical account of the exodus event is essentially a theological interpretation of the birth and formation of the people of Israel. Again and again Israel portrays itself as powerless and unfaithful while Yahweh is the One "merciful and gracious, slow to anger, and abounding in steadfast love and faithfulness" (Exod 34:6).

Understanding the above assists us in viewing the significance of many of the details encountered in the exodus narratives. Readers will find in these pages accounts which involve highly extraordinary circumstances, what modern readers might call "miracles." Examples include the marvelous events which plagued Egypt, the parting of the waters at the sea, and the wondrous ways in which God is said to have provided food and water in the wilderness. The biblical writers expressed their faith in terms of these signs and wonders. They wanted to focus readers' attention on the divine Mystery whom they believed to be freeing and nurturing Israel through these events. Therefore, they "heightened" their accounts of these events in order to emphasize that it was God who was directing history, not Israel. They wrote of the parting of the waters in order to say "*God* saved us from the Egyptians at the sea." It was not themselves and not some accident of history but God. Different writers tell the details of the sea event in different ways but the message is clear: "*God* saved us at the sea!" The "miraculous" ways in which that conviction is articulated must not distract the reader from the basic religious truth which the writers sought to convey. The stories are meant to point to the One who is present in history in powerful and mysterious ways. This is the One in whom Israel's faith rested and whose graciousness and mercy Israel sought to proclaim through the exodus and Sinai stories.

Literary Sources

The complexity of the Book of Exodus derives not only from the multiplicity of literary forms which it incorporates (see above) but also from the fact that it represents the work of different writers from various stages of Israelite history. The literary sources which together comprise the final text of the Book of Exodus are the same as those found in the other Pentateuchal books: the Yahwist source (J), dating from the early period of the United Monarchy; the Elohist source (E), thought to have originated in the northern kingdom during the middle of the ninth century B.C.; the Deuteronomic source (D), derived from a circle which was prominent during the latter part of the seventh century B.C. and which was active through the next hundred years; and the Priestly source (P), dating from the exilic or early post-exilic period. The respective sources must be viewed as collective witnesses to four different theological circles dating from different periods of Israel's history and not as the literary creations of four single individuals. Thus, to say that the Yahwist wrote an account of Israel's story which ranged from the creation of humanity to the inheritance of the land is to say that we have an account from the tenth century B.C. about Israel's early tradition as it was recorded and passed on by a particular theological circle. Another theological interpretation of much of the same material emerged later from circles in the north (i.e., the Elohist). A third theological interpretation came somewhat later and a fourth was recorded and interwoven with the earlier versions during the exilic or post-exilic period. Thus, the Book of Exodus is a tapestry consisting of heavy strains of Yahwistic and Priestly tradition. Somewhat less complete contributions were made by the Elohist and only a few fragmentary additions come from a Deuteronomic hand.

For a further discussion of the literary sources behind the Book of Exodus, see other books within *Old Testament Message*, Vol. 1, pp. 31-33; Vol. 2, pp. 14-17; and Vol. 4, pp. 1-5.

Recognition of this process of biblical composition helps readers to understand repetitions and inconsistencies which appear in the texts from time to time. Perhaps more importantly it offers insight into ancient notions about religious tradition. The biblical writers took certain freedoms with their records of past events. God's saving presence among their ancestors somehow spoke to them of God's saving presence among later generations as well. The past was not ancient history sealed in a sterile museum case for observation and veneration. Rather, early generations transmitted faith to their children and that faith was articulated anew in light of the lived experience of the dynamic presence of God among the later generations. The process continued through Israel's history. Thus, the Book of Exodus bears the fingerprints of different generations of faith as told by the literary sources represented in the book.

Significance

Because the Exodus and Sinai events are only a part of Israel's early creed, a total perspective on the Book of Exodus means that it should be read along with the entire Pentateuchal tradition. Having said that, however, we hasten to add that the exodus-Sinai story has had such profound religious impact on all of Judaeo-Christianity that it allows us to speak of its superlative uniqueness within the biblical tradition.

Commenting on the significance of the exodus story is akin to attempting to preach on Christian worship on Easter Sunday. What words does one use to convey the power of the foundational religious experience of a people? The exodus story is the prism which countless generations of believers have used to shed light upon who they are and to interpret their own experience with the Mystery. The passage from bondage to freedom is ancient yet ever new. It is the story of all God's people. In some foundational way the exodus story tells who God is. For Israel Yahweh is the One who "brought us up out of Egypt, that house of bondage." A major concern of the first fifteen chapters of the Book of Exodus is to voice Israel's conviction that its liberation from oppression was not the work of human pride or selfishness but the commitment of a divine Mystery zealous for justice and for relationship. It was in the context of the exodus event that Israel learned God's name.

While the first major complex of traditions in the Book of Exodus feature the liberation from bondage, the second complex, the Sinai story, features bonding, i.e., the formalization of a covenantal relationship, a relationship founded not in fear but in trust. Israel was free at last and responded to God's invitation to live freely by binding itself to the One who invites freedom through the observance of the law. The rest of the Hebrew tradition witnesses to a persistent struggle to be faithful to this relationship which Israel entered at the mountain of Sinai.

Between the exodus and the Sinai stories lay the brief interlude about Israel's journey through the wilderness. There we see a people who had left a bonded way of being-in-relation, a way based in servitude and security. At Sinai they would commit themselves to a new way of being-in-relation, a way based in risk and trust. The wilderness was the place in between. It was the place for learning about the alternative to which they were called and a place to be formed and nurtured in that alternative possibility of relationship.

Our Commentary on Exodus

We are unable to cover the entire texts of Exodus, Leviticus, and Numbers in a commentary of this size and must therefore be selective about the texts chosen for consideration. From the Book of Exodus we shall treat the story of Israel's bondage and deliverance (Exod 1:1—15:21), the wilderness traditions (Exod 15:22—18:27), and the narratives which are localized at Sinai (Exod 19-20, 24, 32-34) together with the concluding chapter of the Book of Exodus (Exod 40). We set aside the legal materials which constitute the so-called Covenant Code (Exod 20:22—23:33) and the Priestly law which appears in Exod 25-31 and 35-39. For more complete treatment readers are directed to those commentaries on the Book of Exodus which are listed under "Suggestions for Further Reading" at the end of this volume.

THE BEGINNINGS
1:1—2:25

The Book of Exodus begins with a presentation of the background of Israel's going out from Egypt. In some ways the two introductory chapters also foreshadow the great redemptive event which will be narrated. The biblical writers present a power-wielding Pharaoh whose fear is brought to expression in a three-stage program of oppression for the people of Israel (1:8-14, 15-21, 22). His program for the death of the Hebrew boys is ultimately established as national policy and the participation of all Egyptians is demanded. At every turn, however, Pharaoh's death-dealing initiatives are undermined by life-bearing processes: by the mysteriously increased strength of the people, by the decisions of the midwives, and by the deliverance of Moses through the cooperative efforts of his mother and Pharaoh's daughter. What the women do for Moses, God will subsequently do for all Israel. Likewise, in the narrative about Moses' exodus from Egypt the biblical writers foreshadow in a general way the subsequent exodus of all Israel.

This opening section of the Book of Exodus begins and ends with hints of new eras, new realities. Thus, the brief summary of the ancestral traditions of the Book of Genesis (1:1-7) is followed by an announcement that "there arose a

new king over Egypt. . . " (1:8). Likewise, the end of the unit
(2:23-25) abounds with hints of a dramatic change of events:
the death of the king, the people's first protest of their
bondage, and the first notice of the Divinity's attentiveness.

In simple ways these introductory chapters set forth the
tension which is resolved in the chapters which follow.
Clearly, the matter at hand is a struggle of life and death
proportions. Israel's abundant life is stalked by a fearful,
death-dealing tyrant. The points of tension are rooted in
clearly perceptible beginnings. That is to say, the origins of
both oppression and liberation are precisely identified. We
learn that bondage and liberation are not the products of the
inevitable course of events in human society. According to
the writers of Exod 1-2 they have their basis in conscious
decisions made by individuals. The personal is political. The
oppressive policies have their beginnings in Pharaoh's fear.
Liberation has its beginnings in the decisions of the midwives, Moses' mother and Pharaoh's daughter not to participate in Pharaoh's oppressive ways. Moses identifies with
the oppressed and undertakes his own exodus. And, it is this
very concrete and specific instance of political struggle
which caught the divine concern: "God heard. . .and God
remembered. . .and God saw. . .and God knew. . . " (2:24-
25).

ISRAEL'S BONDAGE
1:1-14

1   These are the names of the sons of Israel who came to
Egypt with Jacob, each with his household: ²Reuben,
Simeon, Levi, and Judah, ³Issachar, Zebulun, and Benjamin, ⁴Dan and Naphtali, Gad and Asher. ⁵All the offspring of Jacob were seventy persons; Joseph was already
in Egypt. ⁶Then Joseph died, and all his brothers, and all
that generation. ⁷But the descendants of Israel were fruitful and increased greatly; they multiplied and grew
exceedingly strong; so that the land was filled with them.

⁸Now there arose a new king over Egypt, who did not
know Joseph. ⁹And he said to his people, "Behold, the

people of Israel are too many and too mighty for us. [10]Come, let us deal shrewdly with them, lest they multiply, and, if war befall us, they join our enemies and fight against us and escape from the land." [11]Therefore they set taskmasters over them to afflict them with heavy burdens; and they built for Pharaoh store-cities, Pithom and Ra-amses. [12]But the more they were oppressed, the more they multiplied and the more they spread abroad. And the Egyptians were in dread of the people of Israel. [13]So they made the people of Israel serve with rigor, [14]and made their lives bitter with hard service, in mortar and brick, and in all kinds of work in the field; in all their work they made them serve with rigor.

The opening verses of the Book of Exodus recapitulate the overall thrust of the Genesis traditions and at the same time provide the background for the events to follow. The list of names which initiates the story presents Israel as the family, the "sons of Israel," which grew out of the ancestral narratives in the Book of Genesis (cf. similar listings in Gen 35:23-26 and 46:8-27). But, with the passage of time and generations, the *family* Israel grows into the *people* Israel (v. 9). The turning point in the eras is signalled by the notice of the death of Joseph (cf. the last line of the Book of Genesis, Gen 50:26) "and all his brothers, and all that generation" (v. 6), the record of an early source (possibly the Yahwist) in an introduction otherwise fashioned by the Priestly writer (vv. 1-5, 7). Having signalled the end of the era in v. 6, the combined tradition sets the context for the age to follow by noting the strength of the people Israel whose home was now Egypt (v. 7). Israel's great strength is expressed in terminology which resembles the words of God's blessing pronounced over the first human couple (Gen 1:28: "be fruitful and multiply"), over the new humanity begun in Noah (Gen 9:1: "be fruitful and multiply"), and in the people God initiated in Abraham (Gen 17:2, 6: I will "multiply you exceedingly" and "I will make you exceedingly fruitful"). Thus, when the Priestly writer says in verse 7 that "the descendants of Israel were fruitful and increased greatly;

they multiplied and grew exceedingly strong," the tradition asserts that Israel had grown up in accord with God's words of blessing to its forebears.

Exod 1:8-14 consists of an early (possibly Yahwist) narrative in vv. 8-12 supplemented by the Priestly addition of vv. 13-14. Verse 8 very clearly signals passage to a new era which sparks in the reader the anticipation of a change in direction. Immediately we learn that the multiplication of Israel in accord with God's blessing posed a threat to the power of Egypt's ruler. Thereafter the action ensues quickly. The king of Egypt expresses his fear (v. 9) and invites his people to join him in acting out of that fear (v. 10). Without a hint of hesitation, the Pharaoh's fear is given structural embodiment. One man's fear gives rise to social policy: "they set taskmasters over them to afflict them with heavy burdens" (v. 11). In verse 12 the early source marks the conclusion of the first stage of oppression in words which hearken back to the Priestly writer's witness of v. 7. Oppressive efforts which arose out of fear were thwarted insofar as the exact opposite result took place. We are told that "the more they were oppressed, the more they multiplied" (v. 12). This, in turn, precipitated greater fear which now forms the background for the Priestly writer's record of oppression (vv. 13-14). The counter-productivity of the oppressive measures ironically concludes the narrative about one stage of oppression even as it forms the context for actions which now assume life and death proportions.

PHARAOH AND THE MIDWIVES
1:15-22

¹⁵Then the king of Egypt said to the Hebrew midwives, one of whom was named Shiphrah and the other Puah, ¹⁶"When you serve as a midwife to the Hebrew women, and see them upon the birthstool, if it is a son, you shall kill him; but if it is a daughter, she shall live." ¹⁷But the midwives feared God, and did not do as the king of Egypt commanded them, but let the male children live. ¹⁸So the

king of Egypt called the midwives, and said to them, "Why have you done this, and let the male children live?" [19]The midwives said to Pharaoh, "Because the Hebrew women are not like the Egyptian women; for they are vigorous and are delivered before the midwife comes to them." [20]So God dealt well with the midwives; and the people multiplied and grew very strong. [21]And because the midwives feared God he gave them families. [22]Then Pharaoh commanded all his people, "Every son that is born to the Hebrews you shall cast into the Nile, but you shall let every daughter live."

It appears probable that the story of the midwives (1:15-21) at one time circulated independently of the material which surrounds it in the present form of the text. This proposal helps to explain why reference to the oppressor changes from "Pharaoh" (1:11, 22; 2:1-10) to "king of Egypt" (1:15-21; cf. v. 19). It might also account for the slight difference between the king's instruction for the midwives to kill newborn boys belonging to the Hebrews (1:16) and the Pharaoh's command for all his people to cast Hebrew boys into the Nile (1:22). In addition, viewing the story of the midwives as an originally independent tradition offers a possible resolution to the puzzling situation in the present text according to which, on the one hand, the Hebrew people are apparently so numerous that they are a threat to the security of the Egyptian political power structure (1:8-14) and, on the other hand, the Hebrews are few enough to be served by only two midwives (1:15-21). In terminology and content, then, the story of the midwives appears to stand apart from the material in Exod 1:8-14 and 2:1-10. (Some regard it as belonging to the Elohist writer.) In its present context the story of Pharaoh's command to the midwives represents a stage of oppression which stands between hard labor (1:8-14) and a nationwide attempt to eradicate the Hebrew baby boys (1:22)

In several respects the story of the midwives features elements common to tales attributed to Israel's sages.

Divine intervention in human affairs recedes into the background as human beings pursue their own personal destinies while making decisions which direct the course of their communal history. Some of the characters in the story appear more as typical figures than as actual historical personages. The cleverness of the midwives' response to the oppressor outwits the oppressor's "shrewdness" (cf. v. 10). And finally, the midwives are characterized by their "fear of God," a prominent virtue in wisdom circles (cf. Prov 1:7; 10:27; 14:26).

More needs to be said about the midwives' "fear of God" since the story takes its direction from this and not, as we might expect, from the king's word. In Israel's wisdom tradition the expression "fear of God" bears strong ethical connotations (see Prov 2:1-22; 8:13; 14:2; 15:33; 16:6). Persons who feared God were those who acted according to a moral imperative or standard. This standard was learned through examination both of human experience (Prov 19:6-7; 20:4, 14, 19, 25; 23:1-3, 29-35; 24:30-34) and of the processes of nature (Prov 6:6-7; 26:20-22; 27:18; 28:3). There, by means of keen perception and wise reflection, one could observe common patterns which in turn were thought to reflect a fundamental order in the universe. The wise, i.e., ones who feared God, were those who not only discerned this order but who also brought their actions and lives into harmony with it. Those who feared God, therefore, were respectful of and faithful to a fundamental order of things which was wisely discerned through reflection on experience.

Shiphrah and Puah were, by profession, women who assisted people in life. Commitment to the pattern they perceived while assisting in birthing processes caused them to act according to a life-affirming order which meant disobeying the oppressor's death-dealing command. Thus we are told "the midwives feared God" (v. 17).

It is striking that the writer has recorded the names of the two midwives in a story where many other details are omitted. Whatever the reason for this, knowledge of the names invites the reader to a familiarity with Shiphrah and Puah which contrasts with a sense of alienation from the nameless oppressor. The tyrant is cast as a type while Shiphrah and Puah are individuals whose names the reader knows. The ambiguous description, "the Hebrew midwives," or "mid-wives of the Hebrews" continues to hold scholars in debate about the nationality of the two.

This seemingly simple little story abounds in irony. In order to establish his own security, one of the most powerful persons in the world needs and orders the cooperation of two relatively powerless persons. The king directs profes-sional life-bearers to serve death, not life. The directive, moreover, is selective: only male children need be killed. The presupposition seems to be that females pose no threat to the oppressor's power. Yet, in the end, it is women who render the oppressor's plan unsuccessful by their refusal to participate in it. The irony continues: a potential death story abounds in birth and life (1:20-21). The climax of the story appears in the play on words which appears in the midwives' response to the oppressor's confrontation regarding their disobedience. To his query about why they allowed the male children to live Shiphrah and Puah responded that Hebrew women are *hayot*, i.e., they embody abundant, indomitable life which renders death-dealing efforts powerless (1:19). The midwives express this, however, in a covert way which presumably is accepted by the king: the Hebrew women deliver before midwives arrive. In this affirmation of the Hebrews' life-giving power, the tradition notes that "Hebrew women are not like Egyptian women," a remark in which Israelite readers must have taken great delight!

The story of the midwives is about human commitment, courage and ingenuity. It does not tell so much about what God does as about what seemingly powerless persons are capable of being and doing. A tyrant's plan to secure power by means of death is undermined by the life-bearing service of two women who act according to a more fundamental order which their experience as midwives had taught them.

This unit comes to an end with a brief statement of Pharaoh's command which constitutes the third stage of oppression: a nationwide effort to break the strength of the

Hebrews (v. 22). It is possible that in an early form of the tradition, this verse followed vv. 8-12. As the final text took shape, however, it appears as the final and most comprehensive of Pharaoh's three-stage measures of oppression.

IN THE COMPANY OF WOMEN
2:1-10

2   Now a man from the house of Levi went and took to wife a daughter of Levi. ²The woman conceived and bore a son; and when she saw that he was a goodly child, she hid him three months. ³And when she could hide him no longer she took for him a basket made of bulrushes, and daubed it with bitumen and pitch; and she put the child in it and placed it among the reeds at the river's brink. ⁴And his sister stood at a distance, to know what would be done to him. ⁵Now the daughter of Pharaoh came down to bathe at the river, and her maidens walked beside the river; she saw the basket among the reeds and sent her maid to fetch it. ⁶When she opened it she saw the child; and lo, the babe was crying. She took pity on him and said, "This is one of the Hebrews' children." ⁷Then his sister said to Pharaoh's daughter, "Shall I go and call you a nurse from the Hebrew women to nurse the child for you?" ⁸And Pharaoh's daughter said to her, "Go." So the girl went and called the child's mother. ⁹And the Pharaoh's daughter said to her, "Take this child away, and nurse him for me, and I will give you your wages." So the woman took the child and nursed him. ¹⁰And the child grew, and she brought him to Pharaoh's daughter, and he became her son; and she named him Moses, for she said, "Because I drew him out of the water."

Events described in this narrative presuppose knowledge of the oppressive situation described in chapter 1 of Exodus. The decision of Moses' mother to hide him is understandable only if the reader is aware that the lives of all newborn Hebrew boys were threatened. The fact that Moses is saved by being placed in the reeds of the river (2:3) might have been intended as an ironic sequel to Pharaoh's command that all newborn Hebrew males be cast into the Nile (1:22). In any case, obstacles to Pharaoh's oppressive measures continue and intensify as readers view events surrounding the deliverance of one individual. In this incident a boy's biological mother and his adoptive mother are brought together by his sister and through their combined efforts the one through whom God will eventually rescue the Hebrews is himself rescued.

This infancy narrative arose long after Moses had come to be the overtowering figure of the entire exodus story. In retrospect the Israelites assigned remarkable beginnings to the man who mediated God's plan for them. In doing so, the biblical writer borrowed a general outline and some details from a legend about the beginnings of another great figure, Sargon, a prominent Mesopotamian monarch from the second half of the third millennium B.C. According to legend, Sargon was born in secret. His mother constructed a protective basket of bulrushes for the boy, sealed its lid with bitumen, and cast the basket into the Euphrates River. A man who came to draw water from the river found the child, took him, and raised him as a son. Sargon was later discovered by the goddess Ishtar whose patronage led him to the royal throne.

The similarities between Exod 2:1-10 and Sargon's story are clear. The births of both Sargon and Moses are shrouded in secrecy. Both children are placed in baskets (the descriptions of which are strikingly similar) and placed in rivers. Likewise, both are objects of good fortune in that they are rescued and well cared for. Ultimately, both rise to prominent public positions.

Whatever the original intent of the Sargon legend, it provided the biblical writer with a vehicle for introducing Moses as the one who from the very beginning was the object of special care.

It has been proposed in recent scholarship that some of the details of this story also reflect legal custom. In the ancient world when a mother did not wish to nurse her child or if she was unable to, a nursing woman was contracted to nurture her infant. In these cases a legal contract was drawn up, its usual pattern including a declaration regarding the length of service, a statement of work conditions, specific instructions for nourishment as well as a statement of wages for service and fines for breach of contract. During the period designated in the contract, the nursing woman was responsible for raising the child and acting as its guardian. It is possible that this story of Moses' infancy, especially the details of Exod 2:9, are to be understood against the background of this practice in ancient Near Eastern life.

If the writer of this story relied upon the Sargon legend and/or upon ancient nursing contracts for a general outline and some details, it is also true that the borrowed features were freely adapted and interwoven with elements which are new. The biblical writer's most unique contribution to this story is seen in the three female characters. Unlike the mother in the Sargon legend, Moses' mother does not disappear after placing the child in the river. She recedes into the background only to emerge later and become Moses' nurse-guardian. The biblical writer delights readers with the double irony that not only is Moses nursed by his biological mother but the woman is even paid a salary (presumably out of Pharaoh's budget) for her service!

The introduction of Moses' sister into the story (vv. 4, 7-8) is another unique feature in the biblical story. Post-biblical tradition identified this girl with Miriam who appears alongside Moses and Aaron in other texts (e.g., Num 12:1-15; 26:59; 1 Chr 6:3; Micah 6:4) although there is no explicit suggestion here that this girl is the biblical Miriam. In this story the sister functions as a bridge between the traditions about saving Moses' life and providing for his nourishment, an intermediary between the biological mother and the adoptive mother. She stations herself to watch over Moses and she intervenes at the appropriate moment. The fact that she is there to counsel Pharaoh's daughter and that her suggestion is accepted gives her the appearance of the traditional sagelike court advisor in this interaction among women.

Finally, the writer of this story casts a compassionate, decisive, and courageous portrait of Pharaoh's daughter. The child of the oppressor sees the child of the oppressed and is moved to pity. She acts in contradiction to her father's oppressive policy and it appears that she did so consciously and deliberately for the writer mentions that she recognized the baby as belonging to the Hebrews (v. 6). Furthermore, the writer suggests that she deliberately intended that the child's earliest growth and nourishment take place within a Hebrew orientation when she agreed to the sister's suggestion that the nurse secured for the child be a Hebrew woman (v. 7). It is the princess who adopts the child, initiating the extreme irony that the one who would lead the oppressed from Pharaoh's control grew up under Pharaoh's own roof.

Given this portrait of a princess who aligned herself more with the Hebrews than with her father, the reader is not surprised when the writer casts Pharaoh's daughter as speaking the language of the Hebrews. The explanation of Moses' name which the writer placed on her lips derives from the Hebrew and not from the Egyptian tongue. The text says that Pharaoh's daughter called the child Moses because the name (*mosheh* in Hebrew) sounds like the Hebrew word *mashah* ("draw out"). The explanation given in v. 10 rests on a passive form of the root ("I drew him out") although the form of the name is more properly the active participle ("one who draws out"). In reality, the name Moses is probably of Egyptian origin, a short form of a name which typically combined a deity's name with a particle meaning "child of" or "born of" (e.g., Tut-moses, "child of the god Tut," or Ra-mses, "child of the god Ra"). If the meaning given in v. 10 is inaccurate by contemporary etymological standards, still it provides an opportunity for the writer to introduce another point of irony in this story. Attentive readers of the Hebrew text recognize the foreshadowing here. They know that the child whom Pharaoh's daughter "drew out" is more properly regarded as the "one who draws out." Indeed, Moses was well named!

In sum, the writer of Exod 2:1-10 seems to have drawn

upon some already existing material to communicate a unique and profound message. The one who grew up to become deliverer of the Hebrews himself first had to be delivered. God's direction of history in these events is inseparable and indistinguishable from the course of action taken by the three females in the story. As in the story of the midwives (1:15-21) so here a potential death-dealing situation is transformed into a story of life, nurture and growth by persons who made conscious and deliberate choices. The tradition's presupposition in creating this story is that remarkable people have remarkable beginnings and, in turn, the biblical writer accounts for the beginnings of Israel's most remarkable figure by recounting the remarkable deeds done by ordinary women whose decisions changed the course of history.

MOSES' EXODUS
2:11-22

[11]One day, when Moses had grown up, he went out to his people and looked on their burdens; and he saw an Egyptian beating a Hebrew, one of his people. [12]He looked this way and that, and seeing no one he killed the Egyptian and hid him in the sand. [13]When he went out the next day, behold, two Hebrews were struggling together; and he said to the man that did the wrong, "Why do you strike your fellow?" [14]He answered, "Who made you a prince and a judge over us? Do you mean to kill me as you killed the Egyptian?" Then Moses was afraid, and thought, "Surely the thing is known." [15]When Pharaoh heard of it, he sought to kill Moses.

But Moses fled from Pharaoh, and stayed in the land of Midian; and he sat down by a well. [16]Now the priest of Midian had seven daughters; and they came and drew water, and filled the troughs to water their father's flock. [17]The shepherds came and drove them away; but Moses stood up and helped them, and watered their flock. [18]When they came to their father Reuel, he said, "How is it that you have come so soon today?" ¹⁹They said, "An Egyptian delivered us out of the hand of the shepherds, and even drew water for us and watered the flock." ²⁰He said to his daughters, "And where is he? Why have you left the man? Call him, that he may eat bread." ²¹And Moses was content to dwell with the man, and he gave Moses his daughter Zipporah. ²²She bore a son, and he called his name Gershom; for he said, "I have been a sojourner in a foreign land."

The ultimate goal of the writer in Exod 2:11-22 is to move Moses from Egypt to Midian which is the setting for his initial and profound encounter with God (Exod 3). The writer narrates this passage in three brief scenes. These incidents also demonstrate significant aspects of the character of the adult Moses.

In the events narrated in vv. 11-22 Moses is characterized by the same allegiance to the Hebrews and the same courage which characterized the community of women who were responsible for him in infancy. He intervened when he saw an Egyptian beating a Hebrew (vv. 11-12). He intervened when he saw strife between two Hebrews (vv. 13-15a). Finally, he intervened on behalf of the Midianite women who were harrassed by shepherds at the well (vv. 15b-22).

The biblical writer omits comment on the ethical dimension of the measures taken by Moses against the Egyptian who, in turn, was using physical violence against a Hebrew (vv. 11-12). Rather, the writer's interest in these two verses is concentrated on Moses' identity with the Hebrew people. In saying that "one day...he (Moses) went out to his people..." (v. 11) and again "When he went out the next day..." (v. 13), the writer portrays a continuing pattern, a stance adopted by Moses in his adult life, i.e., that although Moses had been brought up in Pharaoh's palace he allied himself with the oppressed Hebrews. In saying that Moses "went out" (both in v. 11 and in v. 13) the biblical writer uses the same Hebrew verb which later is used of the exodus itself. One interpreter thus observes that Moses' "going out" to his people was the first stage of his own exodus. Having

grown up, Moses "went out" from the oppressive posture of
Pharaoh's household even as he "went out" to identification
with the oppressed. In making this point the writer carefully
and explicitly identifies the abused Hebrew as one with
whom Moses belonged like a brother ("one of his people"; v.
11). Verses 11-12 then relate an incident which ultimately
will lead to Moses' flight from Egypt. Moses' departure
from loyalty to Egyptian ways prepares the reader for his
departure from the land itself.

The second of the three incidents of Exod 2:11-22 shows
that Moses' passion for justice was not limited to the oppression of the Hebrews by the Egyptians. In intervening in the
struggle between the two Hebrews, Moses' confronts the
guilty party. The writer uses technical, legal terminology in
referring to the man who did the wrong, a clear indication
that the incident was no mere difference of opinion but a
case in which injustice had been done. When Moses asked
the unjust Hebrew to account for his action, the man was
unable to explain himself. His only recourse was to seek to
undermine Moses' authority by questioning his credentials:
"Who made you a prince and a judge over us?" (v. 14a).
Moses, acting on his own, is unable to establish a just
situation. Only later, when he returns to Egypt from Midian
as a mediator of divine power will his intervention on behalf of
the powerless be successful. In the unjust Hebrew's second
question to Moses: "Do you mean to kill me as you killed
the Egyptian?" (v. 14b), the narrator witnesses that injustice
reaches across ethnic and political differences to align itself
with other injustice. That is to say, the speaker shows himself to have greater loyalty to the oppressive Egyptian of vv.
11-12 than to his fellow Hebrew.

In the third incident in this narrative (vv. 15b-22), the
writer hastens to show that, just as injustice breeds alliances
which transcend other boundaries, so does the passion for
justice. Moses is forced to flee to Midian but he carried with
him a willingness to intervene when he encounters the struggle of the Midianite priest's daughters with the shepherds.
Contrary to the hostile response of the unjust Hebrew,
Moses' action in Midian meets with a response of warm

hospitality (vv. 20-21). The writer uses this opportunity to repeat a conventional scene wherein the biblical hero's wife is first encountered at a well (cf. Gen 24:1-67 and 29:1-30).

With this final incident, the writer succeeds in portraying Moses in Midianite territory. The setting for his encounter with God is thus finalized. However, when Moses gives his son a name derived from the word for "stranger" or "sojourner" (v. 22), he attests to his primary alliance with the Hebrews and the reader is cautioned that Midian is not a permanent home for Moses. As Moses went out from Egypt, so he will return to lead the Hebrews through a similar passage. Thus, in this account of Moses' flight to Midian the writer foreshadows the exodus of the entire people held in bondage by Pharaoh.

THE CRY UNDER BONDAGE
2:23-25

> [23]In the course of those many days the king of Egypt died. And the people of Israel groaned under their bondage, and cried out for help, and their cry under bondage came up to God. [24]And God heard their groaning, and God remembered his covenant with Abraham, with Isaac and with Jacob. [25]And God saw the people of Israel, and God knew their condition.

This text, usually attributed to the Priestly writer, directs the reader's attention from Midian back to Egypt by recalling the oppression of the Hebrews. More significantly, it marks a turning point in the action of the exodus story.

In the expression, "In the course of those many days" (v. 23), the author alludes to an indefinite period of time during which the Hebrews were oppressed. The notice of the king's death in an indirect way reminds the reader of the opening of the story where the beginnings of oppression are linked with the accession of a new king (1:8). But, if the notice of the king's death points to what has passed, it also initiates in the reader a sense of hopeful anticipation that a new reign, a new era, will soon begin.

For the first time we are told that the oppressed cried out under their bondage. The cry of the oppressed proves to be the turning point in their situation. God began the redemptive action only when the oppressed voiced knowledge of the injustice being done to them. The naming and protest of injustice is the beginning of deliverance. Having voiced the cry, the humans who have been featured thus far in the exodus story are gone and the writer portrays an immediate and intense response on the part of the Divinity. The focus of the story now shifts to God's involvement in the struggle against bondage and oppression.

THE CALL OF THE FIRE
3:1—4:17

In this section of the Book of Exodus we meet one of the most engaging stories of the biblical tradition. It narrates the first of many encounters between God and Moses. The lengthy dialogue between the two has its setting at the "mountain of God," a holy place revered by generations of believers. There a mysterious fire sustained only by a wilderness shrub reached out and drew Moses to itself. From the fire issued word, a voice speaking in multifaceted ways. It told of its personal experience. It spoke of the commitment which rose out of that experience, i.e., its decision to offer a life and a way of relating which was an alternative to what Pharaoh offered. It bid Moses to enter into its own dynamic vision and commitment and, in the face of the mediator's hesitations, it coaxed Moses. Moreover, it told its name.

In this story readers of the text are invited to join Moses at Horeb and, like Moses, to draw near to the mysterious fire in order to catch a glimpse of God's imagination which bears an alternative to oppression. At the same time readers, with Moses, will hear a clear and persistent call to be claimed by that vision and let it offer direction for their own mission.

The text represents the combined accounts of the Yahwist

and Elohist writers. Generally speaking, the lines which refer to the Divinity as "Lord" (3:2-4a, 5, 7-8, 16-22; 4:1-15, 17) probably reflect the hand of the Yahwist while the title "God" signals the contribution of the Elohist (3:1, 4b, 6, 9-15; 4:16).

When one takes an overall look at this unit and views it in comparison with other narratives in Scripture wherein an individual is specially called to become a mediator of God's redemptive activity in Israel, it is possible to see a common pattern. These "call narratives" typically contain the following elements: (a) divine confrontation (Exod 3:1-4a; cf. Judg 6:11b-12a and Jer 1:4); (b) an introductory word by the Divinity (Exod 3:4b-9; cf. Judg 6:12b-13 and Jer 1:5ab); (c) the divine commissioning of the individual (Exod 3:10; cf. Judg 6:14 and Jer 1:5c, 9-10); (d) an objection voiced by the one called (Exod 3:11; cf. Judg 6:15 and Jer 1:6); (e) a reassurance by the Divinity (Exod 3:12a; cf. Judg 6:16 and Jer 1:7-8); and (f) a sign given by the Divinity (Exod 3:12; cf. Judg 6:17). Thus, the overall structure of Exod 3:1-12 represents a literary construction which is more or less typical for biblical accounts of the calls of God's mediators. After 3:12, the encounter between Moses and God is carried forward by a series of questions (3:13; 4:1, 10, 13) wherein Moses voices additional objections to his call. These, in turn, are followed by responses (usually including reassurance) by God (3:15; 4:2-9, 11-12, 14-16). Thus, in this particular instance elements (d) and (e) of the typical call narrative pattern are repeated several times.

Recognition that this story flows according to a typical pattern suggests that it is best understood as something other than a biographical account. Scholars agree that this story, like the other biblical call narratives, was probably designed to legitimate that Moses, like other leaders, acted in response to God's commission and not on his own initiative. Thus, this story asserts that Moses' mission is authorized by God. It presents his public credentials.

The story of Moses' call begins in the Divinity's profound self-revelation which is joined with the divine commissioning and Moses' repeated attempts to resist the call. Several elements in this are noteworthy. First of all, the initiative in the relationship belongs to the Divinity. The Divinity is present in a special way and the Divinity, not Moses, initiates the dialogue. Secondly, the purpose of the Divinity's presence and word is not focused on Moses but rather on the larger community. In other words, the dialogue initiated by God does not have as its purpose the closer relationship between God and Moses. Rather, it constitutes a commission which directs Moses to the needs of the community. Finally, the account witnesses to Moses' resisting of the divine call which in turn elicits from the Divinity a reassurance of divine presence and a sign of God's presence in power. In Exodus chapters 3 and 4 this part of the typical structure of the call narrative is repeated over and over again. The expansion of these particular elements makes a strong statement about the depth of Moses' struggle to answer God's call and the patient but persistent resolve of God to move forward in freeing activity through this specially chosen individual.

THE BURNING BUSH
3:1-12

> **3** Now Moses was keeping the flock of his father-in-law, Jethro, the priest of Midian; and he led his flock to the west side of the wilderness, and came to Horeb, the mountain of God. ²And the angel of the Lord appeared to him in a flame of fire out of the midst of a bush; and he looked, and lo, the bush was burning, yet it was not consumed. ³And Moses said, "I will turn aside and see this great sight, why the bush is not burnt." ⁴When the Lord saw that he turned aside to see, God called to him out of the bush, "Moses, Moses!" And he said, "Here am I." ⁵Then he said, "Do not come near; put off your shoes from your feet, for the place on which you are standing is holy ground." ⁶And he said, "I am the God of your father, the God of Abraham, the God of Isaac, and the God of

Jacob." And Moses hid his face, for he was afraid to look at God.

⁷Then the Lord said, "I have seen the affliction of my people who are in Egypt, and have heard their cry because of their taskmasters; I know their sufferings, ⁸and I have come down to deliver them out of the hand of the Egyptians, and to bring them up out of that land to a good and broad land, a land flowing with milk and honey, to the place of the Canaanites, the Hittites, the Amorites, the Perizzites, the Hivites, and the Jebusites. ⁹And now, behold, the cry of the people of Israel has come to me, and I have seen the oppression with which the Egyptians oppress them. ¹⁰Come, I will send you to Pharaoh that you may bring forth my people, the sons of Israel, out of Egypt." ¹¹But Moses said to God, "Who am I that I should go to Pharaoh, and bring the sons of Israel out of Egypt?" ¹²He said, "But I will be with you; and this shall be the sign for you, that I have sent you: when you have brought forth the people out of Egypt, you shall serve God upon this mountain."

In the first verse of this story the writer establishes the setting. The Elohist characteristically uses the word "Horeb" to refer to Sinai. Moses' profound encounter with God and his special vocation take place at the mountain site where later the entire people will meet God. There were a variety of traditions with regard to the name of the Midianite priest who was Moses' father-in-law. The source represented here knew him as Jethro (cf. Exod 4:18; 18:1) although elsewhere he was known as Reuel (Exod 2:18) and Hobab (Num 10:29; Judg 4:11).

The story about the burning bush serves as the "divine confrontation" part of the typical structure of a call narrative. Viewed apart from the rest of this structure, however, the account looks very similar to other biblical stories which tell how a particular site came to be regarded as a holy place. In ancient Israel certain places were hallowed because it was believed that the Divinity at one time had been present there in a special way. Thus, tradition told that the shrine at

Shechem was first established after God appeared to Abraham there (Gen 12:6-8). Likewise, the foundation of the sanctuary at Bethel is traced to a special encounter with God which Jacob had there (Gen 28:10-22; see also Josh 5:13-15). Sinai-Horeb was a sacred place in Israel's tradition, then, not only because it was the site of the covenant but because, even prior to that, God was specially present there to Moses.

Moses appears to be going about an ordinary day's activity of shepherding when his attention was caught by the extraordinary, the bush which was burning but was not consumed. He was not searching for God; yet he was attuned enough to the mysterious within his surroundings to let it capture his attention when it presented itself. When Moses turned to investigate the fire, he did not yet know he was in the presence of God. He was aware, however, that he was in the presence of Mystery and he gave himself to it. The personhood of the Mystery was clear only when Moses was addressed and it was this word which allowed Moses to realize that the Mystery was Holy.

In verse 6 the Mystery is identified as the God of Abraham, the God of Isaac, and the God of Jacob. With these words, the divine mystery is identified with past religious tradition as the Promise-Maker who had formed bonded relationships with the ancestors of the Hebrews. Verses 7 and 8 make clear that that relationship is now taking dramatic new directions. God has seen the oppression in Egypt and has heard the cries of injustice and has initiated a movement of deliverance which will ultimately lead to inheritance of the land promised long ago. The arena for divine presence and activity now at this moment in history is the Hebrews' struggle for liberation.

In Exod 3:9 we have the Elohist's version of what the Yahwist had recorded in vv. 7-8. In verse 10 the Divinity commissions Moses to mediate the divine involvement in this situation. In vv. 11-12 a pattern of Moses' objection and God's reassurance appears for the first of five times in Exod 3:1—4:17. According to the stereotyped structure of the call narrative, the one called responds with an objection. Here Moses' protest appears to be a sincere recognition of his lack of credentials for such a mission. In God's response Moses is given his credentials: God is with him. The dynamic which will confront Pharaoh and free the slaves does not depend on Moses' ability or authority but is rooted securely in God's being there in the confrontation and in the struggle. The sign that this is true is that Moses' mission will be successful, i.e., Moses one day will return to worship at this very same site.

NAMING THE FIRE
3:13-15

> [13]Then Moses said to God, "If I come to the people of Israel and say to them, 'The God of your fathers has sent me to you,' and they ask me, 'What is his name?' what shall I say to them?" [14]God said to Moses, "I Am Who I Am." And he said, "Say this to the people of Israel, 'I Am has sent me to you.'" [15]God also said to Moses, "Say this to the people of Israel, 'The Lord, the God of your fathers, the God of Abraham, the God of Isaac, and the God of Jacob, has sent me to you': this is my name for ever, and thus I am to be remembered throughout all generations.

Carefully placed between two somewhat lengthy expositions of the divine plan with regard to the slaves (vv. 7-12 and vv. 16-22) stand these three verses which have long captured the interest of biblical interpreters. The lines raise many questions: are we to understand from Moses' statement in v. 13 that the Hebrews in Egypt did not know God's name? How are we to understand that, in the present text, vv. 14 and 15 both appear to be answers to the questions cited in v. 13? What is the meaning of the divine name according to this particular narration? Finally, why does the name-gift appear at this particular juncture in the larger exodus story?

Before pursuing these topics, a word about names and naming in ancient Israel is in order. In modern society, it sometimes happens that persons are given names which do not bear any essential connection to the person's unique qualities or character. In these cases, if the person's name has a specific meaning it is because the bearer, by the uniqueness of his or her life, gives the name a meaning. The person, as it were, lives a meaning into the name which otherwise might be merely an identification tag.

This view of names stands in contrast to the notion that one's name is in some way descriptive of who one really is. In this perception to tell one's name to another is to offer more than an identification tag. In the ancient world to tell one's name was to give the other access to one's energy and potential. It was necessary to know the name of another in order to have a relationship with that person. This was true of divine-human relationships as well as of human relationships. Devotees had to know a deity's name in order to call upon the power and presence of that deity. Thus, when Jacob (Gen 32:22-32) and Manaoh (Judg 13:17-20) encountered the Divinity in special ways and asked its name, each request was denied. Presumably the Divinity sought not to make its potential accessible to these human beings.

It is noteworthy that in Exod 3:13-15 Moses puts the desire to know the divine name on the lips of the people in Egypt. What is the significance of the question when it is posed by the community to whom Moses would announce God's plan? Moses was regarded in some circles as a prophetic figure. One criterion for distinguishing true from false prophets had to do with the deity's name. If the prophet spoke in Yahweh's name, that one was regarded as a true prophet. Thus, if the questions of 3:13 were posed by the community when Moses announced God's plan of liberation, perhaps the community was essentially testing whether Moses was indeed functioning as a true spokesperson for God. If he presented himself as operating in Yahweh's name, the community knew his word was reliable.

Having said this, we must ask further regarding Moses' question: "What shall I tell them?" Does Moses not know Yahweh? Is this a new Divinity, previously unknown to Moses? Is this Moses' first knowledge of the God Yahweh?

Or is Moses here searching through the ambiguity of his own experience, treading deeper into its Mystery? Perhaps a clue to answering these questions can be found in the answer which is given to Moses in verse 15. There the name Yahweh ("Lord" in the RSV translation) is identified with the God of the Fathers, i.e., the God of Israel's ancestors. But that One known in the promise-fulfillment experience of the Hebrews' past now bears a new name. The Mystery's former function now gives way to something so dramatically new as to warrant a new name. The One traditionally present to the ancestors and their families in a promise-fulfillment experience is now the One who subverts and overthrows the oppressive society sponsored by Pharaoh and calls the Hebrews to a new life marked by trust and freedom. Thus, while Moses may have known this same deity before, he has not known God to do these kinds of things before. This leads him to ask that the Mystery identify itself.

Some scholars see verse 14 as a later insertion which was intended to convey the significance of the new name associated with the God of the exodus. Hence, the name Yahweh was thought to have been related to the Hebrew root *hayah* which bears the sense of "being." The answer given in v. 14, *'ehyeh 'asher 'ehyeh*, is variously translated by scholars as present ("I am who I am"), future ("I will be who I will be") or causative ("I will cause to be what is"). Although biblical scholarship is not in perfect agreement on the exact translation of v. 14, it is one in warning against understanding the name as denoting an abstract, static notion of "being" since this is foreign to the Hebrew way of thinking. Rather, the root *hayah* denotes a dynamic sense of being present, being there. This had led some to render *'ehyeh 'asher 'ehyeh* as "I shall be there, as who I am, I shall be there." This translation not only seeks to be faithful to the etymology given in v. 14 but it is consistent with the broader context (see "I shall be with you" in v. 12). According to this understanding, the new name Yahweh is regarded as a pledge on God's part to be dynamically present to the people.

At the same time, the particular form given in v. 14 also insures the freedom of the Divinity. That is to say, it does not give Israel control of the deity through total knowledge of the Mystery. When God said, "I shall be there, *as who I am*, I shall be there," God guarded the divine freedom. Presence was promised but God's particular *way* of being present was not handed over. Thus, believers could never control, never dictate, never be absolutely certain what form God's dynamic presence-in-power would take. God would be present in mystery and freedom. In preserving the Mystery ("as who I am"), God gave Israel a name the meaning of which they would have to continue to search out. The arena for this unfolding significance was to be their own history ("I shall be there"). To search out the meaning of God's name, Israel was called into the mystery of its own experience, its own name.

Israel knew it would never exhaust or know completely the name. Certainly it was not given into their control. Thus, while the pledge of divine presence contained in the name was a source of confidence for Israel, the mystery and freedom borne in it never allowed Israel to be perfectly comfortable.

INSTRUCTIONS FOR THE MISSION
3:16-22

> [16]Go and gather the elders of Israel together, and say to them, 'The Lord, the God of your fathers, the God of Abraham, of Isaac, and of Jacob, has appeared to me, saying, "I have observed you and what has been done to you in Egypt; [17]and I promise that I will bring you up out of the affliction of Egypt, to the land of the Canaanites, the Hittites, the Amorites, the Perizzites, the Hivites, and the Jebusites, a land flowing with milk and honey."' [18]And they will hearken to your voice; and you and the elders of Israel shall go to the king of Egypt and say to him, 'The Lord, the God of the Hebrews, has met with us; and now, we pray you, let us go a three days' journey into the wilderness, that we may sacrifice to the Lord our God.' [19]I know that the king of Egypt will not let you go

unless compelled by a mighty hand. [20]So I will stretch out my hand and smite Egypt with all the wonders which I will do in it; after that he will let you go. [21]And I will give this people favor in the sight of the Egyptians; and when you go, you shall not go empty, [22]but each woman shall ask of her neighbor, and of her who sojourns in her house, jewelry of silver and of gold, and clothing, and you shall put them on your sons and on your daughters; thus you shall despoil the Egyptians."

This unit comes to us from the hand of the Yahwist. Before the combination of Yahwist and Elohist traditions, these verses followed verses 7-8. Thus, originally the announcement of the divine plan was followed by these specific instructions regarding how Moses was to enter into God's dynamic involvement in Israel's liberation.

According to the Yahwist, Moses first had to report to the elders of Israel what he himself had heard (compare vv. 16b-17 with Exod 3:7-8) and then go to the king of Egypt along with a delegation of elders. Moses' role in the Yahwist source is like that of a prophetic messenger, delivering the words which the Divinity placed in his mouth (vv. 16-17, 18). The message Moses is sent to announce is that *Yahweh* will bring Israel out of Egypt.

In casting Moses in the role of messenger, the Yahwist presents a slightly different view from that of the Elohist (3:9-12). According to the latter Moses is instructed by God to go directly and presumably alone to Pharaoh (v. 10). In the Elohist's work, it is *Moses* who brings Israel out of Egypt (vv. 10, 11, 12). As such, he is more of a mediator of God's saving presence than a messenger.

Verses 18-22 contain a foreshadowing of some of the details of how Yahweh's plan will unfold. Thus, the thought of Exod 3:18 reappears in Exod 5:3. Exod 3:19-20, by way of preview, offers a brief summary of the plagues. Exod 3:21-22 foretells details which reappear in the narration of events surrounding the exodus as recorded in Exod 11:2-3 and 12:35-36.

Just as the Elohist writer had presented the commissioning of Moses as followed immediately by an objection on his part (3:9-12, 13-15), so here too the Yahwist's account of Moses' mission (vv. 16-22) is followed by an objection.

OBJECTION AND RESPONSE
4:1-9

4 Then Moses answered, "But behold, they will not believe me or listen to my voice, for they will say, 'The Lord did not appear to you.'" ²The Lord said to him, "What is that in your hand?" He said, "A rod." ³And he said, "Cast it on the ground." So he cast it on the ground, and it became a serpent; and Moses fled from it. ⁴But the Lord said to Moses, "Put out your hand, and take it by the tail" — so he put out his hand and caught it, and it became a rod in his hand — ⁵"that they may believe that the Lord, the God of their fathers, the God of Abraham, the God of Isaac, and the God of Jacob, has appeared to you." ⁶Again, the Lord said to him, "Put your hand into your bosom." And he put his hand into his bosom; and when he took it out, behold, his hand was leprous, as white as snow. ⁷Then God said, "Put your hand back into your bosom." So he put his hand back into his bosom; and when he took it out, behold, it was restored like the rest of his flesh. ⁸"If they will not believe you," God said, "or heed the first sign, they may believe the latter sign. ⁹If they will not believe even these two signs or heed your voice, you shall take some water from the Nile and pour it upon the dry ground; and the water which you shall take from the Nile will become blood upon the dry ground."

The commission narrative from here through Exod 4:17 is carried along by a series of Moses' objections to his vocation (vv. 1, 10, 14). In this particular unit Moses' objection is cloaked as skepticism. He believed his mission to be impossible because he doubted that Israel would believe that he was sent by God. This objection is forestalled patiently and resolutely by the signs God provided Moses, signs which underscore his authenticity as Yahweh's messenger.

In refusing to believe Yahweh's statement that he would be accepted by the Israelites, Moses embodies stark contrast to much of what has gone before. Yahweh had outlined the divine plan (vv. 16-22) as a sure thing. There was no doubt about its success. Moses, on the other hand, doubts the very first step of the plan. In Moses' view, God's sweeping plan for the Israelites would never get off the ground because his fellow Israelites would not trust that Moses' mission came from God. In response, the Divinity insures against such a stumbling block. Yahweh offers Moses three signs which were to be used to dissolve any such disbelief: the rod-serpent, the leprous hand healed, and, if these wonders failed to convince, Moses was instructed about a further sign he could perform, i.e., turning water from the Nile into blood.

Some of these signs bear similarity to events which indeed are recorded in the narratives which follow. Hence, the sign of water from the Nile turning to blood seems to anticipate the plague recorded in Exod 7:14-24. Likewise, the sign of the rod turning into a serpent is similar to the sign recorded in Exod 7:9-12 (note, however, that in Exod 7:9-12 the sign is done before Pharaoh, not Israel, and that it is performed by Aaron, not Moses).

Indeed, it appears that what is rehearsed here between Yahweh and Moses will later be acted out between Moses (as Yahweh's messenger) and Pharaoh. God's word of commission and command is enough neither for Moses nor for Pharaoh. Just as God's command to "let my people go" will need to be aided by signs and wonders before Pharaoh, so with Moses and with Israel signs are needed to validate the sureness of the call to liberation. Freedom is such a daring and dangerous venture. Those called to it need to be coaxed and reassured.

FURTHER OBJECTIONS, FURTHER RESPONSES
4:10-17

[10]But Moses said to the Lord, "Oh, my Lord, I am not eloquent, either heretofore or since thou hast spoken to thy servant; but I am slow of speech and of tongue." [11]Then the Lord said to him, "Who has made man's mouth? Who makes him dumb, or deaf, or seeing, or blind? Is it not I, the Lord? [12]Now therefore go, and I will be with your mouth and teach you what you shall speak." [13]But he said, "Oh, my Lord, send, I pray, some other person." [14]Then the anger of the Lord was kindled against Moses and he said, "Is there not Aaron, your brother, the Levite? I know that he can speak well; and behold, he is coming out to meet you, and when he sees you he will be glad in his heart. [15]And you shall speak to him and put the words in his mouth; and I will be with your mouth and with his mouth, and will teach you what you shall do. [16]He shall speak for you to the people; and he shall be a mouth for you, and you shall be to him as God. [17]And you shall take in your hand this rod, with which you shall do the signs."

The final sections of this extended narrative about the commission of Moses are, like the foregoing sections, carried forward by additional objections raised by Moses. The objection voiced in Exod 4:10 recalls the one already cited in Exod 3:11. Both represent Moses as feeling unqualified for what God was asking of him. As earlier so here too, God assures Moses of the divine presence on the mission: "I will be your mouth and teach you what you should speak." The basis for Moses' mission thus is again shifted from his personal qualifications and credentials to the dynamic presence-in-power of the Divinity in this exodus mission.

In the last of Moses' five objections to his call (Exod 4:13) it might well be that we have reached the real core of the matter. It is possible that all along Moses has been attempting to articulate his reluctance about his vocation. In other

words, perhaps what lay behind those objections wherein
Moses pointed to his inadequacies ("This mission won't
work because...") was a basic unwillingness to get involved
("I don't want to do this"). It is possible that Moses for the
first time here faces himself and expresses a truly honest
response: "...send, I pray, some other person."

Exod 4:13-16 is viewed by nearly all scholars as a secondary addition to the original story. Its chief purpose is to
introduce Aaron into the narrative. Aaron's role is that of
Moses' mouthpiece and God promises to be with both of
them. Aaron is described here as Moses' "brother." It is
difficult to know what was intended by this. It is probable
that the kinship terminology was utilized to designate
Aaron as Moses' "associate" in the exodus process (cf. Exod
15:20 where Miriam is described as Aaron's "sister"). Whatever the case, the extended account of Moses' call (Exod
3:1—4:17) comes to a close with Moses' having evoked from
God a promise of companionship.

The narrative of Moses' call, beginning with Exod 3:1,
then, is a tapestry composed of alternating threads of God's
recital of the divine plan for the redemption which is about
to take place and Moses' reluctance to enter into this movement in the capacity of God's envoy. It is the story of divine
initiative and invitation, on the one hand, and human difficulty in responding, on the other hand. It is the story of
newness (represented in God's new name and Moses' new
mission) but a newness which is continuous with God's
gracious dealings with Israel's ancestors.

SETTING THE FOCUS
4:18—7:7

This section of the Book of Exodus can be regarded as consisting of three passages. The first (4:18-31) functions as a transition between Moses' call in Midian (3:1—4:17) and the initiation of his mission in Egypt (5:1). The second (5:1—6:1) is the reader's first indication that the movement from bondage to freedom, the "call of the fire," involves arduous struggle and pain. This sets the stage for the long and somewhat drawn out plague narratives which begin in 7:8. Finally, the third text (6:2—7:7) forms an inclusion with 3:1—4:17 insofar as it narrates another account of the gift of the name as well as the call and commission of Moses. Following as it does the ominous message about struggle (5:1—6:1), this second account of the call reasserts God's view of the matters at hand even as it recalls God's commitment to save and God's call for Moses to engage and mediate the divine decision to save. As such 6:2—7:7 not only points back to what has gone before but also offers a confident and challenging perspective from which believers might read the plague narratives which follow.

Taken together, these passages set in proper focus our approach to the exodus movement. They take us back from the open wilderness to the strictures of Pharaoh's world.

They reacquaint us with the pain described in Exodus chapters 1-2. At the same time, they call us to confidence in the face of struggle and faith in the Mystery whose name and resolve we know.

MOSES' RETURN TO EGYPT
4:18-31

18Moses went back to Jethro his father-in-law and said to him, "Let me go back, I pray, to my kinsmen in Egypt and see whether they are still alive." And Jethro said to Moses, "Go in peace." 19And the Lord said to Moses in Midian, "Go back to Egypt; for all the men who were seeking your life are dead." 20So Moses took his wife and his sons and set them on an ass, and went back to the land of Egypt; and in his hand Moses took the rod of God. 21And the Lord said to Moses, "When you go back to Egypt, see that you do before Pharaoh all the miracles which I have put in your power; but I will harden his heart, so that he will not let the people go. 22And you shall say to Pharaoh, 'Thus says the Lord, Israel is my first-born son, 23and I say to you, "Let my son go that he may serve me"; if you refuse to let him go, behold, I will slay your first-born son.'"

24At a lodging place on the way the Lord met him and sought to kill him. 25Then Zipporah took a flint and cut off her son's foreskin, and touched Moses' feet with it, and said, "Surely you are a bridegroom of blood to me!" 26So he let him alone. Then it was that she said, "You are a bridegroom of blood," because of the circumcision.

27The Lord said to Aaron, "Go into the wilderness to meet Moses." So he went, and met him at the mountain of God and kissed him. 28And Moses told Aaron all the words of the Lord with which he had sent him, and all the signs which he had charged him to do. 29Then Moses and Aaron went and gathered together all the elders of the people of Israel. 30And Aaron spoke all the words which the Lord had spoken to Moses, and did the signs in the sight of the people. [31]And the people believed; and when they heard that the Lord had visited the people of Israel and that he had seen their affliction, they bowed their heads and worshiped.

Exod 4:18-31 consists of four short segments which begin with Moses in Midian and end with his reunion with Israel in Egypt.

The first incident to be narrated is Moses' taking leave of his father-in-law (vv. 18-20). A close reading shows some unevenness in the passage possibly reflecting a conflation of materials stemming from different oral or written traditions. In v. 18, Moses' speech to Jethro and Jethro's response ("Go in peace") suggest to the reader that Moses is about to be on his way, presumably alone (cf. Exod 18:2-6) and probably with the rod of God in his hand (v. 20b). Yahweh's command for Moses to go back to Egypt which appears in the following verse (v. 19) thus strikes the reader as somewhat superfluous and obstructive in the context of a movement which already appeared to be under way. Yahweh's words recall the tradition of the threat to Moses' life which appeared in Exod 2:15. Verse 20 portrays Moses as taking along his wife and sons which is consistent with the witness of Exod 4:24-26 although to this point the reader has been introduced to only one of Moses' sons (Exod 2:22).

The second incident recorded in this unit (vv. 21-23) constitutes a frequently used literary device whereby the writer foreshadows or previews events which lie ahead. The verses summarize in capsule form the events which are to come. Yahweh's claim on Israel as "first-born son" sets the scene for the dramatic struggle detailed in the following chapters wherein Yahweh and Pharaoh struggle for Israel's allegiance. More specifically, there is a hint of the final plague (Exod 11) in Yahweh's warning that the price Egypt will have to pay for refusal to permit Israel's liberation is the blood of its own "first-born."

The third part of this section (vv. 24-26) records a problematic and mysterious incident the meaning of which continues to intrigue biblical interpreters. The text is problematic for several reasons. First of all, it is not known for certain who is intended by the pronoun "him" in v. 24 ("sought to kill him"). Generally, it has been taken to mean Moses although it is difficult to know why Yahweh would want to take the life of one so recently commissioned as an envoy. Secondly, v. 25 clearly describes the circumcision of Moses' son by the mother. In saying that she touched Moses' "feet" with the foreskin, the writer euphemistically suggests that she applied the foreskin to Moses' genitals. The significance of such a gesture and the meaning of Zipporah's statement ("Surely you are a bridegroom of blood to me!") are both very obscure. The elusiveness of the expression even seems to go back to biblical times for the last line of v. 26 is clearly intended to interpret the expression for readers unfamiliar with it. Finally, in addition to the textual problems, readers are understandably puzzled by the portrait of God suggested in these verses.

Scholars regard this text as reflecting very ancient times and primitive custom. Most simply admit that a full explanation of the meaning of the incident is no longer possible. It might be that at one level of development this story was told to demonstrate some connection between circumcision and marital customs. At another level the story might have served to point out the importance of circumcision. It might also have sought to explain how the custom of circumcising children arose. None of these possibilities, however, clearly explains the text as it now stands.

The concluding incident of chapter 4 (vv. 27-31) is Moses' meeting with Aaron and their preparation for mediating God's activity. Just as God told Moses that Aaron would be given as his spokesperson (4:13-16), so here we are told that "Aaron spoke all the words which the Lord had spoken to Moses" (4:30a). The notation that Aaron also performed signs (v. 30b) comes as something of a surprise since to this point only Moses has been given power to perform signs as an authentication that he was indeed sent by God (4:2-9, 17).

The final verse in chapter 4 clearly and succinctly describes the success which met Moses and Aaron's initial acts. The people believed the words and signs and, having heard that God was aware of their awful situation, they worshipped.

LIBERATION: NOT THROUGH REQUEST, NOT THROUGH REASONING
5:1—6:1

5 Afterward Moses and Aaron went to Pharaoh and said, "Thus says the Lord, the God of Israel, 'Let my people go, that they may hold a feast to me in the wilderness.'" ²But Pharaoh said, "Who is the Lord, that I should heed his voice and let Israel go? I do not know the Lord, and moreover I will not let Israel go." ³Then they said, "The God of the Hebrews has met with us; let us go, we pray, a three days' journey into the wilderness, and sacrifice to the Lord our God, lest he fall upon us with pestilence or with the sword." ⁴But the king of Egypt said to them, "Moses and Aaron, why do you take the people away from their work? Get to your burdens." ⁵And Pharaoh said, "Behold, the people of the land are now many and you make them rest from their burdens!" ⁶The same day Pharaoh commanded the taskmasters of the people and their foremen, ⁷"You shall no longer give the people straw to make bricks, as heretofore; let them go and gather straw for themselves. ⁸But the number of bricks which they made heretofore you shall lay upon them, you shall by no means lessen it; for they are idle; therefore they cry, 'Let us go and offer sacrifice to our God.' ⁹Let heavier work be laid upon the men that they may labor at it and pay no regard to lying words."

¹⁰So the taskmasters and the foremen of the people went out and said to the people, "Thus says Pharaoh, 'I will not give you straw. ¹¹Go yourselves, get your straw wherever you can find it; but your work will not be lessened in the least.'" ¹²So the people were scattered abroad throughout all the land of Egypt, to gather stubble for straw. ¹³The taskmasters were urgent, saying, "Complete your work, your daily task, as when there was

straw." ¹⁴And the foremen of the people of Israel, whom Pharaoh's taskmasters had set over them, were beaten, and were asked, "Why have you not done all your task of making bricks today, as hitherto?"

¹⁵Then the foremen of the people of Israel came and cried to Pharaoh, "Why do you deal thus with your servants? ¹⁶No straw is given to your servants, yet they say to us, 'Make bricks!' And behold, your servants are beaten; but the fault is in your own people." ¹⁷But he said, "You are idle, you are idle; therefore you say, 'Let us go and sacrifice to the Lord.' ¹⁸Go now, and work; for no straw shall be given you, yet you shall deliver the same number of bricks." ¹⁹The foremen of the people of Israel saw that they were in evil plight, when they said, "You shall by no means lessen your daily number of bricks." ²⁰They met Moses and Aaron, who were waiting for them, as they came forth from Pharaoh; ²¹and they said to them, "The Lord look upon you and judge, because you have made us offensive in the sight of Pharaoh and his servants, and have put a sword in their hand to kill us."

²²Then Moses turned again to the Lord and said, "O Lord, why hast thou done evil to this people? Why didst thou ever send me? ²³For since I came to Pharaoh to speak in thy name, he has done evil to this people, and thou hast not delivered thy people at all."   **6** But the Lord said to Moses, "Now you shall see what I will do to Pharaoh; for with a strong hand he will send them out, yea, with a strong hand he will drive them out of his land."

Having briefly narrrated the transition which brought Moses back from the wilderness and into Egypt, the writer now presents the first of many meetings with Pharaoh and the struggle which ensues as a result of Pharaoh's refusal to let Israel go. Pharaoh declares that his refusal is based on his not "knowing Yahweh" (5:2). Thus the biblical writer introduces a motif which will recur in the plague narratives (see Exod 8:10, 22; 9:29).

In verse 3 Moses and Aaron use words quite similar to those of Exod 3:18 in requesting that the people be allowed to leave Egypt. The request only results in Pharaoh's determination to increase the oppression of the Hebrews. His design is to keep them busy, drain their energies, diffuse the likelihood of their reflecting on their situation and giving in to restless imagination about allegiance to anyone but himself (vv. 4-19). Moses and Aaron remain in the background as the officers of the people try to reason with Pharaoh regarding the intensified oppression. Being turned away by Pharaoh, the Hebrew officers rebuke Moses and Aaron for bringing this greater evil upon the people (vv. 20-21). The likelihood of the successful implementation of God's decision to free the slaves appears exceedingly dim at this juncture; not only Pharaoh but the slaves themselves reject the mission announced by Moses and Aaron.

In the narrative of 5:1-21 the biblical writer poignantly sets before us what appears to be an inevitable stage in the movement toward liberation and redemption. On the one hand, we see the intransigence of the oppressor. To deliberately hold others in bondage is not a careless, vacillating enterprise. Those in bondage are really *bound*, held firmly, and any suggestion or hint of loosening those bonds instinctively causes the oppressor to tighten the grip. Passage out of such bondage does not take place as the result of a simple request nor is it accomplished through human reasoning and negotiation. Bondage involves a firm commitment on the part of the oppressor and movement out of it must be undertaken through struggle, conflict.

On the other hand, this narrative demonstrates that the struggle demanded by the process of liberation initially brings discomfort, probably pain, to those who are bound, just as the pulling and twisting necessary to untie ropes around one's hands might lead one bound to protest: "Leave the bonds for the unloosening process is too painful." This is the response of the slaves following the initial confrontation with Pharaoh (5:20-21). It is this same pain which Moses brings to Yahweh (5:22-23). In God's response (6:1) we see that Pharaoh's determination is matched by the divine resolve to free Israel from Pharaoh's oppressive grip.

Thus the writers delineate the unyielding and mutually exclusive claims being made upon Israel. The unit opens and closes with God's resolve. Pharaoh's resolve is described in the intervening verses. The stage is set for the bitter and prolonged struggle between Yahweh and Pharaoh which is recounted in the narratives about the plagues. This, however, is delayed by a second account of Moses' call and commission which has been inserted in Exod 6:2—7:7.

GOD'S NAME AND GOD'S CALL REPEATED
6:2—7:7

²And God said to Moses, "I am the Lord. ³I appeared to Abraham, to Isaac, and to Jacob, as God Almighty, but by my name the Lord I did not make myself known to them. ⁴I also established my covenant with them, to give them the land of Canaan, the land in which they dwelt as sojourners. ⁵Moreover I have heard the groaning of the people of Israel whom the Egyptians hold in bondage and I have remembered my covenant. ⁶Say therefore to the people of Israel, 'I am the Lord, and I will bring you out from under the burdens of the Egyptians, and I will deliver you from their bondage, and I will redeem you with an outstretched arm and with great acts of judgment, ⁷and I will take you for my people, and I will be your God; and you shall know that I am the Lord your God, who has brought you out from under the burdens of the Egyptians. ⁸And I will bring you into the land which I swore to give to Abraham, to Isaac, and to Jacob; I will give it to you for a possession. I am the Lord.'" ⁹Moses spoke thus to the people of Israel; but they did not listen to Moses, because of their broken spirit and their cruel bondage.

¹⁰And the Lord said to Moses, ¹¹"Go in, tell Pharaoh king of Egypt to let the people of Israel go out of his land." ¹²But Moses said to the Lord, "Behold, the people of Israel have not listened to me; how then shall Pharaoh

listen to me, who am a man of uncircumcised lips?" ¹³But the Lord spoke to Moses and Aaron, and gave them a charge to the people of Israel and to Pharaoh king of Egypt to bring the people of Israel out of the land of Egypt.

¹⁴These are the heads of their fathers' houses: the sons of Reuben, the first-born of Israel: Hanoch, Pallu, Hezron, and Carmi; these are the families of Reuben. ¹⁵The sons of Simeon: Jemuel, Jamin, Ohad, Jachin, Zohar, and Shaul, the son of a Canaanite woman; these are the families of Simeon. ¹⁶These are the names of the sons of Levi according to their generations: Gershon, Kohath, and Merari, the years of the life of Levi being a hundred and thirty-seven years. ¹⁷The sons of Gershon: Libni and Shimei, by their families. ¹⁸The sons of Kohath: Amram, Izhar, Hebron, and Uzziel, the years of the life of Kohath being a hundred and thirty-three years. ¹⁹The sons of Merari: Mahli and Mushi. These are the families of the Levites according to their generations. ²⁰Amram took to wife Jochebed his father's sister and she bore him Aaron and Moses, the years of the life of Amram being one hundred and thirty-seven years. ²¹The sons of Izhar: Korah, Nepheg, and Zichri. ²²And the sons of Uzziel: Mishael, Elzaphan, and Sithri. ²³Aaron took to wife Elisheba, the daughter of Amminadab and the sister of Nahshon; and she bore him Nadab, Abihu, Eleazar, and Ithamar. ²⁴The sons of Korah: Assir, Elkanah, and Abiasaph; these are the families of the Korahites. ²⁵Eleazar, Aaron's son, took to wife one of the daughters of Putiel; and she bore him Phinehas. These are the heads of the fathers' houses of the Levites by their families.

²⁶These are the Aaron and Moses to whom the Lord said: "Bring out the people of Israel from the land of Egypt by their hosts." ²⁷It was they who spoke to Pharaoh king of Egypt about bringing out the people of Israel from Egypt, this Moses and this Aaron.

²⁸On the day when the Lord spoke to Moses in the land of Egypt, ²⁹the Lord said to Moses, "I am the Lord; tell

Pharaoh king of Egypt all that I say to you." [30]But Moses said to the Lord, "Behold, I am of uncircumcised lips; how then shall Pharaoh listen to me?"   7 And the Lord said to Moses, "See, I make you as God to Pharaoh; and Aaron your brother shall be your prophet. [2]You shall speak all that I command you; and Aaron your brother shall tell Pharaoh to let the people of Israel go out of his land. [3]But I will harden Pharaoh's heart, and though I multiply my signs and wonders in the land of Israel, [4]Pharaoh will not listen to you; then I will lay my hand upon Israel and bring forth my hosts, my people the sons of Israel, out of the land of Egypt by great acts of judgment. [5]And the Egyptians shall know that I am the Lord, when I stretch forth my hand upon Egypt and bring out the people of Israel from among them." [6]And Moses and Aaron did so; they did as the Lord commanded them. [7]Now Moses was eighty years old, and Aaron eighty-three years old, when they spoke to Pharaoh.

This narrative reasserts, even in the face of struggle and pain, the divine call to exodus. It follows the renewed witness to oppression and the full recognition of the enhanced pain which is entailed in the struggle for liberation. It also extends courage and sustenance for the challenge which accompanied the gift of the divine name.

This is a second account of events already reported in Exod 3:1—4:17. As such it contains a slightly different version of the gift of the divine name as well as another account of the commissioning of Moses and a summarizing overview of the divine plan of events which are about to take place.

Signs of Priestly composition abound in these verses. One indication is found in the two divine monologues (6:2-8 and 7:1-5). In typical Priestly fashion these lengthy divine statements are followed by notices that things happened according to God's word (6:9a and 7:6). The "not listening" mentioned in Exod 6:9 is also a motif which recurs with reference to Pharaoh in the Priestly redaction of the plagues (see 7:22; 8:15, 19; 9:12). A second indication of Priestly composition is the reference to God as "God Almighty" (*El Shaddai*) in 6:3. A third is the attention given to Aaron. Exod 6:14-25 is a family genealogy which must have origi-nally belonged to the high priestly family since it focuses on the family of Levi and within that narrows even further to trace an increasingly exclusive line to Aaron, his son and grandson. Priestly focus upon Aaron is also evident in 6:30—7:2 where the objection which is part of the stereo-typed structure of call narrative (see above on 3:1—4:17) has been used to add equal attention to the commission and role of Aaron alongside Moses in the exodus event. Finally, it is typical of the Priestly writer to record the ages of Israel's great heroes at the time of their appearance in God's great plan of saving history (7:7; cf. Gen 5:1-32; 7:6, 11; 9:29; 11:10-26; 16:16; 17:1; etc.)

In contrast to the account of Exod 3:1—4:17, the Priestly writer sets the call and commissioning of Moses in Egypt, not Midian. Whereas in the earlier account the signal of divine involvement had been the burning bush, here the divine authority is rooted solely in the Divinity's word. Particularly striking is the recurring formula of God's self-revelation: "I am the Lord" (6:2, 6, 7, 8, 29; 7:5). The words convey more than mere information. They somehow bear the power and authority and mystery of the divine presence itself.

Exod 6:3 is the Priestly writer's version of the tradition about the gift of the divine name, Yahweh, to Moses (cf. Exod 3:13-15). According to this writer, a new era in God's relationship with Israel is signalled by the fact that the God who had previously been addressed as God Almighty (*El Shaddai*) now is called by a new name. The Priestly writer stresses the continuity between the Promise-Maker of ages past and Yahweh who now acts to bring the promise to fulfillment by freeing the oppressed. It is one God now being faithful to an ancient promise in a new and unprecedented way (cf. Gen 17:1).

The Priestly writer also stresses continuity with the past by including the genealogy of Exod 6:14-25. It legitimates the leadership of Moses and Aaron by relating them to their roots. The list begins much like that of Gen 46:8-27, but soon focuses exclusively on the Aaronic line. The function of the genealogy in this context is to stress that the chosen and commissioned leaders of this exodus movement are truly Israelite, i.e., true descendants of one of the sons of Jacob. The text shows signs that the genealogy was artificially inserted into an already-existing narrative for Exod 6:28-30 basically restate the content of those verses which preceded the introduction of Aaron and Moses and their roots (cf. 6:10-12).

Finally, in Exod 7:1-7 the Priestly writer anticipates the full exodus movement, complete with details which will be borne out in the following chapters. If readers keep these verses in mind as they proceed through the narratives about the plagues and the exodus event, it will be clear to them that all happened in accord with God's word and that is the theological message which the Priestly writer intended to convey.

THE STRUGGLE
7:8—11:10

The early chapters in the Book of Exodus set the scene for subsequent events: the Hebrews cried out under the weight of their Egyptian bondage and God involved the Divine Self in loosening the bonds, a process which Moses was chosen to mediate. The stage is thus set for the next step, summoning Pharaoh to abide by God's decision. Exod 7:8—11:10 describes struggle: God's persistent imperative that Pharaoh let go of the Hebrews, Pharaoh's persistent refusal to do so, and the resulting disasters which plague the Egyptians.

On the one hand, much attention in biblical scholarship has been given to show that the plagues are best understood as natural phenomena associated with the annual flooding of the Nile River in Egypt. According to this view, the "supernatural" or miraculous element in the plagues lay not so much in the marvelous character of the events themselves as in God's direction and use of the courses of nature for the welfare of the chosen people. On the other hand, it is important to recognize that "natural" and "supernatural" are more clearly distinct categories for modern believers than for ancient peoples. That nature operated according to its own set of laws was an idea unknown in ancient times. Thus, while a modern person might view the annual flooding of the Nile as a natural event, an ancient believer would have been less inclined to distinguish such an event from God's work in the world.

A survey of the plague narratives (Exod 7:8—11:10) indicates that the ten individual stories show remarkable likenesses to one another in structure, motif, and phraseology. These recurring features suggest that the narratives are not so much eyewitness records of spectacular events which took place in ancient Egypt as they are artificially constructed literary pieces intended to serve a message about the divine struggle for human liberation. While the length and redundancy of the plague narratives make for somewhat tedious reading, the writers may be suggesting something of the character of redemption itself, i.e., that the movement from bondage to freedom does not happen quickly or easily. It entails real conflict with real people whose self-interest is served by perpetuating the bondage of others. The texts make clear that Pharaoh heard and understood God's command. Every possible opportunity was given for him to align his policy with God's movement in the human arena; but evil has a profound grip. The unrelenting hardness of Pharaoh's heart is matched only by God's uncompromising commitment to human liberation. Hence, the length and violence of the struggle which is recounted in these stories.

The greater part of the plague narratives comes from the hand of the Yahwist. According to this narrative strand, the pollution of water with blood (7:14-18, 20b-21a, 23-24) was followed by plagues of frogs (7:25; 8:1-4, 8-15), flies (8:20-32), the death of cattle (9:1-7), hail (9:13-35), locusts (10:1-20), and darkness (10:21-29). The final blow was the death of the firstborn in Egyptian households (11:1-8).

The Yahwist's version of the plagues is carried forward by a series of dialogues between God and Moses and between Moses and Pharaoh. With a few exceptions, the accounts follow this pattern:

1) The Lord instructs Moses to approach Pharaoh and initiate dialogue with him saying, "Thus says the Lord."

2) The word of the Lord which Moses is to deliver to Pharaoh characteristically includes the Lord's demand, "Let my people go, that they may serve me." This command is followed by a threat of the plague which will take place should Pharaoh refuse.

3) The Lord sends the plague and its effects are described.

4) In the face of the effects of the plague, Pharaoh calls Moses to negotiate. Pharaoh appears to concede in promising to let the people go if Moses will intercede for the removal of the plague.

5) Moses intercedes and the plague is removed.

6) Pharaoh's heart is hardened when the disaster brought on by the plague is removed. The Yahwist concludes the story with the observation that Pharaoh did not let the people go. This line sets the scene for the sequence to begin again in the subsequent plague story.

In the Yahwist's version of the plagues, Moses' activity has similarities with the work of prophetic figures. He introduces his announcement of God's commands to Pharoah with a messenger formula ("Thus says the Lord") which often appears on the lips of prophetic figures (1 Kgs 21:19; Jer 2:2, 5; 6:6, 9, 16, 21, 22; Amos 1:3, 6, 9, 11, 13; 2:1, 4, 6). Moses' announcement of the plagues before they occur and his intercession with God for their abatement are additional prophetic characteristics (cf. 1 Kgs 13:1-6; 17:17-24; 20:13-21; Isa 7:18-25; 8:5-8; 42:14-17; Amos 7:1-3, 4-6; Jer 14:1-9, 19-22; 18:20).

In addition to a common structure and a common view of Moses' role, the Yahwist's version of the plagues is characterized by the appearance of two motifs. The first is the notice that one of the purposes of the plagues is "knowing Yahweh" (see 8:10, 22; 9:29; 11:7). This motif is initiated by the Yahwist's account of Pharaoh's response to Moses the very first time the two met. When Moses delivered Yahweh's command, Pharaoh said: "Who is the Lord, that I should heed his voice and let Israel go? I do not know the Lord, and moreover I will not let Israel go" (5:2). A second motif which the Yahwist frequently records is that the Lord made a distinction between the Egyptians and Israelites in Egypt

(8:22; 9:4, 6; 9:26; 11:7). Although these two motifs recur several times, the Yahwist does not follow a rigid pattern in their use. That is to say, although they appear frequently in the overall account, they are not necessarily present in each individual plague story. The reader also notes that rigid linguistic formulas are not present in the appearance of these motifs.

Like the Yahwist's plague stories, the other major contribution to the overall narrative, that of the Priestly writer, also bears distinguishing characteristics. The two plague stories which are commonly viewed as coming whole and entire from the Priestly hand are the plagues of gnats (8:16-19) and boils (9:8-12). These two stories share this pattern:

1) God commands Moses to initiate actions through which the plague will be effected.
2) The instructions are followed and the plague ensues.
3) A reference to Egyptian magicians.
4) Pharaoh's heart is hardened and he did not listen. Thus, the stage is set for the next plague story.

It is noteworthy that the magicians appear only in the Priestly account of the plague. Likewise, although Aaron appears from time to time in the Yahwist's account of the plagues, he appears more consistently and prominently in the Priestly version. The Priestly writer presents the plagues as coming about through some action of Moses and/or Aaron whereas in the Yahwist's account the plagues come directly from the Divinity. The Priestly writer concludes his accounts of the gnats and boils by saying that all happened according to God's word which turns the reader's attention back to the Priestly introduction to the plague narratives in Exod 7:1-7.

Familiarity with these characteristics of P's plague stories enables the reader to detect the same writer's additions to stories originally told by the Yahwist. For example, in Exod 7:19-20a, 21b-22 one recognizes the Priestly hand in the major role played by Aaron in effecting the plague, the presence of the magicians, and the familiar extension of the notation about Pharaoh's hardened heart, i.e., that "he would not listen...as the Lord had said." A second clear instance of the Priestly writer's addition to a Yahwist story appears in the account of the second plague (7:25—8:15). Although most of the story belongs to the Yahwist, the prominence of Aaron and the presence of the magicians in Exod 8:5-7 signals a Priestly addition as does the concluding line, that Pharaoh "hardened his heart, and would not listen to them; as the Lord had said" (8:15b).

The Priestly writer's hand can be found in the programmatic introduction to the plagues account which appears in 7:1-7 and in the concluding summary which appears in 11:9-10. In these texts the Priestly writer states his understanding of the purpose of the plagues: Pharaoh's not listening was known ahead of time by God (7:4) and was used so that God's wonders could be multiplied (11:9).

Some scholars detect characteristics of Elohist writing in a few of the plague stories. The Elohist's contribution to these chapters, however, is so minimal and fragmentary that we shall forego a treatment of it here. Additional presentations of the plague tradition can be found in Ps 78:44-51 and Ps 105:28-36.

Finally, before examining the individual plague stories it might be well to view the overall portraits of the chief actors of this struggle. The portrait of Pharaoh is drawn in broad outline, almost artificially, as a vague silhouette. He has no name, no specific place on the timeline of Egypt's history. His lack of personal characteristics makes it difficult for later generations of readers to feel sympathy or compassion or any sense of identity with Pharaoh. Thus readers are offered no basis for emulating him.

At the same time the narratives make clear that the God of the plagues is not a Divinity arbitrarily bent on destruction. Instead, God is the One who is zealous and uncompromising with regard to the welfare of the oppressed. The Divinity repeatedly calls for Pharaoh to join in mediating God's saving work in the world.

The lengthy narratives about the struggle between Yahweh and Pharaoh invite readers' consideration of the mystery of human resistance to the activity wherein God frees persons for the Divine Self. Furthermore, the theologians who passed on these stories invite believers to view the struggle for human liberation as a locus for "knowing Yahweh" and for experiencing the power of God.

PRELUDE
7:8-13

> 8And the Lord said to Moses and Aaron, 9"When Pharaoh says to you, 'Prove yourselves by working a miracle,' then you shall say to Aaron, 'Take your rod and cast it down before Pharaoh, that it may become a serpent.'" 10So Moses and Aaron went to Pharaoh and did as the Lord commanded: Aaron cast down his rod before Pharaoh and his servants, and it became a serpent. 11Then Pharaoh summoned the wise men and the sorcerers; and they also, the magicians of Egypt, did the same by their secret arts. 12For every man cast down his rod, and they became serpents. But Aaron's rod swallowed up their rods. 13Still Pharaoh's heart was hardened, and he would not listen to them; as the Lord had said.

Between the programmatic introduction to the overall plague narratives (7:1-7) and the account of the first plague (7:14-24) we find a brief prelude which sets in relief the two sides of the opposition which will be presented in the following chapters. The Priestly writer's hand is evident in the prominence given to Aaron, the presence of the magicians, and the concluding formula that Pharaoh did not listen "as the Lord had said." At issue in these verses is the question of credentials. However, the writer hints at what is to follow when he shows that nothing is proved by the working of a miracle. The stumbling block throughout the plague narratives is not any uncertainty on Pharaoh's part that Moses truly represents God's demands. Rather, the consistent stumbling block is Pharaoh's hardened heart.

WATER POLLUTION: THE FIRST PLAGUE
7:14-24

¹⁴Then the Lord said to Moses, "Pharaoh's heart is hardened, he refuses to let the people go. ¹⁵Go to Pharaoh in the morning, as he is going out to the water; wait for him by the river's brink, and take in your hand the rod which was turned into a serpent. ¹⁶And you shall say to him, 'The Lord, the God of the Hebrews, sent me to you, saying, "Let my people go, that they may serve me in the wilderness; and behold, you have not yet obeyed." ¹⁷Thus says the Lord, "By this you shall know that I am the Lord: behold, I will strike the water that is in the Nile with the rod that is in my hand, and it shall be turned to blood, ¹⁸and the fish in the Nile shall die, and the Nile shall become foul, and the Egyptians will loathe to drink water from the Nile." ' " ¹⁹And the Lord said to Moses, "Say to Aaron, 'Take your rod and stretch out your hand over the waters of Egypt, over their rivers, their canals, and their ponds, and all their pools of water, that they may become blood; and there shall be blood throughout all the land of Egypt, both in vessels of wood and in vessels of stone.' "

²⁰Moses and Aaron did as the Lord commanded; in the sight of Pharaoh and in the sight of his servants, he lifted up the rod and struck the water that was in the Nile, and all the water that was in the Nile turned to blood. ²¹And the fish in the Nile died; and the Nile became foul, so that the Egyptians could not drink water from the Nile; and there was blood throughout all the land of Egypt. ²²But the magicians of Egypt did the same by their secret arts; so Pharaoh's heart remained hardened, and he would not listen to them; as the Lord had said. ²³Pharaoh turned and went into his house, and he did not lay even this to heart. ²⁴And all the Egyptians dug round about the Nile for water to drink, for they could not drink the water of the Nile.

It is possible that the starting point for this story, the pollution of Egypt's water supply by blood, was a redness in the water associated with the annual flooding of the Nile River. Whatever the case, the concern of the biblical writer was to tell of God's insistence upon freedom for the Hebrews and of Pharaoh's refusal to cooperate. Accordingly, in verse 17 we are told that the plague took place in order that Pharaoh might know Yahweh, although this purpose was not accomplished. Pharaoh's distance even from the needs of his own people is clearly set forth here when the narrator says that Pharaoh paid no attention to the negative effects of the plague while his people searched for water to drink (vv. 23-24).

The appearance of the messenger formula ("Thus says the Lord") along with the stereotyped command ("Let my people go") and the motif of "knowing Yahweh" suggest that the bulk of this account of the first plague comes from the Yahwist's hand. However, traces of the Priestly strand can be seen in verses 19-20a and in 21b-22 where a prominent part in effecting the plague is assigned to Aaron, the magician motif occurs, and an explicit connection is made between Pharaoh's hardness of heart and his not listening "as the Lord had said." In these short segments the Priestly writer heightened the wonder of the event by saying that not only the Nile but all of Egypt's waters were polluted by the plague.

While the picture of Egyptian magicians using secret arts against their own people might seem humorous, their success as narrated here underlines the fact that Yahweh's struggle with Pharaoh was in every way a real struggle and as such was marked by ambiguity and tension.

FROGS: THE SECOND PLAGUE
7:25—8:15

²⁵Seven days passed after the Lord had struck the Nile. **8** Then the Lord said to Moses, "Go in to Pharaoh and say to him, 'Thus says the Lord, "Let my people go, that they may serve me. ²But if you refuse to let them go,

behold, I will plague all your country with frogs; ³the Nile shall swarm with frogs which shall come up into your house, and into your bedchamber and on your bed, and into the houses of your servants and of your people, and into your ovens and your kneading bowls; ⁴the frogs shall come up on you and your people and on all your servants.""'" ⁵And the Lord said to Moses, "Say to Aaron, 'Stretch out your hand with your rod over the rivers, over the canals, and over the pools, and cause frogs to come upon the land of Egypt!'" ⁶So Aaron stretched out his hand over the waters of Egypt; and the frogs came up and covered the land of Egypt. ⁷But the magicians did the same by their secret arts, and brought frogs upon the land of Egypt.

⁸Then Pharaoh called Moses and Aaron, and said, "Entreat the Lord to take away the frogs from me and from my people; and I will let the people go to sacrifice to the Lord." ⁹Moses said to Pharaoh, "Be pleased to command me when I am to entreat, for you and for your servants and for your people, that the frogs be destroyed from you and your houses and be left only in the Nile." ¹⁰And he said, "Tomorrow." Moses said, "Be it as you say, that you may know that there is no one like the Lord our God. ¹¹The frogs shall depart from you and your houses and your servants and your people; they shall be left only in the Nile." ¹²So Moses and Aaron went out from Pharaoh; and Moses cried to the Lord concerning the frogs, as he had agreed with Pharaoh. ¹³And the Lord did according to the word of Moses; the frogs died out of the houses and courtyards and out of the fields. ¹⁴And they gathered them together in heaps, and the land stank. ¹⁵But when Pharaoh saw that there was a respite, he hardened his heart, and would not listen to them; as the Lord had said.

Like the account of the first plague, this story is the result of mixed authorship. Most of 7:25—8:4 and 8:8-15 bears the marks of the Yahwist writer, for example in the use of the messenger formula, the command to "Let my people go," the "knowing Yahweh" motif, Moses' intercessory activity, and the first hint of a concession on Pharaoh's part. On the other hand, the role exercised by Aaron and the presence of the magicians in 8:5-7, as well as the final notice of Pharaoh's not listening "as the Lord had said" in 8:15b, suggest that the Priestly writer made additions to the basic narrative of the Yahwist.

It is reasonable to believe that the annual flooding of the Nile provided a situation ripe for the breeding of multitudes of frogs. Thus it is possible that, as with the first plague, the event narrated here had its starting point in regular processes of nature. Here, the writers say, Yahweh countered Pharaoh's obstinacy with the frog menace although the Egyptian magicians were able to do the same.

For the first time in the plague narratives, the divine struggle for human liberation appears to move closer to a resolution when Pharaoh agrees to let the slaves go in return for the removal of the plague. Moses responded at once to Pharaoh's concession. He separated the "knowledge of Yahweh" from the wonder of the plague (cf. 7:17) and linked it instead with God's graciousness in causing the disappearance of the frog menace at a time set by Pharaoh himself. However, God's concession in removing the plague did not result in Pharaoh's "knowing Yahweh" but in his renewed hardness of heart. Thus, the scene is set for the continuation of the struggle.

GNATS: THE THIRD PLAGUE
8:16-19

> [16]Then the Lord said to Moses, "Say to Aaron, 'Stretch out your rod and strike the dust of the earth, that it may become gnats throughout all the land of Egypt.'" [17]And they did so; Aaron stretched out his hand with his rod, and struck the dust of the earth, and there came gnats on man and beast; all the dust of the earth became gnats throughout all the land of Egypt. [18]The magicians tried by their secret arts to bring forth gnats, but they could

not. So there were gnats on man and beast. [19]And the magicians said to Pharaoh, "This is the finger of God." But Pharaoh's heart was hardened, and he would not listen to them: as the Lord had said.

This brief account belongs wholly to the Priestly writer and may originally have represented an alternate tradition of what is now the fourth plague. That is to say, the present text may simply be a variant of the Yahwist's story of the plague of flies (8:20-32). The narrative succinctly presents the command to be given to Aaron, his fulfillment of the command which thereby sparked the plague of gnats, the presence of the magicians, and Pharaoh's hardness of heart expressed in the Priestly writer's customary manner.

What is new here in the progression of Yahweh's struggle with Pharaoh is the ineffectiveness of the Egyptian magicians' secret arts. Their powerlessness leads the magicians to the recognition of God, though their testimony regarding this does not touch Pharaoh's hardened heart and he did not listen "as the Lord had said."

FLIES: THE FOURTH PLAGUE
8:20-32

[20]Then the Lord said to Moses, "Rise up early in the morning and wait for Pharaoh, as he goes out to the water, and say to him, 'Thus says the Lord, "Let my people go, that they may serve me. [21]Else, if you will not let my people go, behold, I will send swarms of flies on you and your servants and your people, and into your houses; and the houses of the Egyptians shall be filled with swarms of flies, and also the ground on which they stand. [22]But on that day I will set apart the land of Goshen, where my people dwell, so that no swarms of flies shall be there; that you may know that I am the Lord in the midst of the earth. [23]Thus I will put a division between my people and your people. By tomorrow shall this sign be."'" [24]And the Lord did so; there came great

swarms of flies into the house of Pharaoh and into his servants' houses, and in all the land of Egypt the land was ruined by reason of the flies.

[25]Then Pharaoh called Moses and Aaron and said, "Go, sacrifice to your God within the land." [26]But Moses said, "It would not be right to do so; for we shall sacrifice to the Lord our God offerings abominable to the Egyptians. If we sacrifice offerings abominable to the Egyptians before their eyes, will they not stone us? [27]We must go three days' journey into the wilderness and sacrifice to the Lord our God as he will command us." [28]So Pharaoh said, "I will let you go, to sacrifice to the Lord your God in the wilderness; only you shall not go very far away. Make entreaty for me." [29]Then Moses said, "Behold, I am going out from you and I will pray to the Lord that the swarms of flies may depart from Pharaoh, from his servants, and from his people, tomorrow; only let not Pharaoh deal falsely again by not letting the people go to sacrifice to the Lord." [30]So Moses went out from Pharaoh and prayed to the Lord. [31]And the Lord did as Moses asked, and removed the swarms of flies from Pharaoh, from his servants, and from his people; not one remained. [32]But Pharaoh hardened his heart this time also, and did not let the people go.

This narrative begins much like that of the first plague story (cf. 7:15). Characteristics of the Yahwist's treatment of the plagues permeate the account. Like the preceding narratives, this story may have stemmed from regular processes of nature though the Yahwist was concerned to incorporate it into his story of God's continuing efforts at securing human freedom.

A motif which the Yahwist introduced here for the first time and which will come to its culmination in Yahweh's "passing over" the Hebrews' houses during the death of the firstborn is the distinction which God made between the chosen people and Egypt. This explains why Israel was untouched by the disasters plaguing the Egyptians. The

Yahwist offers this "setting apart" as yet one more way whereby Pharaoh might come to "know Yahweh."

Pharaoh's concession to Moses' demand (8:25-28) recalls 8:8 although here the motif is developed considerably. Moses is a shrewd negotiator who does not succumb to Pharaoh's invitations to compromise. Hopes for a resolution to Yahweh's struggle with Pharaoh are raised by Pharaoh's decision to release the slaves to worship in the wilderness. These hopes are dampened, however, by Moses' ominous recollection of the untrustworthy nature of Pharaoh's concession on the earlier occasion (see 8:29b). What Moses suspected came to be and once again a plague story ended where it began, with Pharaoh's obstinate refusal to cooperate with God's designs.

CATTLE: THE FIFTH PLAGUE
9:1-7

> **9** Then the Lord said to Moses, "Go in to Pharaoh, and say to him, 'Thus says the Lord, the God of the Hebrews, "Let my people go, that they may serve me. ²For if you refuse to let them go and still hold them, ³behold, the hand of the Lord will fall with a very severe plague upon your cattle which are in the field, the horses, the asses, the camels, the herds, and the flocks. ⁴But the Lord will make a distinction between the cattle of Israel and the cattle of Egypt, so that nothing shall die of all that belongs to the people of Israel."'" ⁵And the Lord set a time, saying, "Tomorrow the Lord will do this thing in the land." ⁶And on the morrow the Lord did this thing; all the cattle of the Egyptians died, but of the cattle of the people of Israel not one died. ⁷And Pharaoh sent, and behold, not one of the cattle of the Israelites was dead. But the heart of Pharaoh was hardened, and he did not let the people go.

While several characteristic elements of the Yahwist's plague narratives are missing (e.g., the "knowing Yahweh" motif, Pharaoh's concession, Moses' intercession), the "separation" motif is augmented in this brief account of the plague which struck the cattle of the Egyptians but did not touch the cattle of the Israelites. Tension mounts in Yahweh's struggle with Pharaoh as this story moves beyond menacing plagues (water pollution, insects, frogs) to the death of "all the cattle" of the Egyptians.

BOILS: THE SIXTH PLAGUE
9:8-12

[8]And the Lord said to Moses and Aaron, "Take handfuls of ashes from the kiln, and let Moses throw them toward heaven in the sight of Pharaoh. [9]And it shall become fine dust over all the land of Egypt, and become boils breaking out in sores on man and beast throughout all the land of Egypt." [10]So they took ashes from the kiln, and stood before Pharaoh, and Moses threw them toward heaven, and it became boils breaking out in sores on man and beast. [11]And the magicians could not stand before Moses because of the boils, for the boils were upon the magicians and upon all the Egyptians. [12]But the Lord hardened the heart of Pharaoh, and he did not listen to them; as the Lord had spoken to Moses.

This is the second of two plague narratives which come entirely from the hand of the Priestly writer (cf. 8:16-19). As in other Priestly accounts of the plagues, the magicians are present. Here, however, they are stripped of special powers. These masters of secret arts are themselves struck with boils just like the rest of the Egyptians. The notice that it was the Lord who hardened Pharaoh's heart coincides with the view which the Priestly writer set forth in his programmatic introduction to the plague narratives (7:1-7, especially v. 3). It reflects the writer's conviction that nothing takes place apart from Yahweh's control.

HAIL: THE SEVENTH PLAGUE
9:13-35

¹³Then the Lord said to Moses, "Rise up early in the morning and stand before Pharaoh, and say to him, 'Thus says the Lord, the God of the Hebrews, "Let my people go, that they may serve me. ¹⁴For this time I will send all my plagues upon your heart, and upon your servants and your people, that you may know that there is none like me in all the earth. ¹⁵For by now I could have put forth my hand and struck you and your people with pestilence, and you would have been cut off from the earth; ¹⁶but for this purpose have I let you live, to show you my power, so that my name may be declared throughout all the earth. ¹⁷You are still exalting yourself against my people, and will not let them go. ¹⁸Behold, tomorrow about this time, I will cause very heavy hail to fall, such as never has been in Egypt from the day it was founded until now. ¹⁹Now therefore send, get your cattle and all that you have in the field into safe shelter; for the hail shall come down upon every man and beast that is in the field and is not brought home, and they shall die."'" ²⁰Then he who feared the word of the Lord among the servants of Pharaoh made his slaves and his cattle flee into the houses; ²¹but he who did not regard the word of the Lord left his slaves and his cattle in the field.

²²And the Lord said to Moses, "Stretch forth your hand toward heaven, that there may be hail in all the land of Egypt, upon man and beast and every plant of the field throughout the land of Egypt." ²³Then Moses stretched forth his rod toward heaven; and the Lord sent thunder and hail, and fire ran down to the earth. And the Lord rained hail upon the land of Egypt; ²⁴there was hail, and fire flashing continually in the midst of the hail, very heavy hail, such as had never been in all the land of Egypt since it became a nation. ²⁵The hail struck down everything that was in the field throughout all the land of Egypt, both man and beast; and the hail struck down

every plant of the field, and shattered every tree of the field. [26]Only in the land of Goshen, where the people of Israel were, there was no hail.

[27]Then Pharaoh sent, and called Moses and Aaron, and said to them, "I have sinned this time; the Lord is in the right, and I and my people are in the wrong. [28]Entreat the Lord; for there has been enough of this thunder and hail; I will let you go, and you shall stay no longer." [29]Moses said to him, "As soon as I have gone out of the city, I will stretch out my hands to the Lord; the thunder will cease, and there will be no more hail, that you may know that the earth is the Lord's. [30]But as for you and your servants, I know that you do not yet fear the Lord God." [31](The flax and the barley were ruined, for the barley was in the ear and the flax was in bud. [32]But the wheat and the spelt were not ruined, for they are late in coming up.) [33]So Moses went out of the city from Pharaoh, and stretched out his hands to the Lord; and the thunder and the hail ceased, and the rain no longer poured upon the earth. [34]But when Pharaoh saw that the rain and the hail and the thunder had ceased, he sinned yet again, and hardened his heart, he and his servants. [35]So the heart of Pharaoh was hardened, and he did not let the people of Israel go; as the Lord had spoken through Moses.

There is much similarity between the structure, motifs, and terminology of this account and other plague narratives recorded by the Yahwist. This is true with regard to the command ("Let my people go") introduced by the messenger formula ("Thus says the Lord"), the threat, plague, Pharaoh's concession, and Moses' intercession. Several new elements, however, also appear here. Verses 14-16 (which some scholars regard as a gloss) offer an explanation for the continuation of these seemingly unsuccessful plagues. Here a unique interpretation is given to the "knowing Yahweh" motif. Whereas in previous stories this motif was connected with the sending of a plague (7:17), the removal of a plague (8:10), and the distinction God made between Israel and

Egypt (8:22), here God is known in the restraint which the divine power has exercised thus far with regard to the Egyptians. Thus graciousness, and not divine powerlessness, accounts for the prolongation of the plagues.

A second element which appears here for the first time may also be a gloss. In verses 19-21 we encounter distinctions between the Egyptians who "feared the word of the Lord" and those who did not. For the first time God's judgment is linked with personal decisions made by Egyptians other than Pharaoh.

A gloss of a different nature appears in verses 31-32. We have in these verses a rather studied explanation of exactly what was ruined by the hail and why. The lines offer readers a reasonable explanation of how it was that there were any plants left for the locusts of the next plague to destroy.

Finally, for the first time in the plague narratives Pharaoh's failure to cooperate with God's action is described as sin (vv. 27, 34).

LOCUSTS: THE EIGHTH PLAGUE
10:1-20

10 Then the Lord said to Moses, "Go in to Pharaoh; for I have hardened his heart and the heart of his servants, that I may show these signs of mine among them, ²and that you may tell in the hearing of your son and of your son's son how I have made sport of the Egyptians and what signs I have done among them; that you may know that I am the Lord."

³So Moses and Aaron went in to Pharaoh, and said to him, "Thus says the Lord, the God of the Hebrews, 'How long will you refuse to humble yourself before me? Let my people go, that they may serve me. ⁴For if you refuse to let my people go, behold, tomorrow I will bring locusts into your country, ⁵and they shall cover the face of the land; and they shall eat what is left to you after the hail, and they shall eat every tree of yours which grows in the field, ⁶and they shall fill your houses, and the houses of all your

servants and of all the Egyptians; as neither your fathers nor your grandfathers have seen, from the day they came on earth to this day.'" Then he turned and went out from Pharaoh.

⁷And Pharaoh's servants said to him, "How long shall this man be a snare to us? Let the men go, that they may serve the Lord their God; do you not yet understand that Egypt is ruined?" ⁸So Moses and Aaron were brought back to Pharaoh; and he said to them, "Go, serve the Lord your God; but who are to go?" ⁹And Moses said, "We will go with our young and our old; we will go with our sons and daughters and with our flocks and herds, for we must hold a feast to the Lord." ¹⁰And he said to them, "The Lord be with you, if ever I let you and your little ones go! Look, you have some evil purpose in mind. ¹¹No! Go, the men among you, and serve the Lord, for that is what you desire." And they were driven out from Pharaoh's presence.

¹²Then the Lord said to Moses, "Stretch out your hand over the land of Egypt for the locusts, that they may come upon the land of Egypt, and eat every plant in the land, all that the hail has left." ¹³So Moses stretched forth his rod over the land of Egypt, and the Lord brought an east wind upon the land all that day and all that night; and when it was morning the east wind had brought the locusts. ¹⁴And the locusts came up over all the land of Egypt, and settled on the whole country of Egypt, such a dense swarm of locusts as had never been before, nor ever shall be again. ¹⁵For they covered the face of the whole land, so that the land was darkened, and they ate all the plants in the land and all the fruit of the trees which the hail had left; not a green thing remained, neither tree nor plant of the field, through all the land of Egypt. ¹⁶Then Pharaoh called Moses and Aaron in haste, and said, "I have sinned against the Lord your God, and against you. ¹⁷Now therefore, forgive my sin, I pray you, only this once, and entreat the Lord your God only to remove this death from me." ¹⁸So he went out from Pharaoh, and entreated the Lord. ¹⁹And the Lord turned a very strong

west wind, which lifted the locusts and drove them into the Red Sea; not a single locust was left in all the country of Egypt. [20]But the Lord hardened Pharaoh's heart, and he did not let the children of Israel go.

The narrative recounting the eighth plague presents familiar content fashioned according to the Yahwist's established pattern. The pattern, however, is not merely repeated here. It is interwoven with unique features which attest to the artistry of the writers and which serve a plot which grows in complexity and tension as it nears its end.

Exod 10:1b-2 (which may be a late gloss added to the Yahwist's story) offers yet another interpretation of the reason for the plagues. Here the "knowing Yahweh" motif is given a new direction. Yahweh claims to have "made sport of" the Egyptians not so much for the Egyptians to know the Divine Self but in order that Israel itself might know Yahweh and that this would be the subject of Israel's proclamation about Yahweh from generation to generation.

Another new development occurs when, according to 10:7, Pharaoh's servants plead with him to concede to Yahweh's demands. The servants echo the "How long?" of Moses and Aaron (v. 3) and commend to Pharaoh a course of action ("Let the men go") which approximates Yahweh's demand even though it does not measure up to its fullness which includes women and children ("Let my people go"). This plea on the part of his servants leads Pharaoh to initiate negotiations with Moses once again even amidst repeated reminders of Pharaoh's obstinacy (Exod 10:1, 3, 7b). However, just as in Exod 8:25-28, Pharaoh tried to negotiate the release on his own terms (Exod 10:8-11). In response Moses and Aaron insist that Yahweh does not make distinctions among the chosen people. All are called to service. Hopes for an immediate resolution to the struggle are lost when Yahweh's two spokespersons are thrown out of Pharaoh's presence.

Several elements in this story heighten the tension of the overall plague narratives and may subtly turn our attention to what is yet to happen. The east wind which brings the locusts (10:13) will be echoed in the east wind which later will turn the sea into dry land allowing the Hebrews to cross (Exod 14:21). Attention to the event at the sea may also be occasioned by the notice that, following Pharaoh's apparent concession (10:16-17) and Moses' intercession (10:18), the locusts were driven into the Red Sea. Finally, the writer may have intended some irony when he makes Pharaoh refer to the plague of locusts as a "death" (10:17). In a short time that word will take on new meaning for the tyrant (see Exod 11). The end of this narrative resembles that of other plague stories recorded by the Yahwist. Exod 10:20 explicitly records that Pharaoh did not let the people go (cf. 8:32; 9:7).

DARKNESS: THE NINTH PLAGUE
10:21-29

21Then the Lord said to Moses, "Stretch out your hand toward heaven that there may be darkness over the land of Egypt, a darkness to be felt." 22So Moses stretched out his hand toward heaven, and there was thick darkness in all the land of Egypt three days; 23they did not see one another, nor did any rise from his place for three days; but all the people of Israel had light where they dwelt. 24Then Pharaoh called Moses, and said, "Go, serve the Lord; your children also may go with you; only let your flocks and your herds remain behind." 25But Moses said, "You must also let us have sacrifices and burnt offerings, that we may sacrifice to the Lord our God. 26Our cattle also must go with us; not a hoof shall be left behind, for we must take of them to serve the Lord our God, and we do not know with what we must serve the Lord until we arrive there." 27But the Lord hardened Pharaoh's heart, and he would not let them go. 28Then Pharaoh said to him, "Get away from me; take heed to yourself; never see my face again; for in the day you see my face you shall die." 29Moses said, "As you say! I will not see your face again."

While it may be that the starting point for this narrative was an annual occurrence in the spring when terrible hot winds carried enough dust and sand off the desert to darken the sky, it is clear that the biblical writer puts the event in the service of Israel's account of the struggle between Yahweh and Pharaoh. While the story bears a structure and motif like other Yahwist plague stories, it also carries a heightened sense of struggle pressing toward resolution. On the one hand, the plague leads Pharaoh to greater concessions than he has been willing to allow up to now. The reader wonders if this time Moses will agree to the conditions set by Pharaoh, i.e., that all the people may go but their possessions be left behind. Or, having watched Pharaoh come so far as to allow Israel to go, the reader hopes that ultimately the tyrant will concede regarding possessions also.

On the other hand, verses 28-29 suggest an ending albeit not an anticipated resolution. With the threat of death Pharaoh appears to bring all discussion on the matter to a halt. The note of finality which marks the end of this narrative necessitates some drastic new measure by Yahweh. It is clear that repetition of the established pattern would not be successful and indeed that such an attempt would endanger Moses' life.

DEATH OF EGYPT'S FIRSTBORN:
THE TENTH PLAGUE
11:1-10

11 The Lord said to Moses, "Yet one plague more I will bring upon Pharaoh and upon Egypt; afterwards he will let you go hence; when he lets you go, he will drive you away completely. [2]Speak now in the hearing of the people, that they ask, every man of his neighbor and every woman of her neighbor, jewelry of silver and of gold." [3]And the Lord gave the people favor in the sight of the Egyptians. Moreover, the man Moses was very great in the land of Egypt, in the sight of Pharaoh's servants and in the sight of the people.

⁴And Moses said, "Thus says the Lord: About midnight I will go forth in the midst of Egypt; ⁵and all the first-born in the land of Egypt shall die, from the first-born of Pharaoh who sits upon his throne, even to the first-born of the maid-servant who is behind the mill; and all the first-born of the cattle. ⁶And there shall be a great cry throughout all the land of Egypt, such as there has never been, nor ever shall be again. ⁷But against any of the people of Israel, either man or beast, not a dog shall growl; that you may know that the Lord makes a distinction between the Egyptians and Israel. ⁸And all these your servants shall come down to me, and bow down to me, saying, 'Get you out, and all the people who follow you.' And after that I will go out." And he went out from Pharaoh in hot anger. ⁹Then the Lord said to Moses, "Pharaoh will not listen to you; that my wonders may be multiplied in the land of Egypt."

¹⁰Moses and Aaron did all these wonders before Pharaoh; and the Lord hardened Pharaoh's heart, and he did not let the people of Israel go out of his land.

The continuation of the plague tradition at the beginning of chapter eleven of Exodus comes as something of a surprise following, as it does, what appears to be a total breakdown of communication at the end of chapter ten. The resumption of the pattern which heretofore had yielded no resolution might lead the reader to expect no new result from this plague too. The content of verse 1, however, assures us that, although this plague might appear to be like the rest, in fact it will be different. The struggle between Yahweh and Pharaoh has indeed come to a point of resolution. Verses 2 and 3 confirm that the time for deliverance is at hand for conditions are now realized which Yahweh had described at the burning bush as belonging to the exodus event itself (see Exod 3:21-22).

Moses' announcement which appears in Exod 11:4-8a presumably is made to Pharaoh (see 11:8b). It is introduced with the same messenger formula which has marked the Yahwist's version of the foregoing plague stories. The hand of the Yahwist writer is also signalled by the appearance, indeed, the linking of two motifs prominent in the Yahwist's strand of the plague stories, i.e., Yahweh's distinction between the Israelites and the Egyptians and "knowing Yahweh" (v. 7).

A unique feature which sets this story apart from the other plague accounts is the absence of Moses' announcement of God's command to Pharaoh, "Let my people go." There no longer appears to be any opportunity for Pharaoh to decide. Moses simply announces that the death of the firstborn will take place and that it will ultimately result in the exodus. In addition, the fact that the story of Exod 11:1-10 comes to completion only in Exod 12:29-39 also leads us to connect the story of the tenth plague with the passover/exodus story which is to come. Thus, this story bears elements in common both with what precedes and with what follows it. As such it functions as the bridge between Yahweh's struggle with Pharaoh and Yahweh's victory over Pharaoh as demonstrated in the exodus event. The story of the death of Egypt's firstborn, then, is a turning point in the overall narrative of Exod 1-15.

The Priestly writer has appended a conclusion to the plague narratives in Exod 11:9-10. Essentially the Priestly writer summarizes here what he had stated in his introduction to the plague stories (see Exod 7:1-7). According to this writer, Yahweh was in control of matters throughout the struggle. It was Yahweh's doing that Pharaoh had not listened. God used this as an opportunity to multiply divine wonders.

PASSAGE: REDEMPTION AND RITUAL
12:1—13:16

If readers come to the end of chapter 11 with a heightened sense of expectation that Yahweh's struggle with Pharaoh is on the verge of a definitive resolution, the material which follows will come as something of a surprise. In Exodus 12:1—13:16 we are presented with the unlikely situation that, at this critical juncture, the Hebrew community paused to receive rather elaborate instruction regarding the ritual celebration of the event about to take place. In addition, we are told that the community conducted the rituals as commanded. Tucked in the middle of this concern for ritual is the Yahwist's modest account of the tenth plague which resulted in the exodus from Egypt (Exod 12:29-39).

Exodus 12:1—13:16 is a complex block of material in that it contains legislation for three originally separate festivals all of which at some stage of Israelite religion came to be connected with the exodus from Egypt. The three festivals are passover, unleavened bread, and the offering of the firstborn. Further complexity arises from the realization that the legislation given here derives, not from a single period, but from three separate sources of tradition representing a span of about five hundred years of religious practice. Thus the legislation for passover which appears in Exod 12:21-23 derives from an early source (possibly the Yahwist) and to that has been attached Deuteronomic legislation for the same feast (12:24-27a). Priestly legislation for passover both prefaces the earlier traditions (12:1-13) and follows them (12:43-49). Likewise, Deuteronomic directives for celebrating the feast of unleavened bread appear in Exod 13:3-10 although the Priestly writer had already addressed this topic in Exod 12:14-20. Finally, Exod 13:1-2 contains Priestly legislation for the offering of the firstborn while earlier legislation offered by the Deuteronomic tradition appears later in the chapter (13:11-16). Non-legislative units of material which appear in this section are the Yahwist's account of the tenth plague and the exodus from Egypt (12:29-39) and Priestly editorial summaries (12:28; 12:40-42; 12:50-51).

The Israelite feast of passover (*pesah*) probably had its beginnings in a rite observed by shepherds in the spring of the year as they prepared to migrate with their flocks to new grazing land. Scholars have suggested that the focal point of the observance was the smearing of blood of a sacrificial animal, a ritual designed to insure the safety and fertility of the flock during this time of passage. It has been further suggested that the shepherds, having prepared to leave, ate the sacrificial animal in haste. Some have connected this rite with the night of the first full moon of springtime.

Although this rite was probably practiced by the Hebrews' nomadic ancestors long before the time of the coming out of Egypt, it took on new meaning as later generations of Israelites continued the traditional ritual but reinterpreted it in light of Yahweh's deliverance from Egypt. Accordingly, Yahwistic worshippers viewed the ritual smearing of blood as a symbol of God's protection not of the flocks but of the people themselves as they undertook the passage from slavery to freedom.

Likewise, the feast of unleavened bread probably originated as an agricultural festival and only later was "historicized," i.e., given a meaning which was based not in nature religion but in an historical event. It is believed that at the beginning of the barley harvest in the spring farmers refrained for a time from profaning the new grain by mixing leaven with it. At some stage, certainly after they were an agricultural people themselves, the Israelites reinterpreted this harvest feast in light of Yahweh's deliverance from Egypt. The feasts of unleavened bread and passover were easily joined to one another since both were spring festivals and both had come to be associated with the event of the exodus from Egypt.

Finally, it appears to have been widespread custom in the ancient world to offer the firstborn of the womb to the deities. The firstborn was thought to embody most completely the best features of the parent generation. Consecrating this firstborn (through ritual sacrifice, destruction, or redemption) testified to the belief that all life belongs to the Sacred. One witnesses to this by setting aside the first and best for the Divinity. Because of the story of the death of the firstborn at the time of the coming out of Egypt, the customary practice of offering firstborn was easily reinterpreted and linked with the exodus event. In this way it also came to be associated with the feasts of passover and unleavened bread.

In sum, through their common association with one historical event, i.e., the deliverance from Egypt, the three originally independent rituals of passover, unleavened bread, and the offering of the firstborn came to be linked with one another. The complex traditions of Exod 12:1—13:16 represent various stages of development in the combination of these festivals with one another and with the exodus event which they had come to symbolize. For a proper understanding of Exod 12:1—13:16, then, readers must recognize that in the text as it now stands late cultic practices have been anachronistically linked with the narrative about the exodus event itself.

The text of Exod 12:1—13:16 testifies to a bond between redemption and ritual. Familiarity with passover ritual (smearing of blood, offering of firstborn) shaped the writer's design of the story about the events of the night of

exodus (see Exod 12:29-39). At the same time, later generations of worshippers ritually repeated those events seeking
thereby to make present again God's redeeming power in
their own lives.

PASSOVER
12:1-13

12 The Lord said to Moses and Aaron in the land of
Egypt, [2]"This month shall be for you the beginning of
months; it shall be the first month of the year for you.
[3]Tell all the congregation of Israel that on the tenth day of
this month they shall take every man a lamb according to
their fathers' houses, a lamb for a household; [4]and if the
household is too small for a lamb, then a man and his
neighbor next to his house shall take according to the
number of persons; according to what each can eat you
shall make your count for the lamb. [5]Your lamb shall be
without blemish, a male a year old; you shall take it from
the sheep or from the goats; [6]and you shall keep it until
the fourteenth day of this month, when the whole assembly of the congregation of Israel shall kill their lambs in
the evening. [7]Then they shall take some of the blood, and
put it on the two doorposts and the lintel of the houses in
which they eat them. [8]They shall eat the flesh that night,
roasted; with unleavened bread and bitter herbs they
shall eat it. [9]Do not eat any of it raw or boiled with water,
but roasted, its head with its legs and its inner parts.
[10]And you shall let none of it remain until the morning,
anything that remains until the morning you shall burn.
[11]In this manner you shall eat it: your loins girded, your
sandals on your feet, and your staff in your hand; and you
shall eat it in haste. It is the Lord's passover. [12]For I will
pass through the land of Egypt that night, and I will smite
all the first-born in the land of Egypt, both man and
beast; and on all the gods of Egypt I will execute judg-
ments: I am the Lord. [13]The blood shall be a sign for you,

upon the houses where you are; and when I see the blood, I will pass over you, and no plague shall fall upon you to destroy you, when I smite the land of Egypt.

The Priestly writer's prescriptions for the celebration of passover are considerably more elaborate than the more ancient legislation which is now placed after it in Exod 12:21-27. According to the Priestly writer, the passover meal was to consist of roasted lamb, unleavened bread, and bitter herbs. Specifications regarding the choice of the lamb and its preparation are minute and exact, as are directives for the time and manner in which the meal is to be eaten. Besides the ritual meal, the Priestly writer legislates for the smearing of blood on the doorposts (12:7). In Exod 12:13 the Priestly writer interprets this blood ritual as a means whereby Yahweh distinguished between Israelite and Egyptian houses during the tenth plague. However, in the more ancient account of the narrative about the tenth plague (Exod 11:4-8 and Exod 12:29-39) the Yahwist writer did not draw an explicit connection between Yahweh's "passing over" of Israelite houses and the blood smeared on doorposts.

At the conclusion of the legislation, the Priestly writer gives his interpretation of the festival which had been celebrated by countless generations of his nomadic ancestors and their neighbors. Because the Lord "passed over" the houses of Israel during the tenth plague, Israel keeps "passover" for the Lord.

UNLEAVENED BREAD
12:14-20

[14]"This day shall be for you a memorial day, and you shall keep it as a feast to the Lord; throughout your generations you shall observe it as an ordinance for ever. [15]Seven days you shall eat unleavened bread; on the first day you shall put away leaven out of your houses, for if any one eats what is leavened, from the first day until the

seventh day, that person shall be cut off from Israel. [16]On the first day you shall hold a holy assembly; no work shall be done on those days; but what every one must eat, that only may be prepared by you. [17]And you shall observe the feast of unleavened bread, for on this very day I brought your hosts out of the land of Egypt: therefore you shall observe this day, throughout your generations, as an ordinance for ever. [18]In the first month, on the fourteenth day of the month at evening, you shall eat unleavened bread, and so until the twenty-first day of the month at evening. [19]For seven days no leaven shall be found in your houses; for if any one eats what is leavened, that person shall be cut off from the congregation of Israel, whether he is a sojourner or a native of the land. [20]You shall eat nothing leavened; in all your dwellings you shall eat unleavened bread."

These verses represent Priestly legislation for the feast of unleavened bread. Two series of prescriptions appearing in vv. 14-16 and in vv. 18-20 are linked by the writer's statement of the meaning of the feast which appears in the center of the passage, v. 17. The fact that passover is never mentioned supports the view that the feast of unleavened bread was originally independent of passover. The feast of unleavened bread is said to have lasted for seven days (12:15, 19), a feature which also distinguishes it from passover, a meal eaten hastily during one night (12:10-11). Passover and unleavened bread are brought together by the one historical event which each of them eventually came to commemorate. Thus, the center of this passage, the statement of meaning in 12:17, supplies the point of contact between the originally independent feasts of unleavened bread and passover. Likewise, the calendar notice of 12:18 makes the beginning of the observance of unleavened bread coincide with the date of passover (cf. 12:2, 6).

MORE ANCIENT PASSOVER LEGISLATION
12:21-28

> [21]Then Moses called all the elders of Israel, and said to them, "Select lambs for yourselves according to your families, and kill the passover lamb. [22]Take a bunch of hyssop and dip it in the blood which is in the basin, and touch the lintel and the two doorposts with the blood which is in the basin; and none of you shall go out of the door of his house until the morning. [23]For the Lord will pass through to slay the Egyptians; and when he sees the blood on the lintel and on the two doorposts, the Lord will pass over the door, and will not allow the destroyer to enter your houses to slay you. [24]You shall observe this rite as an ordinance for you and for your sons for ever. [25]And when you come to the land which the Lord will give you, as he has promised, you shall keep this service. [26]And when your children say to you, 'What do you mean by this service?' [27]you shall say, 'It is the sacrifice of the Lord's passover, for he passed over the houses of the people of Israel in Egypt, when he slew the Egyptians but spared our houses.'" And the people bowed their heads and worshipped.
> [28]Then the people of Israel went and did so; as the Lord had commanded Moses and Aaron, so they did.

The Priestly writer's legislation regarding the celebration of passover (12:1-13) was portrayed as spoken by the Divinity to Moses and Aaron (cf. 12:1). The passover legislation in the present text is portrayed as delivered by Moses and thus in the overall text may be regarded as Moses' interpretation of God's instruction (12:1-13) regarding the festival.

Verses 21-23 are commonly regarded as stemming from the Yahwist. It is noteworthy that the legislation here is concerned only with a blood ritual. There is no mention of a meal. The prescriptions of vv. 21-22 are followed by the interpretation given to the ritual by the Yahwist. As in the Priestly version (12:13), here the blood ritual is connected with the distinction God made between Israelite and Egyptian houses at the time of the tenth plague (12:23).

The Deuteronomic writer presumably refers to the smearing of blood when he offers legislation for and theology of passover in 12:24-27. His concern is not so much with the rite itself as with its continuation in future generations and its meaning. Like the Yahwist before him (12:23), the Deuteronomist bases the meaning of the rite in God's own saving action. As Yahweh "passed over" us, so all future generations shall keep passover for Yahweh.

At the conclusion of all the ritual traditions of 12:1-27, we recognize the command-fulfillment schema of the Priestly writer when, in 12:28 we are told that all the prescriptions were carried out.

PASSAGE OUT OF EGYPT
12:29-39

29At midnight the Lord smote all the first-born in the land of Egypt, from the first-born of Pharaoh who sat on his throne to the first-born of the captive who was in the dungeon, and all the first-born of the cattle. 30And Pharaoh rose up in the night, he, and all his servants, and all the Egyptians; and there was a great cry in Egypt, for there was not a house where one was not dead. 31And he summoned Moses and Aaron by night, and said, "Rise up, go forth from among my people, both you and the people of Israel; and go, serve the Lord, as you have said. 32Take your flocks and your herds, as you have said, and be gone; and bless me also!"

33And the Egyptians were urgent with the people, to send them out of the land in haste; for they said, "We are all dead men." 34So the people took their dough before it was leavened, their kneading bowls being bound up in their mantles on their shoulders. 35The people of Israel had also done as Moses told them, for they had asked of the Egyptians jewelry of silver and of gold, and clothing; 36and the Lord had given the people favor in the sight of the Egyptians, so that they let them have what they asked. Thus they despoiled the Egyptians.

[37]And the people of Israel journeyed from Rameses to Succoth, about six hundred thousand men on foot, besides women and children. [38]A mixed multitude also went up with them, and very many cattle, both flocks and herds. [39]And they baked unleavened cakes of the dough which they had brought out of Egypt, for it was not leavened, because they were thrust out of Egypt and could not tarry, neither had they prepared for themselves any provisions.

The manner in which this account of the exodus event is told bears likeness to the event itself: it is simple, decisive, and quick. In eleven verses the Yahwist swiftly brings the readers through the passage for which they had longed since the beginning of the Book of Exodus. What the tedious, recurring plagues were unable to accomplish is secured definitively in a single blow which, submerged as it is in the legislative texts, appears almost suddenly and mysteriously, a death in the night.

To be sure, the reader was prepared for this since the event is narrated in terms carefully consistent with what the Yahwist had foreshadowed in Exod 11:1-10. The expulsion appears to be the unanimous wish of Pharaoh and all the Egyptians (12:31-34; cf. 11:1, 8). As predicted, the Israelites leave heavily laden with a share in Egyptian property (12:35-36; cf. 11:2-3 and 3:21-22), a detail which probably arose from the customary practice whereby a freed slave was not to be left empty-handed at the end of the time of service and so was given a certain share in the owner's possessions at the time of departure (see Deut 15:13-14). Finally, the emphasis on the haste of the departure which appears in this narrative (12:33, 39) probably represents an attempt to account for the unleavened bread ritual which had come to be associated with this event.

The Yahwist attempts to describe the exodus community. There is little question that his enumeration, six hundred thousand men (not counting women and children), is a gross exaggeration. As such it is not unlike the tradition of Num 1:17-46. Another detail included here, i.e., the tradition that the exodus group was a "mixed multitude" (12:38), is given more careful attention by contemporary scholars. It is not unlikely that the one common element which was shared by members of the exodus group was not blood kinship or faith but a marginalized social status. In the exodus event God intervened on behalf of those who had no rights in the political establishment in which they found themselves.

CONCLUSION: LOOKING BACK AND LOOKING FORWARD
12:40-42

> [40]The time that the people of Israel dwelt in Egypt was four hundred and thirty years. [41]And at the end of four hundred and thirty years, on that very day, all the hosts of the Lord went out from the land of Egypt. [42]It was a night of watching by the Lord, to bring them out of the land of Egypt; so this same night is a night of watching kept to the Lord by all the people of Israel throughout their generations.

These verses contain a summarizing statement belonging to the Priestly writer. The time span noted here has been used by some scholars as partial evidence in calculating the Hebrews' descent into and exodus from Egypt. Accordingly, if the descent into Egypt coincided with the migration into that area of Hyksos peoples around 1720 B.C., then the exodus can be dated about 1290 B.C. This date would link the exodus event with the reign of Rameses II, a view which would appear to be supported by the notation that one of the store-cities on which the Hebrews labored bore the name of the Pharaoh Rameses (see Exod 1:11).

In addition to the glance backwards over the years passed in Egypt, the Priestly writer presents here a sweeping glance of future generations. This pivotal exodus-moment is to be marked in the future by Israelites who will imitate in their own actions what the Lord did in this momentous event of passage. Ritually they shall continue the event by "keeping watch" for the Lord just as the Lord "kept watch" for them.

PASSOVER LEGISLATION CONTINUED
12:43-51

⁴³And the Lord said to Moses and Aaron, "This is the ordinance of the passover: no foreigner shall eat of it; ⁴⁴but every slave that is bought for money may eat of it after you have circumcised him. ⁴⁵No sojourner or hired servant may eat of it. ⁴⁶In one house shall it be eaten; you shall not carry forth any of the flesh outside the house; and you shall not break a bone of it. ⁴⁷All the congregation of Israel shall keep it. ⁴⁸And when a stranger shall sojourn with you and would keep the passover to the Lord, let all his males be circumcised, then he may come near and keep it; he shall be as a native of the land. But no uncircumcised person shall eat of it. ⁴⁹There shall be one law for the native and for the stranger who sojourns among you."

⁵⁰Thus did all the people of Israel; as the Lord commanded Moses and Aaron, so they did. ⁵¹And on that very day the Lord brought the people of Israel out of the land of Egypt by their hosts.

In Exod 12:1-13 the Priestly writer had legislated for the food for the passover meal, its preparation and its consumption. Here the same writer offers regulations regarding who may participate in the meal. Slaves who have been brought into the family (and thus into the congregation of Israel) may participate while uncircumcised strangers and foreigners are prohibited.

To the legislation of 12:43-49 the Priestly writer appends his familiar summarizing statement, noting that all the commands were fulfilled and the event was thus complete (12:50-51).

OFFERING THE FIRSTBORN
13:1-2

13 The Lord said to Moses, ²"Consecrate to me all the first-born; whatever is the first to open the womb among the people of Israel, both of man and of beast, is mine."

This chapter opens with the Priestly writer's legislation wherein God instructs that the firstborn of all life be set apart for the Divinity. Although it is placed between Priestly legislation for passover (12:43-49) and Deuteronomic legislation for the feast of unleavened bread (13:3-10), the consecration of the firstborn is not explicitly linked with either of the other rituals or with the exodus event.

UNLEAVENED BREAD
13:3-10

³And Moses said to the people, "Remember this day, in which you came out from Egypt, out of the house of bondage, for by strength of hand the Lord brought you out from this place; no leavened bread shall be eaten. ⁴This day you are to go forth, in the month of Abib. ⁵And when the Lord brings you into the land of the Canaanites, the Hittites, the Amorites, the Hivites, and the Jebusites, which he swore to your fathers to give you, a land flowing with milk and honey, you shall keep this service in this month. ⁶Seven days you shall eat unleavened bread, and on the seventh day there shall be a feast to the Lord. ⁷Unleavened bread shall be eaten for seven days; no leavened bread shall be seen with you, and no leaven shall be seen with you in all your territory. ⁸And you shall tell your son on that day, 'It is because of what the Lord did for me when I came out of Egypt.' ⁹And it shall be to you as a sign on your hand and as a memorial between your eyes, that the law of the Lord may be in your mouth; for with a strong hand the Lord has brought you out of Egypt. ¹⁰You shall therefore keep this ordinance at its appointed time from year to year.

These verses portray Moses as prescribing how the feast of unleavened bread is to be kept once Israel settles down in the land. The text's literary style and vocabulary mark it as Deuteronomic. By and large this tradition is in agreement with Priestly legislation for the same feast which already appeared in Exod 12:14-20. The two agree that this is to be a seven-day festival (13:6-7; cf. 12:15, 19). In addition, like the Priestly presentation in chapter 12, this Deuteronomic text never mentions passover although the date for the feast of unleavened bread coincides with the date for the passover observance (13:4; cf. 12:2) and the two feasts find their meaning in the same exodus event (13:8; cf. 12:17). In characteristically Deuteronomic fashion, the writer of these verses underlines the importance of carrying the past forward into the future. The feast is a remembering of a past redemptive event. But in the very act of ritual remembering one makes the redemptive power of the event present again and hands it on to the next generation. The practice of binding this instruction to one's very body (Exod 13:9; cf. Deut 6:8) was a very concrete way used by pious Israelites of later generations to try to stay closely connected to this pivotal redemptive passage.

OFFERING OF THE FIRSTBORN
13:11-16

[11]"And when the Lord brings you into the land of the Canaanites, as he swore to you and your fathers, and shall give it to you, [12]you shall set apart to the Lord all that first opens the womb. All the firstlings of your cattle that are males shall be the Lord's. [13]Every firstling of an ass you shall redeem with a lamb, or if you will not redeem it you shall break its neck. Every first-born of man among your sons you shall redeem. [14]And when in time to come your son asks you, 'What does this mean?' you shall say to him, 'By strength of hand the Lord brought us out of Egypt, from the house of bondage.

¹⁵For when Pharaoh stubbornly refused to let us go, the Lord slew all the first-born in the land of Egypt, both the first-born of man and the first-born of cattle. Therefore I sacrifice to the Lord all the males that first open the womb; but all the first-born of my sons I redeem.' ¹⁶It shall be as a mark on your hand or frontlets between your eyes; for by a strong hand the Lord brought us out of Egypt."

The Deuteronomic writer continues with legislation regarding the consecration of the firstborn. This passage is cast in a fashion very similar to the same writer's legislation for the feast of unleavened bread in the preceding portion of the text. Thus, he sets forth these directives as applying to the time of Israel's settlement in the land (13:11; cf. 13:5). He articulates the meaning of the observance in the familiar schema of the dialogue with the next generation (13:14; cf. 13:8). He requires that believers sign themselves with reminders of the instruction (13:16a; cf. 13:9a). And, finally, he bases the significance of the practice in the exodus event (13:16b; cf. 13:9b).

The directives for the practice of offering the firstborn begin by saying that all firstborn must be set aside (13:12a). However, the writer immediately proceeds to cite exceptions: only males need be offered, unclean animals (e.g., asses) and humans can be ransomed (13:12b-13). In verse 15 the practice is based on what Yahweh had done for Israel, a passage which harmonizes well with the events of the exodus night as reported by the Yahwist in Exod 12:29-39. The rationale for the practice of setting aside the firstborn of animals and humans is strikingly similar to the rationale for the offering of the first fruits of the earth as recorded in Deut 26:5-11. Both texts indicate the Deuteronomic writer's awareness of the profound giftedness of life which ancient Israel experienced in its relationship with Yahweh. Whatever offering Israel gave to God was recognized as nothing more than a token set apart from the superabundance of gifts which Yahweh had already showered upon Israel.

EVENTS AT THE SEA
13:17—15:21

The narrative about the deaths of the firstborn and the consequent expulsion of the Hebrews from Egypt, together with the rituals commemorating the going out of Egypt, might legitimately lead readers to regard the exodus as complete. Yet Exod 13:17—15:21 contains one final encounter between the Egyptians and the Hebrews, between Pharaoh and Yahweh. It is clear that freedom from Egyptian domination is not secured until Yahweh delivered the Hebrews at the sea. At the conclusion of the passage the redeemed are portrayed as celebrating this event in song and dance.

Exod 13:17—15:21 is best viewed as a composite of different versions of one event which have been interwoven like threads of a fine tapestry. Scholars identify the main threads of the narrative tradition as belonging to the Yahwist and Priestly writers, although fragments from the Elohist are also present. The witness about Israel's celebration of the event (15:1-21) is probably the product of generations of worshippers who sang the songs and danced the dance recorded here.

The Yahwist's version of the event at the sea is found in Exod 13:21-22; 14:5b-6, 10a, 11-14, 19b, 21b, 24, 25b, 27b, 28b, 30-31. According to this early tradition, Israel went out from Egypt with a profound sense of God's presence signalled by a cloud during the day and fire at night. Pharaoh and his entourage pursued Israel. When the two groups met at the sea, Israel responded full of fear, regretting ever having begun the flight to freedom. Moses countered their faithlessness with an invitation to "stand firm" in God's presence-in-power. The cloud protected them while a tidal-like wind caused the waters to recede during the night. The Lord then threw the Egyptian army into a panic so that they rushed into the sea bed. When the waters returned to their normal depths, the Egyptians were engulfed in destruction. Israel saw that what Moses said had indeed taken place and they had faith in Yahweh and in Moses.

Most of the remainder of the story (14:1-4, 8-9, 15-18, 21ac, 22-23, 26-27a, 28-29) belongs to the Priestly writer. In this strand the reader learns the tradition that the Egyptians were defeated at the sea through a series of acts executed by Moses at God's command. Moses and the Israelites encamped where God directed. Moses raised his staff over the waters as God directed, the waters split and the sea became a path of dry land bordered by a wall of water on each side. The Israelites passed through with the Egyptians close behind. Deliverance was secured when, in response to Moses' outstretched hand, the waters fell in upon the Egyptians.

A comparison of the two versions of the event reveals several points of contrast in the biblical tradition. The Yahwist characteristically presents the human perspective on the event (Pharaoh's plan, Israel's fear, etc.). God alone acts in bringing about deliverance. For the Yahwist, the people "have only to be still." The Priestly version, on the other hand, presents the divine perspective throughout, carefully showing how everything takes place in accordance with God's previously announced word. (Thus, the word announced in 14:1-4 comes to fulfillment in 14:8-9 while 14:15-18 unfolds into 14:21ac, 22-23 and 14:26 is completed in 14:27a, 28-29) In contrast to the earlier version, the Priestly writer presents the divine work of deliverance as mediated through the actions of Moses. Even Pharaoh acts in accord with God's word although the tyrant is not aware of doing so. According to the Yahwist, God uses the forces of nature (the strong east wind) to accomplish deliverance while the Priestly writer presents the waters standing up like walls, contrary to the usual forces of nature. The Yahwist's story bears elements in common with stereotyped features of Israel's life in the wilderness (for example the "murmuring motif" in vv. 11-12) whereas the Priestly writer utilizes motifs like the hardening of Pharaoh's heart and "knowing Yahweh" to bring the story into closer association with the story of Yahweh's struggle with Pharaoh throughout the plagues. Thus, while the Yahwist may have regarded this deliverance as the initial event of Israel's wilderness journey, the Priestly writer's contribution portrays the event at the sea as the final and definitive part of the overall exodus event.

A final preliminary word must be said about those elements in the text which highlight the military character of the event at the sea. According to Exod 13:18, the people who left Egypt were "equipped for battle." The Egyptian pursuit is portrayed as a full-scale military operation (see 14:6-7). Yahweh's action as described in Exod 14:14 is that of a warrior (cf. Exod 15:3). These and other textual clues suggest that ancient Israel regarded the event at the sea as the first and greatest of a series of battles through which the Divine Warrior secured the life and well-being of the redeemed people. Knowledge of some elements of Israel's "Holy War" tradition sheds light on particular details included by the writers of Exod 13:17—14:31.

The ancient Israelites held to the conviction that Yahweh was present in power with them. Yahweh's presence lent a sacral dimension to Israel's concrete historical experience. Israel experienced God's presence (or absence) most dramatically in those situations where its very life was at stake, e.g., on the battlefield. War, then, was a sacral event because Yahweh was dynamically present as Israel's chief warrior, the Divine Warrior. Just as Israel conducted special preparations and rituals in drawing near to Yahweh's presence at a shrine, so the conduct of war was governed by practices which reflected Israel's belief in its sacral character. When battle appeared imminent, warriors conducted ritual purifications in addition to offering sacrifice or consulting oracles concerning the decision of whether or when to engage the enemy forces. They did not go into battle until they knew Yahweh was ready to march at the head of their armies. With the certainty of Yahweh's presence came certainty about the outcome of the battle. Victory was assured; therefore warriors were exhorted not to fear. Characteristically there was something very extraordinary about the battle (cf. the use of the forces of nature in Judg 5:20-21; Josh 10:10-11; 1 Sam 7:10 or the walls of Jericho in Josh 6). Sometimes this took the form of utter chaos or confusion wherein Israel's enemies actually did something to bring destruction upon themselves. Finally, Israel enforced the ban (*herem*), consecrating the booty of war for the real victor in battle, the Divine Warrior.

Two of these standard features in the presentation of Holy War figure prominently in Exod 13:17—14:31. Certainty about the outcome of any battle enjoined by Israel's Divine Warrior forms the background of Moses' exhortation in 14:13-14: "Fear not, stand firm...The Lord will fight for you, and you have only to be still." The story proceeds to narrate how these words are borne out (see especially Exod 14:25b). Whereas in some other examples of Holy War thought Yahweh puts to use the efforts of Israel's army, here tradition tells us Yahweh did it all. In this sense, the event at the sea is the act *par excellence* of Israel's Divine Warrior.

A second element in this story which is illuminated by viewing it in the context of Holy War thought is a detail cited in Exod 14:24. It is suggested here that through some mysterious action God glanced at the Egyptians rushing headlong into the sea and thus into their own demise. As was mentioned above, mysterious actions causing the enemy to contribute to its own destruction belong to the standard features of texts written within a Holy War framework.

We have discussed several elements of the separate

threads which have come together to form the tapestry of Exod 13:17—14:31. It remains for us now to stand back and view the text as a whole.

One commentator has suggested that the overall effect of Exod 13:17—14:31 is governed by a theological message about God's plan. Viewed as such, the final text of the narrative about the event at the sea can be regarded as consisting of three story units (13:17—14:8; 14:9-14, and 14:15-29) and an epilogue (14:30-31).

THE TWO PLANS
13:17—14:8

[17]When Pharaoh let the people go, God did not lead them by way of the land of the Philistines, although that was near; for God said, "Lest the people repent when they see war, and return to Egypt." [18]But God led the people round by the way of the wilderness toward the Red Sea. And the people of Israel went up out of the land of Egypt equipped for battle. [19]And Moses took the bones of Joseph with him; for Joseph had solemnly sworn the people of Israel, saying, "God will visit you; then you must carry my bones with you from here." [20]And they moved on from Succoth, and encamped at Etham, on the edge of the wilderness. [21]And the Lord went before them by day in a pillar of cloud to lead them along the way, and by night in a pillar of fire to give them light, that they might travel by day and by night; [22]the pillar of cloud by day and the pillar of fire by night did not depart from before the people.

14   Then the Lord said to Moses, [2]"Tell the people of Israel to turn back and encamp in front of Pihahiroth, between Migdol and the sea, in front of Baal-zephon; you shall encamp over against it, by the sea. [3]For Pharaoh will say of the people of Israel, 'They are entangled in the land; the wilderness has shut them in.' [4]And I will harden Pharaoh's heart, and he will pursue them and I will get glory over Pharaoh and all his host; and the Egyptians shall know that I am the Lord." And they did so.

⁵When the king of Egypt was told that the people had fled, the mind of Pharaoh and his servants was changed toward the people, and they said, "What is this we have done, that we have let Israel go from serving us?" ⁶So he made ready his chariot and took his army with him, ⁷and took six hundred picked chariots and all the other chariots of Egypt with officers over all of them. ⁸And the Lord hardened the heart of Pharaoh king of Egypt and he pursued the people of Israel as they went forth defiantly.

The first phase in the overall story about the sea event casts the action in terms of God's plan and Pharaoh's plan. On the one hand, in 13:17-22 events are presented as carefully ordered and controlled by God: "When Pharaoh let the people go, God did not lead them by the way of the Philistines...(v. 17) But God led the people round by the way of the wilderness...(v. 18) and the Lord went before them... (v. 21)." In the divine monologue of 14:1-4 the Lord discloses to Moses what the divine plan is and how it relates to Pharaoh's conduct. On the other hand, 14:5-8 the reader learns the mind of Pharaoh and what governs his action. Thus, by the time the reader reaches 14:8 two contrasting plans, God's and Pharaoh's, have been set in motion. It is also clear to the reader (vv. 4, 8), however, that Yahweh's plan encompasses that of the Pharaoh.

ISRAEL'S VIEW
14:9-14

⁹The Egyptians pursued them, all Pharaoh's horses and chariots and his horsemen and his army, and overtook them encamped at the sea, by Pihahiroth, in front of Baal-zephon.

¹⁰When Pharaoh drew near, the people of Israel lifted up their eyes, and behold, the Egyptians were marching after them; and they were in great fear. And the people of Israel cried out to the Lord; ¹¹and they said to Moses, "Is it because there are no graves in Egypt that you have taken us away to die in the wilderness? What have you

done to us, in bringing us out of Egypt? ¹²Is not this what we said to you in Egypt, 'Let us alone and let us serve the Egyptians'? For it would have been better for us to serve the Egyptians than to die in the wilderness."¹³And Moses said to the people, "Fear not, stand firm, and see the salvation of the Lord, which he will work for you today; for the Egyptians whom you see today, you shall never see again. ¹⁴The Lord will fight for you, and you have only to be still."

The second section of the story focuses upon how the Israelites perceive the two plans which are now unfolding into action. The cry of vv. 11-12 indicates that the Israelites are more keenly attuned to the power of Pharaoh's plan than to God's work. Moses responds (vv. 13-14) by sharing his conviction about the reliable power of God's plan. He intended to encourage Israel by his witness.

MEETING AT THE SEA
14:15-29

¹⁵The Lord said to Moses, "Why do you cry to me? Tell the people of Israel to go forward. ¹⁶Lift up your rod, and stretch out your hand over the sea and divide it, that the people of Israel may go on dry ground through the sea. ¹⁷And I will harden the hearts of the Egyptians so that they shall go in after them, and I will get glory over Pharaoh and all his host, his chariots, and his horsemen. ¹⁸And the Egyptians shall know that I am the Lord, when I have gotten glory over Pharaoh, his chariots, and his horsemen."

¹⁹Then the angel of God who went before the host of Israel moved and went behind them; and the pillar of cloud moved from before them and stood behind them, ²⁰coming between the host of Egypt and the host of Israel. And there was the cloud and the darkness; and the night passed without one coming near the other all night.

²¹Then Moses stretched out his hand over the sea; and

the Lord drove the sea back by a strong east wind all night, and made the sea dry land, and the waters were divided. 22And the people of Israel went into the midst of the sea on dry ground, the waters being a wall to them on their right hand and on their left. 23The Egyptians pursued, and went in after them into the midst of the sea, all Pharaoh's horses, his chariots, and his horsemen. 24And in the morning watch the Lord in the pillar of fire and of cloud looked down upon the host of the Egyptians, and discomfited the host of the Egyptians, 25clogging their chariot wheels so that they drove heavily; and the Egyptians said, "Let us flee from before Israel; for the Lord fights for them against the Egyptians."

26Then the Lord said to Moses, "Stretch out your hand over the sea, that the water may come back upon the Egyptians, upon their chariots, and upon their horsemen." 27So Moses stretched forth his hand over the sea, and the sea returned to its wonted flow when the morning appeared; and the Egyptians fled into it, and the Lord routed the Egyptians in the midst of the sea. 28The waters returned and covered the chariots and the horsemen and all the host of Pharaoh that had followed them into the sea; not so much as one of them remained. 29But the people of Israel walked on dry ground through the sea, the waters being a wall to them on their right hand and on their left.

The third section of the story records the confrontation of the two plans at two levels (cf. the different literary sources). According to one view, God's plan is carried forward directly by the Divinity's action (movement of pillar of cloud, strong east wind, terror strikes the Egyptians) and according to the other view, God's plan is carried forward indirectly through Moses' action (the rod). In this third section, it is clear that Pharaoh's plan has been subsumed under God's. The Lord uses Pharaoh's plan to assist in the accomplishment of the divine plan.

EPILOGUE
14:30-31

> ³⁰Thus the Lord saved Israel that day from the hand of the Egyptians; and Israel saw the Egyptians dead upon the seashore. ³¹And Israel saw the great work which the Lord did against the Egyptians, and the people feared the Lord; and they believed in the Lord and in his servant Moses.

The short epilogue to the story about the event at the sea offers a counterpart to the middle section of the story where the Israelites feared because they could perceive only Pharaoh's plan at work (see especially v. 10). Now, in vv. 30-31, the story has reached a fitting conclusion: the Israelites saw that God's plan had been worked for their welfare. As a result they feared Yahweh.

CELEBRATION
15:1-21

> **15** Then Moses and the people of Israel sang this song to the Lord, saying,
> "I will sing to the Lord, for he has triumphed gloriously;
>   the horse and his rider he has thrown into the sea.
> ²The Lord is my strength and my song,
>   and he has become my salvation;
> this is my God, and I will praise him,
>   my father's God, and I will exalt him.
> ³The Lord is a man of war;
>   the Lord is his name.
>
> ⁴"Pharaoh's chariots and his host he cast into the sea;
>   and his picked officers are sunk in the Red Sea.
> ⁵The floods cover them;
>   they went down into the depths like a stone.
> ⁶Thy right hand, O Lord, glorious in power,
>   thy right hand, O Lord, shatters the enemy.
> ⁷In the greatness of thy majesty thou

overthrowest thy adversaries;
thou sendest forth thy fury, it consumes
them like stubble.
8At the blast of thy nostrils the waters piled up,
the floods stood up in a heap;
the deeps congealed in the heart of the sea.
9The enemy said, 'I will pursue, I will overtake,
I will divide the spoil, my desire shall
have its fill of them.
I will draw my sword, my hand shall destroy them.'
10Thou didst blow with thy wind, the sea covered them;
they sank as lead in the mighty waters.

11"Who is like thee, O Lord, among the gods?
Who is like thee, majestic in holiness,
terrible in glorious deeds, doing wonders?
12Thou didst stretch out thy right hand,
the earth swallowed them.

13"Thou hast led in thy steadfast love
the people whom thou hast redeemed,
thou hast guided them by thy strength
to thy holy abode.
14The peoples have heard, they tremble;
pangs have seized on the inhabitants of Philistia.
15Now are the chiefs of Edom dismayed;
the leaders of Moab, trembling seizes them;
all the inhabitants of Canaan have melted away.
16Terror and dread fall upon them;
because of the greatness of thy arm,
they are still as a stone,
till thy people, O Lord, pass by,
till the people pass by whom thou hast purchased.
17Thou wilt bring them in, and plant
them on thy own mountain,
the place, O Lord, which thou hast made for thy abode,
the sanctuary, O Lord, which thy hands have
established.
18The Lord will reign for ever and ever."
19For when the horses of Pharaoh with his chariots and

his horsemen went into sea, the Lord brought back the waters of the sea upon them; but the people of Israel walked on dry ground in the midst of the sea. [20]Then Miriam, the prophetess, the sister of Aaron, took a timbrel in her hand; and all the women went out after her with timbrels and dancing. [21]And Miriam sang to them: "Sing to the Lord, for he has triumphed gloriously; the horse and his rider he has thrown into the sea."

In these verses we are presented with two traditions about the celebration at the sea which expressed the faith of the redeemed community. The first, 15:1-18, puts on the lips of Moses and the people of Israel a hymn-like song which probably dates from monarchical times. Here the praise of God for the saving event at the sea (vv. 1b-12) has been joined with the praise of God for the gift of the land and for God's abiding presence in the sanctuary (vv. 13-18). The "coming out" (of Egypt) thus was linked with the "coming into" the land. In this profession of faith, as in others, Israel regarded the event at the sea as the first of victories wherein Yahweh secured its life and wellbeing.

The transition which appears in 15:19 sets the context for the second tradition about the celebration at the sea. In 15:20-21 leadership in the celebration is attributed to Miriam. Scholars generally regard this as a more ancient tradition than the celebration recorded in 15:1-18. It may well be that the song of 15:21 is the Bible's oldest witness regarding the event at the sea.

The likeness of Miriam's celebration, with its tambourines, dance and song, to other biblical records (Judg 11:34; 1 Sam 18:6) indicates that the celebration led by Miriam had the character of a victory celebration. Unlike the celebrations attributed to Jephthah's daughter (Judg 11) and to the women greeting Saul and David (1 Sam 18) however, the victorious warrior honored by Miriam was Israel's Divine Warrior. The proper context, then, for viewing Miriam's celebration is not a secular festival but Israel's cult. Miriam's dance and song not only expressed joy at victory. They were also ritual actions and, like all ritual, were intended to capture the event being celebrated, expressing its meaning and keeping it alive. The dramatic movements of dance, accompanied by the words of the song and the sound of the tambourine, somehow expressed the struggle and victory, the fear and exultation, the death and life which Yahweh's battle at the sea entailed.

In 15:20-21 an early writer (perhaps the Yahwist) attributed the cultic celebration of the foundational event in Israelite religion to a woman who is introduced here, for the first time. Miriam is the first to articulate the religious dimension of the event at the sea. In all seven of the biblical texts in which she appears (Exod 15:20-21; Num 12:1-15; 26:59; 1 Chr 6:3; Micah 6:4; Deut 24:8-9; Num 20:1), Miriam is portrayed as a leader in the wilderness community. It is likely that in very early circles of oral tradition she enjoyed much more prominence than what has been handed on to us in the written texts.

The description of Miriam as prophetess is probably anachronistic since authentic prophetic activity is never attributed to her in the biblical texts. The writer seems to have described her in terms of leadership roles exercised by women in later generations. Likewise, the description of Miriam as Aaron's sister probably stems from an editor who sought to bring all liturgical leaders into association with Aaron, the priest who had come to be the figurehead for all cultic personnel in a late period of Israelite religion.

With the text of Exod 15:20-21 the writers appropriately conclude the story of the arduous struggle for freedom. In its faith-filled response Israel recognizes that the journey was God's doing. The Exodus event, together with its climax in the event at the sea, came to be seen as somehow telling the experience of all generations of Israelites. To belong to the people of God was to belong to a group which experienced a marvelous passage from bondage to freedom. To tell Israel's story entailed telling this exodus story. Miriam thus initiated a dance which many generations of believers would join and make their own.

THE SHAPE OF FREEDOM
15:22—18:27

The celebration at the sea marked the end of one stage of life for God's people. They had completed passage out of their bondage to Pharaoh. Now the biblical writers describe the initial phase of their new life of freedom. The setting is the desert, a wild territory easily associated with lack of direction, lack of shape. There the newly freed slaves experienced the reality which was voiced in a popular song several years ago: "Freedom's just another word for nothin' left to lost." Survival was their continuing concern. In addition, the group struggled to find a new self-understanding. Wants were not yet clearly distinguished from necessities. The community lacked effective organization. But, the biblical writers say, God nurtured and sustained the newly redeemed in the wilderness and there God fashioned the motley group into a people.

The narratives about Israel's life in the wilderness are foundational stories. That is to say, they not only describe the life of an early group but of later generations as well. First of all, the new base for Israel's existence is defined. Israel's foundation, the source of its life, is no longer to be found in Pharaoh's slave wages but in Yahweh's gifting presence. Israel learned that its proper posture in relation to this new reality was trust. The wilderness was a school in which Israel first experienced the precariousness of a life based on trust, covenanted life. In addition, the foundations of Israel's organizational existence were set in this wilderness period. Issues centering on the relationship of Moses to other leaders in the community are settled. The institutions of sabbath rest, prophecy, and the administration of justice are traced to this formative period of Israel's existence.

Many of the stories which constitute the wilderness traditions were originally independent of one another. They probably have long histories of transmission both in oral and written stages of the growth of the biblical tradition. In the text which has come down to us originally separate stories have been artificially linked with one another by means of an itinerary. Thus, the narratives have the appearance of being separate incidents at various stopping places along one extended journey from the "coming out" of Egypt to the "coming into" the land. The journey is divided into two stages: in the first the newly freed slaves move from the Red Sea, through the wilderness, to Mount Sinai (Exod 15-18). The second stage takes the Israelites through the wilderness between Mount Sinai and the borders of the Promised Land (Num 10-36). Between these two complexes of narratives appears a huge block of material which is now localized at Mount Sinai (Exod 19—Num 10).

The journey motif is supplemented by other literary and theological motifs which also serve to unify originally separate stories. One recurring motif witnesses to the constancy of God's gifts and fidelity. These are borne out in many diverse situations along the wilderness journey. Another is the "murmuring motif" which again and again presents Israel as remarkably uncourageous in the wilderness. The most consistent complaint which rose out of the different instances of hardship was Israel's regret at ever having left the security which their bondage to Pharaoh had offered.

Contemporary biblical scholarship traces two patterns in the narratives which recount Israel's murmuring in the wilderness. Those stories which follow Pattern I begin with a description of legitimate need experienced by the wanderers (e.g., not having water to drink). This initial need gives rise to a complaint on the part of the people. Moses then intercedes with God on behalf of the community and God responds by graciously providing for its need. This pattern governs two stories along the journey prior to the arrival at Sinai (Exod 15:22-25 and 17:1-7; cf. Num 20:1-13).

Like those of Pattern I, the murmuring stories which belong to Pattern II include a description of the people's complaint and of Moses' intercession with God. However, the stories governed by Pattern II differ in that they do not begin with a legitimate need. Rather, they begin with complaints which rise out of simple dissatisfaction with the conditions in which the people find themselves (e.g., the "worthless food" in Num 21:5). This type of complaint arouses God's anger and punishment. Moses then intercedes with God that the divine wrath not consume the people. God's graciousness is then manifest in relief from the punishment. This pattern appears prominently in stories of life along the journey following the departure from Sinai (Num 11:1-3; 16:41-50; 21:4-9).

The wilderness narratives come primarily from the hands of the Yahwist and Priestly writers. Both sources record stories covering a wide variety of content. Both include the positive theological motif of Yahweh's gracious aid and the negative portrait of rebellious Israel. Both have the two patterns of Israel's murmuring: one which rises out of a situation of real need and the other which merely voices dissatisfaction with the way things are. Both include wilderness stories on the journey prior to the arrival at Sinai (Exod 15-18) and subsequent to Israel's departure from Sinai (Num 10-36).

Segments of the biblical tradition outside these narratives recall Israel's wilderness experience in different ways. Memories of this ancient period were colored by unique experiences and theological reflection on those experiences. On the one hand, those who associated Israel's participation in sin with its life in the land of plenty remembered the wilderness as a time of innocence, a time prior to Israel's capitulation to the seductiveness of the land. They wrote of the wilderness as representative of Israel's most profound, singlehearted experience of being faithful in love with Yahweh. Examples of this view of the wilderness can be found in Deut 32:10-14, Hos 2:14-15, and Jer 2:1-3. On the other hand, those writers who were overwhelmed by the recognition of Israel's sin and its pervasiveness were more prone to think of Israel as having always been sinful. Thus Ezek 20:9-26, Ps 106, Neh 9:16-25 view Israel's time in the wilderness as an early stage of flagrant infidelity and rebelliousness, traits which they say continued throughout Israel's history and which ultimately brought on the action of God which resulted in the Babylonian Exile.

WATER, SWEET WATER
15:22-27

22Then Moses led Israel onward from the Red Sea, and they went into the wilderness of Shur; they went three days in the wilderness and found no water. 23When they came to Marah, they could not drink the water of Marah because it was bitter; therefore it was named Marah. 24And the people murmured against Moses, saying, "What shall we drink?" 25And he cried to the Lord; and the Lord showed him a tree, and he threw it into the water, and the water became sweet.

There the Lord made for them a statute and an ordinance and there he proved them, 26saying, "If you will diligently hearken to the voice of the Lord your God, and do that which is right in his eyes, and give heed to his commandments and keep all his statutes, I will put none of the diseases upon you which I put upon the Egyptians; for I am the Lord, your healer."

27Then they came to Elim, where there were twelve springs of water and seventy palm trees; and they encamped there by the water.

This is one of the simplest of all the wilderness stories. It begins and ends with Israel's movement along its itinerary through the desert. However the incident which is narrated is not attached to the journey itself but to a stopping place along the way. The place is called Marah and the crisis which initiated the story is connected with the meaning of the word from which that place took its name, "bitterness." Thus, at one level the story is aetiological in character. It tells us how Marah got its name.

The structure of the story is clear and unadorned: the thirsty wanderers were brought to the point of murmuring against Moses when water they had reached after three days of travel turned out to be undrinkable. Their complaint rose out of a real need. Moses' immediate response was to intercede with the Lord and the Lord showed Moses how to mediate the divine gracious response to Israel's need. The "healing" of water seems to be based in what was probably a relatively common method of assuring that water was drinkable. The bark or leaves of certain trees were viewed as capable of transforming bad water into water fit for human use (cf. 2 Kgs 2:19-22).

Verses 22-25a, which probably come from the Yahwist source, comprise a simple, rather complete wilderness story. It includes several features which will recur in subsequent narratives: (1) an itinerary notice at the beginning and/or end; (2) a play on the name of the place where the incident is localized; (3) the need-complaint-intercession-gracious response pattern. The central need here, water, brings this story into close relationship with other incidents located at Massah and Meribah (see Exod 17:1-7 and Num 20:1-13) in the wilderness.

The content and structure of verses 25b-26 share little with what typically appears in wilderness narratives. This, plus its literary style and vocabulary, has led scholars to regard it as a later addition which the Deuteronomic writer attached to the rest of the story. There are two points of contact which may have prompted the addition. The first is the notion of healing. The Deuteronomist uses the earlier tradition of God's "healing" the water at Marah as a basis for asserting the Divinity's promise to heal Israel itself in return for the people's obedience. The Deuteronomic theologian transformed a simple story about God's graciousness into an appeal for obedience.

Another possible connection between the earlier story in vv. 22-25a and the addition in vv. 25b-26 is the notion of "proof." The early story about thirst at Marah may have reminded the Deuteronomic writer of the story about thirst at Massah and Meribah (Exod 17:1-7). The narrative of Exod 17:1-7 includes a strong indictment against Israel for having put the Lord "to the proof." (The place-name Massah has its root in a Hebrew stem, *nasah*, which means "to tempt," "to put to the proof.") Because Exod 17:1-7 already shared with the Marah story the crisis occasioned by thirst, it is not unreasonable to suggest that the Deuteronomic writer naturally associated these two stories and hence found it easy to transfer the "proof" motif from the Exod 17 story to the Marah incident. Whereas Exod 17 says that Israel put Yahweh "to the proof" in the wilderness, here in Exod 15 the Deuteronomic writer asserts that in the wilderness Yahweh "proved" Israel by the call to obedience.

The Deuteronomic writer sparked many scholarly questions and theories when he reinterpreted the old Marah story by saying that there God proved Israel with a statute and ordinance. The chief biblical witness, of course, is that Israel did not receive the law until its arrival at Mount Sinai. Yet here the Deuteronomic writer seems to connect the law-giving event with Marah. The easiest explanation for this witness is that it is a simple anachronism. Some scholars, however, have posited that it bears hints of a tradition wherein close associations were made between the law and Kadesh, a major oasis in the wilderness associated with Massah and Meribah (Num 20:1-13; 27:14; Deut 32:51; cf. Gen 14:7) and, by virtue of their parallels with the water incident recorded in Exod 15:22-27, with Marah. Whatever the case, Kadesh was remembered by the Deuteronomic circle as Israel's major center during the wilderness period (see Deut 1:46 and 2:14).

In this simple story of Exod 15:22-27 the biblical writers offer an initial glimpse of life between Israel's exodus from Egypt and its inheritance of the land. On the one hand,

God's provision of sweet water for the wanderers is narrated here as the first of many instances of the divine sustenance and care along the way of the desert sojourn. On the other hand, Israel's murmuring, first reported here as a complaint reflecting a legitimate need, will become full-scale revolt against God and against Moses in the course of the journey.

BREAD FROM HEAVEN
16:1-36

16 They set out from Elim, and all the congregation of the people of Israel came to the wilderness of Sin, which is between Elim and Sinai, on the fifteenth day of the second month they had departed from the land of Egypt. ²And the whole congregation of the people of Israel murmured against Moses and Aaron in the wilderness, ³and said to them, "Would that we had died by the hand of the Lord in the land of Egypt, when we sat by the fleshpots and ate bread to the full; for you have brought us out into this wilderness to kill this whole assembly with hunger."

⁴Then the Lord said to Moses, "Behold, I will rain bread from heaven for you; and the people shall go out and gather a day's portion every day, that I may prove them, whether they will walk in my law or not. ⁵On the sixth day, when they prepare what they bring in, it will be twice as much as they gather daily." ⁶So Moses and Aaron said to all the people of Israel, "At evening you shall know that it was the Lord who brought you out of the land of Egypt, ⁷and in the morning you shall see the glory of the Lord, because he has heard your murmurings against the Lord. For what are we, that you murmur against us?" ⁸And Moses said, "When the Lord gives you in the evening flesh to eat and in the morning bread to the full, because the Lord has heard your murmurings which you murmur against him — what are we? Your murmurings are not against us but against the Lord."

⁹And Moses said to Aaron, "Say to the whole congre-

gation of the people of Israel, 'Come near before the Lord, for he has heard your murmurings.' " [10]And as Aaron spoke to the whole congregation of the people of Israel, they looked toward the wilderness, and behold, the glory of the Lord appeared in the cloud. [11]And the Lord said to Moses, [12]"I have heard the murmurings of the people of Israel; say to them, 'At twilight you shall eat flesh, and in the morning you shall be filled with bread; then you shall know that I am the Lord your God.' "

[13]In the evening quails came up and covered the camp; and in the morning dew lay round about the camp. [14]And when the dew had gone up, there was on the face of the wilderness a fine, flake-like thing, fine as hoarfrost on the ground. [15]When the people of Israel saw it, they said to one another, "What is it?" For they did not know what it was. And Moses said to them, "It is the bread which the Lord has given you to eat. [16]This is what the Lord has commanded: 'Gather of it, every man of you, as much as he can eat; you shall take an omer apiece, according to the number of the persons whom each of you has in his tent.' " [17]And the people of Israel did so; they gathered, some more, some less. [18]But when they measured it with an omer, he that gathered much had nothing over, and he that gathered little had no lack; each gathered according to what he could eat. [19]And Moses said to them, "Let no man leave any of it till the morning." [20]But they did not listen to Moses; some left part of it till the morning, and it bred worms and became foul; and Moses was angry with them. [21]Morning by morning they gathered it, each as much as he could eat; but when the sun grew hot, it melted.

[22]On the sixth day they gathered twice as much bread, two omers apiece; and when all the leaders of the congregation came and told Moses, [23]he said to them, "This is what the Lord has commanded: 'Tomorrow is a day of solemn rest, a holy sabbath to the Lord; bake what you will bake and boil what you will boil, and all that is left over lay by to be kept till the morning.' " [24]So they laid it by till the morning, as Moses bade them; and it did not

become foul, and there were no worms in it. 25Moses said, "Eat it today, for today is a sabbath to the Lord; today you will not find it in the field. 26Six days you shall gather it; but on the seventh day, which is a sabbath, there will be none." 27On the seventh day some of the people went out to gather, and they found none. 28And the Lord said to Moses, "How long do you refuse to keep my command-ments and my laws? 29See! The Lord has given you the sabbath, therefore on the sixth day he gives you bread for two days; remain every man of you in his place, let no man go out of his place on the seventh day." 30So the people rested on the seventh day.

31Now the house of Israel called its name manna; it was like coriander seed, white, and the taste of it was like wafers made with honey. 32And Moses said, "This is what the Lord has commanded: 'Let an omer of it be kept throughout your generations, that they may see the bread with which I fed you in the wilderness, when I brought you out of the land of Egypt.'" 33And Moses said to Aaron, "Take a jar, and put an omer of manna in it, and place it before the Lord, to be kept throughout your generations." 34As the Lord commanded Moses, so Aaron placed it before the testimony, to be kept. 35And the people of Israel ate the manna forty years, till they came to a habitable land; they ate the manna, till they came to the border of the land of Canaan. 36(An omer is the tenth part of an ephah.)

This story contrasts in length and complexity with the simple story of Exod 15:22-27. However, the two stories bear important thematic elements in common, particularly the witness to God's generous care in spite of Israel's murmuring.

Several characteristics in this text suggest that the bulk of it comes from the Priestly source: (1) the use of the word "congregation" to refer to the people of Israel; (2) the rela-tively prominent presence of Aaron alongside Moses; (3) the centrality of the sabbath; (4) the theophany (vv. 9-10); (5) concern for a cultic preservation of the manna tradition (vv.

31-35). The Priestly writer anachronistically retrojected views and practices of his own day into this early period of Israel's life with God.

Unevenness in the flow of the story suggests that it did not come whole and entire from the Priestly hand. For example, Moses and Aaron announce what Yahweh is about to do (vv. 6-8) before God has announced the course of action (vv. 11-12). Different stages of tradition have come together without being perfectly harmonized. The text yields little basis for recognizing specific literary sources with any degree of certainty. Suffice it to say that Exod 16 is a complex literary unit some of which bears strong evidence of Priestly composition. The narrative is an alternate version of an earlier story from J and E about manna and quail which now appears in Numbers 11.

Just as concrete, physical thirst had prompted the murmuring at Marah so here it is real, visceral hunger which leads to complaint. In the present case, however, the expressed complaint is much more radical than a simple "What shall we eat?". For the first time Israel expresses regret over its redemption from slavery. Better to die slaves with full stomachs than to live with the hunger and uncertainty of this freedom.

Verses 4-12 contain a somewhat uneven response to the people's murmuring. Verses 6-12 flow more smoothly from the complaint recorded in v. 3 while vv. 4-5 (often regarded by scholars as belonging to a different literary strand than their context) seem to fit more appropriately with the content of vv. 13-36. Hence, we shall set aside vv. 4-5 for the moment and briefly view the series of statements beginning in verse 6 and culminating in the divine promise of v. 12.

Israel's experience, as reported in Scripture, is rarely one-dimensional. That is to say, the physical-material dimension of life does not operate apart from a sacred or religious dimension and vice versa. A crisis over food is at the same time a crisis of faith. Perhaps this is most clearly reflected in Moses' statement on behalf of himself and Aaron: "Your murmurings are not against us but against the Lord" (v. 8). In the speeches of vv. 6-12 food and faith are

consistently intertwined. Moses and Aaron first address the
faith crisis: "At evening you shall know that it was the Lord
who brought you out of Egypt and in the morning you shall
see the glory of the Lord, because he has heard your murmurings . . . " (vv. 6-7a). It is clear in the following verses that
addressing the faith question will not (perhaps could not)
happen apart from the gift of food; thus there will be a
steady supply (i.e., evening and morning) of food. Finally,
in v. 12 the Divine Self echoes what Moses and Aaron had
already said. Yahweh's promise addresses not only the
hunger but also the underlying doubt about the divine
reliability. As happened throughout the struggles with Pharaoh in Egypt and at the astonishing rescue at the sea, so
through the gift of flesh and bread in the wilderness Israel
will come to know its God, Yahweh.

The remainder of the chapter (vv. 4-5, 13-36) paints in
greater detail the schema according to which the Lord's
sustenance was given, i.e., day by day although allowing for
sabbath rest. The end of v. 4 makes it clear that offering the
gift in this way was God's deliberate choice. The Lord's
gift-giving served as an opportunity for Israel to assume a
responsible lifestyle. The strict measure to be used in gathering this "daily bread" was that it be an amount which
satiated each person's daily food requirement (vv. 16-18).
The people were not to gather provisions for storage (vv.
19-21) except on the sixth day to allow for the sabbath rest
(vv. 22-30).

Much of the beauty of this story can be traced to its care
for detail. The narrator sketches an experience of abundance which is marked by serenity and satiation, good
measure and regularity. As Israel faced life in the wilderness
day after day, God's gifts of food came not too much and
not too little.

Two areas of failure on Israel's part are recorded here. On
the one hand, some Israelites failed in the discipline of living
for the present day. They kept part of their food for the
morrow only to learn that the gift indeed was daily and that
on the morrow it was not fit for eating (v. 20). A second
failure was in the area of rest. Even after the explicit com-

mand to keep sabbath on the seventh day, some people went to work (v. 27). As in the failure in the discipline of "daily-ness," the failure to rest was counter-productive. Moreover, it brought on a harsh restatement of the Lord's will (v. 29).

The Lord's promise of food to satiate Israel's hunger was said to include both flesh and bread. Verse 13 contains the only reference to the provision of flesh (quails) in this story. In the Numbers 11 version of this story the steady diet of manna becomes the basis for murmuring and the Lord responds by promising to send meat *ad nauseam*! The manna provided by Yahweh was clearly desert food, not familiar to later generations who lived off the land. The writers' description of the manna (vv. 14, 31; cf. Num 11:7-9) bears strong resemblance to a phenomenon which continues to appear in the desert even in the present day. Insects which feed on trees bring the secretion of a sweet, sticky substance which solidifies into pellets during the cool of the night but which melts in the heat of the day. The biblical tradition explains how this desert food got its name. Exod 16:15 says that unfamiliarity with this desert phenomenon prompted the wilderness generation of Israelites to ask "What is it?" (in Hebrew, *man-hu'*).

The end of the story of the manna contains a liturgical directive designed to insure that this event not be forgotten by future generations. Accordingly, a jar of manna was placed "before the Lord" (i.e., at the shrine) and "before the testimony" (i.e., before the ark). The Priestly writer creates an anachronism here for in the biblical account there is, as of yet, no shrine and no testimony. The tablets of the law, later kept in the ark at the shrine, had not yet been given. The point, however, is that the experience of God's good-ness in the gift of "daily bread" was regarded as an impor-tant witness for future generations. Josh 5:10-12 corroborates the tradition that Israel was nourished by God with manna throughout the desert sojourn.

According to Exod 16:3 the experience of hunger in the wilderness caused Israel to remember the "good old days" of being well fed in bondage. In their new freedom the Israel-ites had not yet learned where to turn for a new source of

life and sustenance so when they got hungry they remembered and regretted having left Pharaoh's table. Just as the
story opens in "remembering," so it ends. God's gift of
manna in the wilderness is now designated as an object of
remembrance and as such it replaces memories of Pharaoh's
table. When future generations seek sustenance, they shall
recall the "daily bread" of the wilderness, not the "fleshpots"
of Egypt. They are to trust the precarious gifts of freedom,
not the security of bondage (cf. Gen 47:13-26).

The manna, given on God's terms, had to be respected as
such. Israel learned through the experience that "daily
bread" is not to be hoarded or greedily grasped but received
in the same spirit in which it is offered, i.e., as gift. In Exod
16 the Priestly writer used an ancient tradition about God's
nourishing presence in the wilderness to speak about the
meaning of sabbath. Together, the manna and sabbath
traditions are reminders of God's gifts of food and rest. At
the same time they are reminders and challenges for Israel to
live responsibly with its gifts.

WATER FROM THE ROCK
17:1-7

17 All the congregation of the people of Israel moved
on from the wilderness of Sin by stages, according to the
commandment of the Lord, and camped at Rephidim;
but there was no water for the people to drink. ²Therefore
the people found fault with Moses, and said, "Give us
water to drink." And Moses said to them, "Why do you
find fault with me? Why do you put the Lord to the
proof?" ³But the people thirsted there for water, and the
people murmured against Moses, and said, "Why did you
bring us up out of Egypt, to kill us and our children and
our cattle with thirst?" ⁴So Moses cried to the Lord,
"What shall I do with this people? They are almost ready
to stone me." ⁵And the Lord said to Moses, "Pass on
before the people, taking with you some of the elders of

Israel; and take in your hand the rod with which you struck the Nile, and go. 6Behold, I will stand before you there on the rock at Horeb; and you shall strike the rock, and water shall come out of it, that the people may drink." And Moses did so, in the sight of the elders of Israel. 7And he called the name of the place Massah and Meribah, because of the faultfinding of the children of Israel, and because they put the Lord to the proof by saying, "Is the Lord among us or not?"

Like the previous story about hunger and God's gracious gift of manna, the present narrative describes a problem of physical need which prompts a faith crisis. Without reference to the witness of God's care in the previous incidents of thirst (Exod 15:22-27) and hunger (Exod 16:1-36), the problem of thirst stirs up feelings of regret for ever having left Egypt. The faith crisis is poignantly recorded at the end of Exod 17:7: "Is the Lord among us or not?"

This story shares much in common with other wilderness motifs. The thirst here and God's gracious response which is mediated by Moses' action reminds us of the incident at Marah. Likewise, the structure of the present story is identical to that of Exod 15:22-27: a legitimate need is described, the people murmur, Moses intercedes with God, and the miraculous character whereby the need is answered indicates that it is God who sustains the life of Israel in the wilderness.

The story in Exod 17:1-7 bears even closer resemblance to an incident recorded in Num 20:1-13. Though the Numbers account has some unique elements which do not appear in Exod 17, the structure is the same as that described above and the content is parallel. Moreover, the Num 20 version shares with Exod 17 the localization of the event at Meribah.

Scholars are uncertain about the specific literary source represented in Exod 17:1-7. The fact that the pattern of vv. 1c-2 (notice of thirst followed by complaint) is repeated in v. 3 leads one to suspect that different literary traditions have

simply been juxtaposed but the lack of distinguishing criteria makes it difficult to identify the traditions with any of the
standard literary sources.

Whatever the source, the narrative demonstrates the
work of a skillful narrator in the play on words which the
story bears. Just as the name Marah ("bitterness") was
derived from the incident connected with that place (Exod
15:23), so here the narrator coordinates the place names
with the incident which is described. The Hebrew root, *rib*,
means "to argue a case, to dispute, to contend" while the
root, *nasah*, means "to prove, to test." These roots are used
in v. 2 to describe how the people "found fault" (from *rib*)
and put the Lord "to the proof" (from *nasah*). Thus the
place came to be called Massah ("place of testing, proof")
and Meribah ("place of dispute, contention"). The identification of Massah and Meribah with one another is somewhat problematic since in other parts of the biblical
tradition the two appear independent of one another (Deut
6:16; Num 20:13; Ps 81:8; 106:32). In some texts the two are
associated but not explicitly identified with one another
(Deut 33:8; Ps 95:8). One way to view the present reference
is to understand it as referring loosely to the region of
Massah and Meribah, two springs which were part of the
prominent wilderness oasis of Kadesh.

Another problematic element in this story is the connection it makes between the rock and Horeb. Horeb (Sinai), of
course, is the locus for Moses' encounter with God at the
burning bush (Exod 3) and the place of the covenant formalization and gift of the law (Exod 19-24). It is difficult to
reconcile the water-giving rock in the wilderness of Massah
and Meribah with the Mount Horeb which the Israelites
otherwise do not reach until Exod 19.

A play on the words Massah and Meribah gave the
narrator of Exod 17:1-7 ample opportunity to emphasize
the negative stance Israel took in the face of adversity in the
wilderness. They "found fault" (*rib*) and put Yahweh "to the
proof" (*nasah*). Israel is the subject of the proving/testing in
this story whereas in previously narrated incidents in the
wilderness God is said to have proved/tested Israel (Exod

15:25; 16:4). Viewed together, the wilderness journey described thus far constitutes a two-edged sword, an experience of "testing and being tested," both for Yahweh and for Israel. It was a time when loyalties were formed through trial and error.

The precariousness of freedom caused Israel to waver and look with longing to the security of life under Egyptian bondage. Instead they were called to the rock, an unlikely solution to a problem about water. Yet the rod which once struck the sea and made it dry is now used to strike the rock and bring forth water. Once again Israel is sustained in God's mysterious power and love.

THE BATTLE WITH AMALEK
17:8-16

8Then came Amalek and fought with Israel at Rephidim. 9And Moses said to Joshua, "Choose for us men, and go out, fight with Amalek; tomorrow I will stand on the top of the hill with the rod of God in my hand." 10So Joshua did as Moses told him, and fought with Amalek; and Moses, Aaron, and Hur went up to the top of the hill. 11Whenever Moses held up his hand, Israel prevailed; and whenever he lowered his hand, Amalek prevailed. 12But Moses' hands grew weary; so they took a stone and put it under him, and he sat upon it, and Aaron and Hur held up his hands, one on one side, and the other on the other side; so his hands were steady until the going down of the sun. 13And Joshua mowed down Amalek and his people with the edge of the sword.

14And the Lord said to Moses, "Write this as a memorial in a book and recite it in the ears of Joshua, that I will utterly blot out the remembrance of Amalek from under heaven." 15And Moses built an altar and called the name of it, The Lord is my banner, 16saying, "A hand upon the banner of the Lord! The Lord will have war with Amalek from generation to generation."

The absence of distinct criteria makes it difficult to identify this narrative with one of the major literary sources of
the Pentateuch. The story of battle with the Amalekites
bears hints of belonging to very ancient tradition. Literary
and theological motifs which have appeared heretofore in
the wilderness stories are notably absent. There is no murmuring motif and no instance of Yahweh's gracious aid
which sustains Israel through adversity in the wilderness
journey. It appears that the story has not been artificially
shaped to fit the wilderness schema. In fact, there is little
that is explicitly theological in the narrative until notice of
the Lord's intervention in v. 14. Another hint that the story
is relatively untouched by a heavy theological hand is the
manner in which the victory is won, i.e., by Moses' raised
hands. This borders on a magical conception similar to the
ancient view that the outcome of battle could be decided
solely by the pronouncement of a blessing or a curse (cf.
Num 22-24). Finally, the obscurity of the altar connected
with and named for this particular battle also suggests that
this tradition was left relatively untouched by later writers
whose tendency was to connect ancient traditions with
places which had subsequently become prominent holy
places for later generations of Israelites.

The Amalekites were a desert tribe who not only raided
Israel in the wilderness (Exod 17:8-16; cf. Num 13:29; 14:45)
but who also continued to be an enemy to Israel after the
latter's settlement in the land (Judg 6) even into the period of
the monarchy (1 Sam 15, 27, 30). Israel's continuing animosity toward Amalek appears to be justified by the divine
oath of Exod 17:14 and by the saying at the end of Exod
17:16: "The Lord will have war with Amalek from generation to generation." The oath of Exod 17:14 bears close
resemblance to the part of Deut 25:17-19 where the reason
for the oath is more carefully specified (cf. 1 Sam 15:2).

The name of the altar which Moses constructed, "The
Lord is my banner," must at one time have borne a connection with the rest of the story but that particular link has
now been lost. The slogan which is recorded in verse 16 ("a
hand upon the banner of the Lord") is actually unintelligible

in the Hebrew original and the present reading is possible through a slight textual emendation. The emended reading has the effect of expanding on the name of the altar.

Joshua is introduced here in the biblical texts for the first time. He is presented without introduction and without credentials; the writer simply presupposes that readers know who he is and that his reputation as a heroic leader on the battlefield is well known. Another figure, Hur, appears alongside Aaron as he does in Exod 24:14. It is likely that he was a renowned figure in ancient tradition even though only these two pieces of his portrait have survived in the biblical record.

In Exod 17:8-16, then, we are presented with what might be only a remnant of tales once told in ancient circles about Israel's longstanding feud with a group of desert marauders known as the Amalekites. The manner in which Moses is featured lends something of the character of a folktale to this story. The final verses (vv. 14-16) contribute a religious dimension in offering a divine endorsement for Israel's hatred toward Amalek. An ancient story was thus preserved as part of the national and religious record of the divine providence which secured Israel's destiny in the face of its enemies in the wilderness.

FORMATION FOR JUSTICE
18:1-27

18 Jethro, the priest of Midian, Moses' father-in-law, heard of all that God had done for Moses and for Israel his people, how the Lord had brought Israel out of Egypt. ²Now Jethro, Moses' father-in-law, had taken Zipporah, Moses' wife, after he had sent her away, ³and her two sons, of whom the name of the one was Gershom (for he said, "I have been a sojourner in a foreign land"), ⁴and the name of the other, Eliezer (for he said, "The God of my father was my help, and delivered me from the sword of Pharaoh"). ⁵And Jethro, Moses' father-in-law, came with his sons and his wife to Moses in the wilderness where he was encamped at the mountain of God. ⁶And when one told Moses, "Lo, your father-in-law Jethro is coming to you with your wife and her two sons with her," ⁷Moses went out to meet his father-in-law, and did obeisance and kissed him; and they asked each other of their welfare, and went into the tent. ⁸Then Moses told his father-in-law all that the Lord had done to Pharaoh and to the Egyptians for Israel's sake, all the hardship that had come upon them in the way, and how the Lord had delivered them. ⁹And Jethro rejoiced for all the good which the Lord had done to Israel, in that he had delivered them out of the hand of the Egyptians.

¹⁰And Jethro said, "Blessed be the Lord, who has delivered you out of the hand of the Egyptians and out of the hand of Pharaoh. ¹¹Now I know that the Lord is greater than all gods, because he delivered the people from under the hand of the Egyptians, when they dealt arrogantly with them." ¹²And Jethro, Moses' father-in-law, offered a burnt offering and sacrifices to God; and Aaron came with all the elders of Israel to eat bread with Moses' father-in-law before God.

¹³On the morrow Moses sat to judge the people, and the people stood about Moses from morning till evening. ¹⁴When Moses' father-in-law saw all that he was doing for the people, he said, "What is this that you are doing for the people? Why do you sit alone, and all the people stand about you from morning till evening?" ¹⁵And Moses said to his father-in-law, "Because the people come to me to inquire of God; ¹⁶when they have a dispute, they come to me and I decide between a man and his neighbor, and I make them know the statutes of God and his decisions." ¹⁷Moses' father-in-law said to him, "What you are doing is not good. ¹⁸You and the people with you will wear yourselves out, for the thing is too heavy for you; you are not able to perform it alone. ¹⁹Listen now to my voice; I will give you counsel, and God be with you! You shall represent the people before God, and bring their cases to God; ²⁰and you shall teach them the statutes and the decisions, and make them know the way in which

they must walk and what they must do. ²¹Moreover choose able men from all the people, such as fear God, men who are trustworthy and who hate a bribe; and place such men over the people as rulers of thousands, of hundreds, of fifties, and of tens. ²²And let them judge the people at all times; every great matter they shall bring to you, but any small matter they shall decide themselves; so it will be easier for you, and they will bear the burden with you. ²³If you do this, and God so commands you, then you will be able to endure, and all this people also will go to their place in peace."

²⁴So Moses gave heed to the voice of his father-in-law and did all that he had said. ²⁵Moses chose able men out of all Israel, and made them heads over the people, rulers of thousands, of hundreds, of fifties, and of tens. ²⁶And they judged the people at all times; hard cases they brought to Moses, but any small matter they decided themselves. ²⁷Then Moses let his father-in-law depart, and he went his way to his own country.

This account of the meeting with Jethro lacks several of the elements which have appeared heretofore in wilderness narratives. It neither opens nor closes with an itinerary notice about Israel's journey. There is no need on the part of the people and no murmuring. There is no record of God's life-sustaining gifts along the way. Thus, like the story of the battle with Amalek in Exod 17:8-16, the narrative of Exod 18 stands apart from the portrait of life in the wilderness between the sea and Sinai as it is reported in much of Exod 15-17. However, the present chapter does raise issues which recur in stories told about the wilderness journey between Sinai and the land (Num 11-24). For example, the concern for the establishment of legitimate leadership roles within the community which is addressed in Exod 18:13-27 has much in common with parts of Numbers 11. Thus, although Exod 18 has little in common with wilderness motifs which have already appeared, it does offer the first instance of areas of concern which will recur in subsequent wilderness stories.

Exod 18 constitutes one story narrated in two parts. In both parts the central figure is Jethro, Moses' father-in-law, a Midianite priest. Verses 1-12 focus on Jethro's response to the "good news" of Yahweh's great act in freeing Israel from Egyptian oppression. The remainder of the chapter, vv. 13-27, focus on Jethro's activity in effecting a systematic change in the Israelite community which would result in a more efficient administration of justice.

Both parts of the story are complex but scholars generally view them as stemming from the same literary source even though the exact identification of the source is still debated. One noteworthy literary characteristic of this story is repetition. For example, the term "father-in-law" occurs eight times in the first twelve verses and thirteen times in the entire chapter. Reference to God's decisive act in freeing Israel from Egyptian bondage is made five times in the first eleven verses. Verses 25-26 are virtually a repetition of verses 21-22.

The portrait of Jethro in Exod 18 has been the subject of much discussion in those scholarly circles where special interest is given to teasing out an historical thread which might be intertwined with the literary and theological threads of the tapestry of the biblical narrative. The fact that Jethro is represented as presiding at a Yahwist worship service (Exod 18:12) has given rise to the suggestion that Jethro was a worshipper of Yahweh (indeed, a Yahwistic priest) and that it was he who first introduced Moses to the God Yahweh. In support of this view, scholars point to the unusual endorsement implicitly given to Jethro when in Exod 18:13-27 the writer acknowledges that Israel was indebted to him for its system of justice. Jethro was a foreigner whose advice even Moses honored. This picture is supplemented by the witness of Exod 3 that Moses first learned Yahweh's name during the time he was a member of Jethro's household. This evidence has been brought together in what has come to be called the "Kenite Hypothesis," so called because Jethro is elsewhere described as a Kenite (see Judg 1:16; 4:11). Thus has Exod 18 served

as a basis for one theory regarding the possible historical
origins of Yahwism.

The focus on Jethro and Moses' family circle in Exod
18:1-12 affords an opportunity for us to pause and look
back to the beginnings of the exodus.

We recall that Moses was in the wilderness at this "mountain of God" (cf. Exod 18:5) tending his father-in-law's flock
when he first came to know Yahweh and to perceive his own
mission in mediating God's redeeming activity toward
Israel. In an attempt to harmonize the witness of Exod 4:20
which says that Moses' wife and sons accompanied him to
Egypt and the witness of Exod 18:2-5 which suggests that
they stayed with Jethro during Moses' absence, a writer has
inserted an explanatory phrase at the end of Exod 18:2
("after he had sent her away"), suggesting that Zipporah had
gone with Moses but at some time prior to the exodus she
had been sent back to her father's care. Contemporary
readers might be surprised that Jethro, not Zipporah, Gershom or Eliezer, was the object of Moses' affection at this
tender reunion. However, this accords with ancient Near
Eastern custom and with the focus of the rest of the story.

The "family matters" described in Exod 18:2-7 are set
within a religious context (vv. 1, 9-12) which directs our
attention to the exodus event. Exod 18:1 says that Jethro
heard "of all that God had done for Moses and for Israel his
people, how the Lord had brought Israel out of Egypt." This
apparently prompted Jethro to seek out Moses at the mountain of God where he again heard the "good news" but this
time from Moses himself. The Midianite priest's response
was to rejoice (v. 9) and to worship (vv. 10-12). The description of Jethro's worship is probably modeled on later Israelite liturgical practices. He offered sacrifices and shared a
sacred meal "before God" with Aaron, the figurehead of
Israel's priests. Moreover, the confession placed on his lips
in vv. 10-11 shares a common structure ("Blessed be the
Lord who..." followed by a statement of Yahweh's
redemptive acts) with the witness of other biblical texts (Gen
24:27; 1 Kgs 8:56-61) and thus may represent a stereotyped

confessional formula from recurrent worship assemblies.

In the second part of the story, verses 13-27, Jethro's concern is that justice be made accessible to the community in a more efficient manner. At the point of Jethro's intervention, Moses' role in the community seems to be both singular and complex. In v. 15 he is described as the one to whom the community goes "to inquire of God" (i.e., to seek an oracle regarding God's will). Moreover, v. 16a presents Moses as the judge who settles civil disputes within the community while v. 16b represents Moses as the one who pronounces God's will in sacred matters. Jethro sees what is happening and aptly observes that this system leaves Moses sitting alone and all the people standing around "from morning to evening" (v. 14). This is a poor use of resources and it is burdensome for all involved (v. 18). In the face of this, Jethro intervenes with a new policy which is designed to relieve the burden. Simply stated, his advice is to decentralize. Under his proposed plan (the adoption of which Jethro says is God's command; see v. 23) Moses is to mediate between God and Israel (v. 19) and to bear the sacred ordinances (v. 20). In addition, he is to be the one to whom "great matters" are referred (v. 22). In all other instances, however, the gifts of other members of the community should be utilized in dispensing justice. These judges are appointed for groupings "of thousands, of hundreds, of fifties and of tens," units based on procedures of organizations for military purposes.

The story of Exod 18:13-27 probably reflects an effort to legitimate a reorganization in the system of administering justice during the monarchical period in Israel. The story suggests that the system was borrowed from, or shared much in common with, a corresponding Midianite system. The reorganization was intended to expedite the execution of justice within the community. The writer represents the new system as the result of Jethro's advice but also as God's will.

The portrait of Jethro in the last part of Exod 18 fits well with the writer's portrayal of him in the early part of the chapter. The Midianite priest's response to the "good news" of God's activity in freeing Israel from the bondage of Egypt included rejoicing, confessing, and worshipping (vv. 9-12) but it did not stop there. He took it upon himself to facilitate systemic changes which would insure continued and efficient access to the justice mission initiated by Yahweh in the exodus event. The responsibility of mediating God's justice no longer rests solely with Moses but is shared by selected members of the community.

SEALING THE RELATIONSHIP: THE COVENANT AT SINAI 19:1—24:18

The tremendous importance which Israel's religious tradition assigned to the covenant-making at Sinai is indicated by the vast amount of material allotted to it in Scripture. According to the biblical record Israel's experience at Sinai begins in chapter 19 of the Book of Exodus and it is not until Numbers chapter 10 that we are told of the people's departure from this mountain of God. Thus, a significant part of the Pentateuch (over half of the Book of Exodus, the entire Book of Leviticus, and the first ten chapters of the Book of Numbers) is situated within the context of Sinai. Moreover, the Book of Deuteronomy brings the Pentateuch to a close with a rehearsal of Yahweh and Israel's life together where primary attention is given to their encounter at the mountain of God.

When Israel wrote about the Sinai experience, it spoke of an encounter with the Living God through a special theophany (Exod 19), a word-event wherein Israel was taught the responsibilities which flowed out of its relationship with Yahweh (Exod 20-23), and Israel's acceptance under oath of the relationship with all of its ramifications. The covenant which bound Israel to Yahweh was concluded and expressed symbolically in rituals rich with suggestions of shared life (Exod 24). To this story the Priestly circle of tradition attached large quantities of material (Exod 25-31, 35-40; Leviticus; Num 1-10) which it viewed as belonging to the covenantal theology associated with Sinai. Finally, within the context of this solemn event Israel also witnessed to its own infidelity and God's response, a story which dips heavily into the mysteries of human sin and divine compassion (Exod 32-34).

Even a superficial glance at the overall content of the material placed within the context of the Sinai event in the Books of Exodus, Leviticus and Numbers indicates that most of it is law. The word *torah*, rendered "law" in modern English translations, has its starting point in a Hebrew root which means to point out or direct and, by extension, to teach or instruct. Biblical law, then, is best viewed as instruction regarding what it is to live faithfully within the mystery of a faithful God. The law falls within and belongs to the bond which constituted Yahweh's covenant relationship with Israel.

It is significant that the Sinai law was not passed on by lawyers but by storytellers. The biblical writers collected generations of Israel's civil and religious laws, attributed their origin to God, and placed them within the story of salvation history, i.e., within the witness to God's saving deeds. This context provides an enduring reminder that for Israel law was not viewed in and of itself. Rather, it was embraced as continuous with the prior experience of deliverance from Egyptian bondage and as the expression of Israel's commitment to be faithful to that exodus experience.

As Moses had been drawn by the fire in the bush at this mountain of God and approached to hear its voice (Exod 3), so now all of the Israelites take their stand in relation to the fire at Mount Sinai and listen to words which express God's claim on them, a people redeemed by and for the Divine Self. The voice which addressed Moses from the fire had spoken freely and out of divine fidelity. Now, at this new juncture in the exodus story, the voice instructs Israel that its new life of freedom is not to be chaotic and direction-less like the desert wind. Israel's freedom is to be like God's, faithful. Freedom and fidelity, mystery and revelation, are held together for Israel as they had been for Moses, in the gifts of theophany and word.

THEOPHANY
19:1-25

19 On the third new moon after the people of Israel had gone forth out of the land of Egypt, on that day they came into the wilderness of Sinai. ²And when they set out from Rephidim and came into the wilderness of Sinai, they encamped in the wilderness; and there Israel encamped before the mountain. ³And Moses went up to God, and the Lord called to him out of the mountain, saying, "Thus you shall say to the house of Jacob, and tell the people of Israel: ⁴You have seen what I did to the Egyptians, and how I bore you on eagles' wings and brought you to myself. ⁵Now therefore, if you will obey my voice and keep my covenant, you shall be my own possession among all peoples; for all the earth is mine, ⁶and you shall be to me a kingdom of priests and a holy nation. These are the words which you shall speak to the children of Israel."

⁷So Moses came and called the elders of the people, and set before them all these words which the Lord had commanded him. ⁸And all the people answered together and said, "All that the Lord has spoken we will do." And Moses reported the words of the people to the Lord. ⁹And the Lord said to Moses, "Lo, I am coming to you in a thick cloud, that the people may hear when I speak with you, and may also believe you for ever."

Then Moses told the words of the people to the Lord. ¹⁰And the Lord said to Moses, "Go to the people and consecrate them today and tomorrow, and let them wash their garments, [11]and be ready by the third day; for on the third day the Lord will come down upon Mount Sinai in the sight of all the people. [12]And you shall set bounds for the people round about, saying, 'Take heed that you do not go up into the mountain or touch the border of it; whoever touches the mountain shall be put to death; [13]no hand shall touch him, but he shall be stoned or shot; whether beast or man, he shall not live. When the trumpet sounds a long blast, they shall come up to the mountain." [14]So Moses went down from the mountain to the people, and consecrated the people; and they washed their garments. [15]And he said to the people, "Be ready by the third day; do not go near a woman."

[16]On the morning of the third day there were thunders and lightnings, and a thick cloud upon the mountain, and a very loud trumpet blast, so that all the people who were in the camp trembled. [17]Then Moses brought the people out of the camp to meet God; and they took their stand at the foot of the mountain. [18]And Mount Sinai was wrapped in smoke, because the Lord descended upon it in fire; and the smoke of it went up like the smoke of a kiln, and the whole mountain quaked greatly. [19]And as the sound of the trumpet grew louder and louder, Moses spoke and God answered him in thunder. [20]And the Lord came down upon Mount Sinai, to the top of the mountain; and the Lord called Moses to the top of the mountain, and Moses went up. [21]And the Lord said to Moses, "Go down and warn the people, lest they break through to the Lord to gaze and many of them perish. [22]And also let the priests who come near to the Lord consecrate themselves, lest the Lord break out upon them." [23]And Moses said to the Lord, "The people cannot come up to Mount Sinai; for thou thyself didst charge us, saying, 'Set bounds about the mountain, and consecrate it.'" [24]And the Lord said to him, "Go down, and come up bringing Aaron with you; but do not let the priests and the people break through to come up to the Lord, lest he break out against them." [25]So Moses went down to the people and told them.

The narrative about the covenanting at Sinai begins in a deliberate and solemn style which reminds one of a sacred religious festival. It is probable that the depiction of the Sinai meeting with God was influenced by the experience of worshippers who later sought to express the meaning of the primitive event by somehow rehearsing it amidst the smoke and sounding trumpets of Israel's cult. The ritual purification at the foot of the mountain probably reflects the practice of later generations of worshippers.

The literary character of this chapter, like the mountain itself, seems to shift as thoughts are expressed uneasily and uncertainly in jagged juxtaposition. Verses 3-8 hasten to tell the whole covenant story from start to finish whereas the rest of the narrative moves very slowly and cautiously as if on sacred ground. Verse 9 articulates the purpose of the meeting in terms of the validation of Moses' role as mediator, a topic which is not addressed again until Exod 20:18-21. Verses 21-25 portray a rather forgetful Divinity who demonstrates no knowledge of directions which had already been given (cf. v. 21 and vv. 12-13), a slip of memory which Moses has to point out. Amidst concern that the people and the space be properly consecrated for the encounter with God (vv. 10-15 and vv. 21-25) lies the account of the theophany itself (vv. 16-20). The text further communicates the restlessness and excitement of this moment in Israel's history by portraying Moses' repeated trips up and down the mountain in accord with the duties of a zealous mediator.

Tensions in the text also appear in connection with the nature of God's presence and the people's taking their stand in relation to that Mystery. Verse 3 presupposes that the Divinity's presence at the mountain was an abiding one while other lines (vv. 9, 11, 18) suggest that the Divinity came to meet Israel at the mountain but was not at home there. As for the people's response, some lines (vv. 12, 21-25) presuppose that Israel, in its fervor, would rush the mountain. This led to a concern that the sacredness of the divine presence not be violated and precautionary measures were issued. On the other hand, Exod 19:16 and its sequel in Exod 20:18-21 portray the people as trembling at the divine presence. Because they feared God's nearness they begged Moses to act as mediator.

The unevenness in this narrative is best explained by positing that it has been handed down by several writers representing different viewpoints. Either literally or figuratively, different generations of believers in ancient Israel undertook their own pilgrimages to Sinai. Each came away with a unique perspective on the significance of the encounter there. Although biblical scholarship has not reached a consensus regarding the correspondence between the threads of tradition in Exod 19 and the major Pentateuchal literary sources, many agree that for the most part the chapter represents a conflation of Yahwist and Elohist traditions.

The compact unit of Exod 19:3-8 deserves special attention. Scholars generally view it as an editorial insertion contributed by a writer from the Deuteronomic school. Its content includes a proclamation of God's saving presence in the exodus event, here tenderly likened to the movement of an eagle sweeping up and bearing Israel to the Divine Self (v. 4). This graciousness calls for Israel's obedient response which in itself expresses a willingness to bind the relationship between Yahweh and Israel more firmly and so extend it into the future (vv. 5-6). Israel engages God's bonding initiative by swearing on oath to give itself over to Yahweh (v. 8). The structure of this unit has much in common with other texts which speak of covenant (Josh 24; 1 Sam 12). It is likely that in the structure we see an outline of recurring covenant renewal ceremonies as they were celebrated in the ancient Israelite community.

Exod 19:3-8 presents a concise summary of the overall event at Sinai, the details of which are now taken up in the text. Having established with great care God's presence (Exod 19), the biblical writers describe the gift of the law (Exod 20-23) and the formalization of the relationship in the making of the covenant (Exod 24).

THE DECALOGUE
20:1-17

20 And God spoke all these words, saying,

²"I am the Lord your God, who brought you out of the land of Egypt, out of the house of bondage.

³"You shall have no other gods before me.

⁴"You shall not make for yourself a graven image, or any likeness of anything that is in heaven above, or that is in the earth beneath, or that is in the water under the earth; ⁵you shall not bow down to them or serve them; for I the Lord your God am a jealous God, visiting the iniquity of the fathers upon the children to the third and the fourth generation of those who hate me, ⁶but showing steadfast love to thousands of those who love me and keep my commandments.

⁷"You shall not take the name of the Lord your God in vain; for the Lord will not hold him guiltless who takes his name in vain.

⁸"Remember the sabbath day, to keep it holy. ⁹Six days you shall labor, and do all your work; ¹⁰but the seventh day is a sabbath to the Lord your God; in it you shall not do any work, you, or your son, or your daughter, your manservant, or your maidservant, or your cattle, or the sojourner who is within your gates; ¹¹for in six days the Lord made heaven and earth, the sea, and all that is in them, and rested the seventh day; therefore the Lord blessed the sabbath day and hallowed it.

¹²"Honor your father and your mother, that your days may be long in the land which the Lord you God gives you.

¹³"You shall not kill.

¹⁴"You shall not commit adultery.

¹⁵"You shall not steal.

¹⁶"You shall not bear false witness against your neighbor.

¹⁷"You shall not covet your neighbor's house; you shall not covet your neighbor's wife, or his manservant, or his

maidservant, or his ox, or his ass, or anything that is your neighbor's."

The word-event at Sinai begins with a statement of the divine name together with a reference to God's pivotal redemptive act which had brought Israel to this moment. Exod 20:2 presents the *torah*-instruction at Sinai as rising out of and continuous with God's freeing activity. The decalogue issues not from some universal natural law or lawgiver but from the One who is "your God, who brought you out of the land of Egypt, out of the house of bondage." Thus, what could have been a burdensome yoke is presented as a tie that binds Israel to the personal Mystery who frees.

Some scholars have noted that the decalogue flows out of God's self-identification and they conclude from this that we are to understand the laws as continuous with that self-identification. That is to say, the laws of the decalogue are presented as flowing from the righteousness and justice of God's own person. The decalogue, the very core of the life and integrity of the covenant community, must then be regarded as profoundly theocentric. The text bears witness to the notion that the very life of the community is centered in the person of the living and liberating God.

Considerable attention in scholarly discussions has been given to the question of whether or not the text of Exod 20 was modelled after the pattern of political treaties in the ancient Near Eastern world. It has been pointed out that Hittite treaty forms begin with the self-identification of the king who is initiating the treaty and that this is followed by a so-called historical recital in which the great king describes the relationship which has already been formed between himself and his prospective treaty partner. The account of the relationship characteristically highlights the good will which the great king has already demonstrated toward the other. These two sections of the treaty documents preface the stipulations which then spell out the loyalty and fidelity which the great king asks in return. Some scholars have seen this pattern in Exod 20 where the decalogue follows Yahweh's self-identification and a reference to the redemptive event of the exodus. Others, however, point out that the self-identification and reference to past deeds in Exod 20 are too brief to have been modelled on ancient Near Eastern treaties. In addition, they note that other parts of the typical treaty form (such as witnesses to the treaty agreement, a pronouncement of curses and blessings which will follow the fidelity or infidelity of the treaty partners, and instructions regarding the care of the treaty document) are not found in Exod 20 as they are, for instance, in Josh 24.

The self-disclosure of Exod 20:2 is followed by what many contemporary believers refer to as the "ten commandments" or what the Bible itself calls the "ten words" (Exod 34:28; Deut 4:13, 10:4). That such a list enjoyed privileged status even in biblical times is suggested by this special designation and by the fact that it is presented as having been spoken directly by God to the community (cf. the beginning of other law collections such as Exod 20:22, Exod 25:1, Exod 35:1, and Lev 17:1), and by the fact that virtually the same list appears in different levels of tradition (cf. Exod 20, Deut 5, Hos 4:1-3).

The laws which comprise the decalogue are "apodictic" laws. As such they are characterized by the categorical nature of their content, typically expressed in short, straightforward statements. Apodictic law is usually devoid of statement of motivation, elaboration or explanation, and it does not provide for exceptions or specific extenuating features. It characteristically deals with matters of extreme concern, evidenced by the fact that disobedience frequently involves the death penalty or its equivalent, a curse (cf. Exod 21:15; Lev 20:9, 10, 16). Apodictic law addresses matters on which the very life of the community was thought to rest. Sometimes stated in negative formulations, it charts boundary points and aims at protecting core values of the community by categorically ruling out specific acts which were thought to endanger common life. Although they chart the outer limits encircling the community's well-being, apodictic laws do not offer specific guides for what is permissible and desirable within community life. The inner part of the circle is left open. Thus, specific demands and responsibilities are subjects for discussion and further development and understanding. In the words of one scholar, specific procedures for life within the circle of these general policies are "trusted to a healthy feeling for justice." It is probable that originally the "ten words" were similarly-structured prohibitions forming a catechesis of tribal ethos that could easily be remembered and taught because of their simple formulation and because they were readily numbered on the fingers of the hands.

Regardless of the witness of Exod 34:1 and Deut 5:22, contemporary readers would do well not to regard the "ten words" as having been carved in stone. That is to say, these commandments probably were not delivered once for all by God at the mountain at Sinai and forever remained the same. The slight differences between the decalogues of Exod 20 and Deut 5 suggest that the lists were shaped by the faith of generations of believers and in some cases bear the fingerprints of different traditions in the final text. As such the "ten words" reflect human testimony from communities of believers. By the "ten words" Israel rejected those matters which were ruled out by the integrity and wholeness of the covenant community. The "ten words" emerged from a long inspired tradition.

While it is clear that the biblical writers regarded the commandments as numbering a total of ten (Exod 34:28; Deut 4:13; 10:4), post-biblical religious traditions have numbered the individual commandments in different ways. The divergent enumerations depend upon whether the prohibition against other gods (Exod 20:3) is read in conjunction with the prohibition against graven images (Exod 20:4-6) and whether the prohibition against coveting (Exod 20:17) is regarded as a single command or as two. A third point of divergent interpretations rests on whether Exod 20:2 is to be regarded as a command or simply as an introduction to the list which follows.

Briefly stated, Jewish tradition is alone in understanding verse 2 as the first commandment. The prohibitions against other gods and against graven images (vv. 3-6) are then read as one commandment as is the prohibition against coveting (v. 17). Anglican, Greek Catholic and Reformed traditions regard v. 2 as an introduction. The prohibition against other gods (v. 3) is read as the first commandment and separate from the prohibition of graven images (vv. 4-6). The prohibition against coveting (v. 17) is understood to be a single command. Finally, Lutheran and Roman Catholic traditions also regard v. 2 as an introduction to the list of ten commandments. They combine it with the prohibitions against other gods and against graven images (vv. 2-6) which together are viewed as constituting the first commandment. Lutherans and Roman Catholics read v. 17 as two commands. According to this enumeration the ninth commandment prohibits the coveting of a neighbor's spouse and the tenth commandment the coveting of a neighbor's goods. This division is closer to the copy of the decalogue in Deut 5:21.

As we turn our attention to a brief examination of each of the "ten words," the reader will recognize that we have adopted the enumeration shared by Lutherans and Roman Catholics.

The exact intent of the first commandment (Exod 20:3) is not perfectly clear because of the expression which the RSV renders "before me" but which literally means "before my face." Some have suggested that the commandment prohibits the setting up of idols in Yahweh's presence, i.e., in a place of worship. Whatever the case, the core value which it appears to protect is the Oneness which must be at the heart of the covenant community. Israel is bonded with One; its center is One. This is safeguarded by excluding other gods, other primary allegiances. The first "word" thus appears to be a commandment about Israel's radical monotheism. It is not so much addressed to a general intellectual acknowledgement of the existence of only one God as it is a call to absolute, categorical, singular loyalty. The wholeness and integrity of Israel's life, its oneness, demanded that its center be One.

The second commandment (Exod 20:4-6) diverges from several of the others in that it contains material which goes beyond a simple, categorical negative prohibition which may have been the original form of the commandments. Thus, verse 4 begins with a simple prohibition of graven images but then goes on to prohibit any representation of God whatsoever. Verse 5 makes the command even more inclusive by prohibiting as well the worship of other gods. This is followed in verse 6 by a statement of motivation.

This commandment protects God's freedom. A graven image is constructed from lifeless material according to a human blueprint. Once constructed the image remains static; it is moved only by human initiative and according to the needs and wishes of the humans in whose control it rests. Such an image could never represent the One whom Israel experienced as moving in its history in ways which were dynamic and mysterious and free.

As in the second commandment, so in the third commandment (Exod 20:7) it is probable that the motivation clause represents an addition to what was originally a simple, categorical prohibition. Precise definition of the original intent of this prohibition continues to elude modern scholarship. The Hebrew expression which the RSV renders "in vain" is rooted in a semantic range which suggests emptiness, something to which there is no substance or worth, something not grounded in any reality. Given the ancient Near Eastern reverence for the power and mystery which belonged to one's name and the Israelite tradition of the gift of God's name to Moses (cf. the commentary on Exod 3:13-15), it seems appropriate that Israel would seek to insure the sacredness of the name of the One in whom they found life and blessing. This ruled out vain or evil uses of God's name, reserving it instead for solemn and hallowed occasions such as oath-taking and blessing. The third commandment thus prohibits the abuse of sacred sounds by their use in angry or superficial speech.

The fourth commandment (Exod 20:8-11) bears marks of the faith of different generations of believers. Scholars have suggested that the command which now appears in positive formulation originally was a short, negative prohibition like other commands of the decalogue. If this was the case, the original prohibition may have resembled that which now appears in Lev 23:3: "...the seventh day is a sabbath of solemn rest, a holy convocation; you shall do no work...." As it now appears in the text of Exod 20:8-11, the command has grown to include a listing of who is to rest (v. 10); it is expressed in terms used by the Deuteronomic writers. Moreover, verse 11 offers a rationale for sabbath rest which appears to be based on the view of creation recorded by the Priestly writer in Gen 1:1—2:4a. The sabbath command, therefore, more than any of the other commands, reflects a long history of theological reflection upon the practice of resting on the seventh day.

Sacred days and taboo days are known to have been marked by special observance including rest from routine activity by other peoples of the ancient world. Thus in observing sabbath the Israelites may have been adapting non-Yahwistic customs which marked mysteries associated with special moments in the rhythms of the universe. As it is stated in Exod 20:8-11, however, Israelite practice is thoroughly theocentric. As God had rested, so must believers and all those who assist with the labors of believers (children, servants, cattle, strangers). The first and last lines of the commandment refer to the holiness of the day. The Lord hallowed the sabbath (v. 11) and believers are not merely to rest on that day but to "keep it holy" (v. 8).

The fifth commandment (Exod 20:12) shares with the one which precedes it a departure from the style of simple, categorical prohibition. The command is voiced in the positive and includes a statement which describes the reward and hence motivation for its observance. If, as some have suggested, this command was originally voiced in the negative, it probably consisted of something like this: "Do not curse (or abuse) you father or your mother"(cf. Exod 21:15, 17; Lev 20:9). It, like the others, was addressed to a community of adults. As such, it was designed to protect the honor of aged parents against adult offspring who might be abusive toward parents whose most vital years and service had been spent.

The writer affixed a promise to the command: a full life is

the reward for esteem and respect shown to one's parents. Thus to uphold one's parents' welfare is to insure one's own. One enhances the life one has received by revering its bearers.

The sixth commandment (Exod 20:13) initiates a list of several short, categorical prohibitions. Although there is much ambiguity about the precise intent of this prohibition against killing, it appears certain that this commandment seeks to secure the value of human life. To that end, it prohibits murder, the intentional shedding of blood. Israel regarded God's lordship of life as a sacred reality. While it seems true that Israel did actually tolerate the taking of human life in some cases, these instances were carefully monitored and controlled by the community through institutions such as the constraints of blood vengeance, altars and cities of refuge, and so forth. In other words, laws were carefully designed to insure that human life was not taken arbitrarily.

Stated categorically without motivation or qualification, the seventh commandment (Exod 20:14) presumably aimed to safeguard the value of the marital bond. This prohibition of adultery does not address the topic of sexual relations in general. It is specifically concerned with marriage. Israel saw the exclusive claims of the marital relationship as somehow touching upon the core of the life of the entire covenant community.

On the basis of Exod 21:16 and Deut 24:7 some scholars have suggested that the prohibition against stealing which constitutes the eighth commandment (Exod 20:15) represents a secondary development of a commandment which was originally directed against the stealing of persons, i.e., kidnapping. Whatever its original content, as it now stands it does not limit the inclusiveness of what is not to be stolen. Neither things nor persons are to be taken in secret. Twentieth century Western notions of the right to private ownership are foreign to the original context of this commandment. However, Israel did see and attempt to safeguard a connectedness between a person or family and those things or people which made up the person or family's sphere of life. Thus, to steal was to transgress against another's sphere of life and, by extension, to transgress against the person of that other. To do so was regarded by ancient Israel as jeopardizing the integrity of life within the covenant community.

The ninth commandment (Exod 20:16) has its background in ancient Near Eastern legal procedure. It prohibits the twisting of speech before a communal institution of justice in a way which would deny another member of the covenant community access to justice. The commandment does not address itself to lying in general (cf. Hos 4:2). To protect the wholeness of the fabric of community life, Israel had to be able to trust the language of legal testimony which one member bore with regard to another. The commandment attests to a conviction in ancient Israel regarding the bond and mutual service between truth and justice.

In the Roman Catholic and Lutheran traditional lists of the ten commandments, the prohibition against coveting (Exod 20:17) is regarded as two commandments. That is to say, the command against coveting a neighbor's wife has been regarded as separate from the command not to covet a neighbor's belongings. On the other hand, it is also possible to regard the imperative not to covet one's neighbor's "house" (v. 17a) as intended to be inclusive of everything connected with the wholeness of a neighbor's life. Thus, a neighbor's "house" is further defined and specified as wife, manservant, maidservant, ox, and ass (v. 17b). The list is summed up in the concluding phrase: "or anything that is your neighbor's." This commandment bears a close connection with the prohibition against stealing but it is unique among the ten in that it addresses itself to an underlying attitude. The value protected by this prohibition shares much in common with the values which lie at the heart of the preceding commandments. Ancient Israel recognized that the integrity of the covenant community demanded mutual respect for persons, their very life, extensions of that life in one's primary relationships, one's reputation and good name, and one's belongings.

ON MOSES' MEDIATORIAL ROLE
20:18-21

> [18]Now when all the people perceived the thunderings
> and the lightnings and the sound of the trumpet and the
> mountain smoking, the people were afraid and trembled;
> and they stood afar off, [19]and said to Moses, "You speak
> to us, and we will hear; but let not God speak to us, lest we
> die." [20]And Moses said to the people, "Do not fear; for
> God has come to prove you, and that the fear of him may
> be before your eyes, that you may not sin."
> [21]And the people stood afar off, while Moses drew near
> to the thick darkness where God was.

These few verses bear strong resemblance to material
which appeared in Exod 19, so much so that some have
suggested that they were originally placed after Exod 19:18.
The unit begins with reference to theophany in much the
same terms as used in the preceding chapter and it also
recalls the people's fearful response described in Exod
19:16. As in Exod 19:9, there is explicit reflection on Moses'
mediatorial role; Exod 20:19 differs slightly in that the
initiative for Moses' service is said to have arisen with the
people and not with God as the preceding chapter had said.
In verse 20 Moses introduces Israel to the purpose for the
Sinai encounter; ultimately, he says, it is "that you may not
sin."

Regardless of the original placement of these lines, they
serve theological and literary purposes in their present context. First of all, in the present text the law (Exod 20:1-17) is
now enveloped by theophany. The event narrated thus far is
bipolar: there is both Mystery and revelation. The divine
Mystery is shrouded in clouds and smoke yet the divine
word is given clear expression. The law flows out of and
back into the otherness of God and in the process the
covenant community learns what it is to be holy.

Secondly, when read in its present context, verses 18-21
provide an opportunity for the tradition to record that

additional laws were given at Mount Sinai (Exod 20:22—23:33). Unlike the decalogue which is presented as having been spoken directly by God to the community, the additional laws in Exod 20-23 are presented as having been given to Moses, presumably because of the people's fear of God's direct speech. Moses thus acts as the community had called him to do; he mediated the further words of God.

In accord with the original design of this commentary, we forego treatment of the so-called Covenant Code which appears in Exod 20:22—23:33 (see Vol. 4, *Deuteronomy*, by Richard Clifford, S.J., pages 186-191) and proceed directly to the narrative which continues in Exod 24.

THE COVENANT
24:1-18

24 And he said to Moses, "Come up to the Lord, you and Aaron, Nadab, and Abihu, and seventy of the elders of Israel, and worship afar off. ²Moses alone shall come near to the Lord; but the others shall not come near, and the people shall not come up with him."

³Moses came and told the people all the words of the Lord and all the ordinances; and all the people answered with one voice, and said, "All the words which the Lord has spoken we will do." ⁴And Moses wrote all the words of the Lord. And he rose early in the morning, and built an altar at the foot of the mountain, and twelve pillars, according to the twelve tribes of Israel. ⁵And he sent young men of the people of Israel, who offered burnt offerings and sacrificed peace offerings of oxen to the Lord. ⁶And Moses took half of the blood and put it in basins, and half of the blood he threw against the altar. ⁷Then he took the book of the covenant, and read it in the hearing of the people; and they said, "All that the Lord has spoken we will do, and we will be obedient." ⁸And Moses took the blood and threw it upon the people, and said, "Behold the blood of the covenant which the Lord has made with you in accordance with all these words."

⁹Then Moses and Aaron, Nadab, and Abihu, and seventy of the elders of Israel went up, ¹⁰and they saw the God of Israel; and there was under his feet as it were a pavement of sapphire stone, like the very heaven for clearness. ¹¹And he did not lay his hand on the chief men of the people of Israel; they beheld God, and ate and drank.

¹²The Lord said to Moses, "Come up to me on the mountain, and wait there; and I will give you the tables of stone, with the law and the commandment, which I have written for their instruction." ¹³So Moses rose with his servant Joshua, and Moses went up into the mountain of God. ¹⁴And he said to the elders, "Tarry here for us, until we come to you again; and, behold, Aaron and Hur are with you; whoever has a cause, let him go to them."

¹⁵Then Moses went up on the mountain, and the cloud covered the mountain. ¹⁶The glory of the Lord settled on Mount Sinai, and the cloud covered it six days; and on the seventh day he called to Moses out of the midst of the cloud. ¹⁷Now the appearance of the glory of the Lord was like a devouring fire on the top of the mountain in the sight of the people of Israel. ¹⁸And Moses entered the cloud, and went up on the mountain. And Moses was on the mountain forty days and forty nights.

The biblical writers bring the event on Mount Sinai to a close with their accounts of the covenant rituals described in Exod 24:1-11. The remainder of the chapter (vv. 12-18) sets a context for the material which has been added, i.e., the instructions for the construction of the tabernacle (Exod 25-31). Verses 12-18 also help to account for Moses' lengthy absence from the community which in turn is the background and starting point for the building of the golden calf as narrated in Exod 32.

The narrative about the ritual formalization of the covenant relationship reflects at least two distinct traditions. Verses 1-2 contain instructions for an encounter which is narrated in verses 9-11. According to this tradition, the leaders (Moses, Aaron, Nadab, Abihu, and seventy elders) are called apart from the community and, although verse 2 seems to separate Moses from the small group of leaders, it is these "chief men of the people of Israel" who symbolically mark the ratification of Yahweh's covenant bonding with Israel by sharing a meal in the divine presence. This tradition says that these leaders "saw the God of Israel" (v. 10; cf. v. 11), a remarkable assertion in light of the biblical notion that death would come to one who gazed upon God (see, for example, Exod 33:20). The biblical writer appears to acknowledge that this event was exceptional with the note that "he (God) did not lay a hand on the chief men of the people of Israel" (v. 11). The caution of the biblical writer can be seen, however, in the fact that the text avoids a description of the Divine Self and offers instead a description of the floor which supported the Divinity (v. 10).

Exod 24:3-8 contain an alternate tradition regarding the conclusion of the covenant at Sinai. In contrast to vv. 1-2 and 9-11, the setting for the ritual described in vv. 3-8 would appear to be the base of the mountain where the people were. Furthermore, in distinction from the special roles of the "chief men of the people of Israel" in the tradition of vv. 1-2 and 9-11, this account stresses the participation of the entire community while Moses exercised the role of mediator. Another obvious difference between the two traditions is that the ritual meal of vv. 1-2 and 9-11 has been replaced in vv. 3-8 by a ceremony marked by the prominence of word (God's law and the people's oath) and blood (sprinkled first on the altar and then on the people). The structure of the solemn ceremony described in vv. 3-8 almost certainly reflects covenant renewal ceremonies in later Israel's cultic rehearsal of the Sinai event.

The variant traditions regarding the sealing of the covenant at Mount Sinai appear to represent two attempts at capturing the meaning of the bond between Yahweh and Israel. Both ceremonies feature symbols which speak of shared life. In envisioning the meal at the ancient mountain, one tradition tapped the view that the sharing of food somehow symbolizes sharing in the very stuff of life. A shared meal suggests a communion made sacred by virtue of food's inherent connection with life itself (cf. the covenant meal in Gen 31:44-54). Another circle of tradition sought to capture the same covenant relationship by utilizing instead the blood in which life itself was thought to be contained (see Deut 12:23). To share blood is to share life, to become one. In these rituals ancient Israel suggests that in the covenant bond finalized at Mount Sinai Yahweh and Israel came to form a single family, a communion of life.

The final redactor of Exod 24:1-11 tried to lessen the differences between the two traditions by enveloping the service of word and blood (vv. 3-8) with the witness about the sacred meal (vv. 1-2, 9-11). In the final text, then, the tradition featuring the word and blood has the appearance of growing out of the instructions contained in vv. 1-2 and of flowing into and culminating in the communion described in vv. 9-11.

Exod 24:12-18 once again feature Moses' unique role in the bonding between Yahweh and Israel which was solemnized at Mount Sinai. His mediatorial position is secure here, having been steadily built into the witness of the chapters since the arrival at Sinai. For the first time Joshua is presented as accompanying Moses while Aaron and Hur appear together in the capacity of settling issues which might arise in Moses' absence (cf. the linking of Aaron and Hur as Moses' assistants in the war against the Amalekites described in Exod 17:8-13). The ancient account of Moses' ascent to the mountain (vv. 12-15a) is elaborated upon in the Priestly writer's witness of vv. 15b-18. The older tradition contained in vv. 12-15a points forward to the continuation of the narrative in Exod 32 by including Joshua at Moses' side and by telling us that Moses disappeared into the mountain in order to receive the tablets on which the law was written (v. 12; cf. Exod 32:15-16). Even so, the addition by the later Priestly writer points backward to the beginnings of this Sinai encounter by recalling the mysterious elements of the theophany described in Exod 19 (cloud and fire). Taken together, Exod 24:12-18 reach back to the mystery of God's presence and they point forward to the mystery of Israel's failure to live faithfully within its bonded relationship with Yahweh (Exod 32).

Moses' lengthy sojourn into the mountain provides the context wherein biblical tradition inserted instructions about the tabernacle (Exod 25-31). We set aside this material and proceed to an examination of the narrative text which resumes in Exod 32-34.

COVENANT BROKEN
AND RESTORED
32:1—34:35

Amidst several chapters of tradition about the tabernacle (Exod 25-31 and 35-40), the biblical editors have inserted three chapters which speak of Israel's sin against its covenanted God and the restoration of the bonded relationship through God's forgiveness and Moses' mediation.

The story of Exod 32-34 unfolds primarily through a series of dialogues. The text is marked by some inconsistency and considerable repetition, characteristics which suggest that the narrative as it now stands is the product of a long development in the course of which contributions were made by different hands. Generally speaking, the story is thought to belong to early stages of Hebrew thought (perhaps a combination of Yahwist and Elohist traditions), although a Deuteronomic hand probably inserted verses 7-14 into chapter 32 and verses 11-16 in chapter 34. Likewise, tensions within Israel's Priestly circles probably lay behind the incident about the ordination of the Levites (Exod 32:25-29) making it likely that this too represents a later insertion into the overall narrative.

There is a clear movement in the narrative from Israel's sin to God's forgiveness. The sin is said to have arisen from

Israel's demand for a tangible, visible guide whose presence they could be certain of. Basically, it was a failure in trust, a sin which strikes at the heart of covenant. God's forgiveness, on the other hand, is said to have been secured through Moses' persistent intercession, a subject which receives considerable attention in chapters 32 and 33. Literary connections which envelop the movement from sin to forgiveness are to be found in the references to the *torah* tablets. The two intact stones are explicitly brought to the reader's attention at the close of the text immediately preceding Exod 32: "And he gave to Moses, when he had made an end of speaking with him upon Mount Sinai, the two tablets of the testimony, tables of stone, written with the finger of God" (Exod 31:18). They are mentioned again at the inception of Moses' return to the community (Exod 32:15-16). However, upon discovering the sin which had occurred at the foot of the mountain before the golden calf (Exod 32:19), Moses broke the tablets thereby symbolizing the fracture which had taken place in Israel's covenant relationship with Yahweh. Finally, at the end of the story the two tables are reconstructed in the context of the narrative about the restoration of the covenant relationship (Exod 34:1, 28).

In these chapters readers are given a profound statement about ancient Israel's perception of its relationship with Yahweh. To the story of its marvelous encounter with the Living God at Sinai and the formalization of a covenant bond which would carry forward its relationship with that One who had called them out of Egypt (Exod 19-24), Israel adds testimony to its failure in fidelity. The story of the covenant bond at Sinai was regarded as incomplete until Israel had included an account of its sin and God's forgiveness. Here in Exod 32-34, in the middle of chapters about the law, Israel makes clear that its covenant bond with Yahweh was maintained not so much by human fidelity as by divine mercy.

THE GOLDEN CALF
32:1-35

32 When the people saw that Moses delayed to come down from the mountain, the people gathered themselves together to Aaron, and said to him, "Up, make us gods, who shall go before us; as for this Moses, the man who brought us up out of the land of Egypt, we do not know what has become of him." ²And Aaron said to them, "Take off the rings of gold which are in the ears of your wives, your sons, and your daughters, and bring them to me." ³So all the people took off the rings of gold which were in their ears, and brought them to Aaron. ⁴And he received the gold at their hand, and fashioned it with a graving tool, and made a molten calf; and they said, "These are your gods, O Israel, who brought you up out of the land of Egypt!" ⁵When Aaron saw this, he built an altar before it; and Aaron made proclamation and said, "Tomorrow shall be a feast to the Lord." ⁶And they rose up early on the morrow, and offered burnt offerings and brought peace offerings; and the people sat down to eat and drink, and rose up to play.

⁷And the Lord said to Moses, "Go down; for your people, whom you brought up out of the land of Egypt, have corrupted themselves; ⁸they have turned aside quickly out of the way which I commanded them; they have made for themselves a molten calf, and have worshiped it and sacrificed to it, and said, 'These are your gods, O Israel, who brought you up out of the land of Egypt!'" ⁹And the Lord said to Moses, "I have seen this people, and behold, it is a stiff-necked people; ¹⁰now therefore let me alone, that my wrath may burn hot against them and I may consume them; but of you I will make a great nation."

¹¹But Moses besought the Lord his God, and said, "O Lord, why does thy wrath burn hot against thy people, whom thou hast brought forth out of the land of Egypt with great power and with a mighty hand? ¹²Why should

the Egyptians say, 'With evil intent did he bring them forth, to slay them in the mountains, and to consume them from the face of the earth'? Turn from thy fierce wrath, and repent of this evil against thy people. ¹³Remember Abraham, Isaac, and Israel, thy servants, to whom thou didst swear by thine own self, and didst say to them, 'I will multiply your descendants as the stars of heaven, and all this land that I have promised I will give to your descendants, and they shall inherit it for ever.'" ¹⁴And the Lord repented of the evil which he thought to do to his people.

¹⁵And Moses turned, and went down from the mountain with the two tables of the testimony in his hands, tables that were written on both sides; on the one side and on the other were they written. ¹⁶And the tables were the work of God, and the writing was the writing of God, graven upon the tables. ¹⁷When Joshua heard the noise of the people as they shouted, he said to Moses, "There is a noise of war in the camp." ¹⁸But he said, "It is not the sound of shouting for victory, or the sound of the cry of defeat, but the sound of singing that I hear." ¹⁹And as soon as he came near the camp and saw the calf and the dancing, Moses' anger burned hot, and he threw the tables out of his hands and broke them at the foot of the mountain. ²⁰And he took the calf which they had made, and burnt it with fire, and ground it to powder, and scattered it upon the water, and made the people of Israel drink it.

²¹And Moses said to Aaron, "What did this people do to you that you have brought a great sin upon them?" ²²And Aaron said, "Let not the anger of my lord burn hot; you know the people, that they are set on evil. ²³For they said to me, 'Make us gods, who shall go before us; as for this Moses, the man who brought us up out of the land of Egypt, we do not know what has become of him.' ²⁴And I said to them, 'Let any who have gold take it off'; so they gave it to me, and I threw it into the fire, and there came out this calf."

²⁵And when Moses saw that the people had broken

loose (for Aaron had let them break loose, to their shame among their enemies), [26]then Moses stood in the gate of the camp, and said, "Who is on the Lord's side? Come to me." And all the sons of Levi gathered themselves together to him. [27]And he said to them, "Thus says the Lord God of Israel, 'Put every man his sword on his side, and go to and fro from gate to gate throughout the camp, and slay every man his brother, and every man his companion, and every man his neighbor.'" [28]And the sons of Levi did according to the word of Moses; and there fell of the people that day about three thousand men. [29]And Moses said, "Today you have ordained yourselves for the service of the Lord, each one at the cost of his son and of his brother, that he may bestow a blessing upon you this day."

[30]On the morrow Moses said to the people, "You have sinned a great sin. And now I will go up to the Lord; perhaps I can make atonement for your sin." [31]So Moses returned to the Lord and said, "Alas, this people have sinned a great sin; they have made for themselves gods of gold. [32]But now, if thou wilt forgive their sin — and if not, blot me, I pray thee, out of thy book which thou hast written." [33]But the Lord said to Moses, "Whoever has sinned against me, him will I blot out of my book. [34]But now go, lead the people to the place of which I have spoken to you; behold, my angel shall go before you. Nevertheless, in the day when I visit, I will visit their sin upon them."

[35]And the Lord sent a plague upon the people, because they made the calf which Aaron made.

Exod 32-34 has its beginnings in Israel's failure to cope with Moses' long absence from the community. Indeed, Exod 24:18 tells us that Moses was gone "forty days and forty nights," that is to say, a long time. This is the context in which we are told that Israel demanded not a different human leader, as we might expect, but another god ("make us gods who shall go before us"). Aaron immediately answered their request, constructed a calf from their gold jewelry, and announced that a festival would be celebrated around the calf and that it would be "a feast of the Lord," i.e., a festival honoring Israel's god, Yahweh. Verse 6 describes the feast.

In these verses tradition about Israel's apostasy at the foot of Sinai has been cast in terms of a much later event which is connected with Jeroboam I and which is described in 1 Kgs 12:25-33. It was under Jeroboam's leadership that several tribes brought an end to David and Solomon's United Kingdom by establishing their own state in the north, Israel. In an effort to secure his people's loyalty and the strength of his new state, Jeroboam sought to sever his people's ties with religious worship in Jerusalem. To this end, we are told that he constructed calves of gold which were enshrined at Dan and Bethel with the proclamation: "Behold your gods, O Israel, who brought you up out of the land of Egypt" (1 Kgs 12:28). Even though the calf was the symbol for Baal, the Canaanite deity hailed for prowess in love and war, Jeroboam's announcement makes it appear likely that he intended that the golden calves be used in the worship of Yahweh, not Baal. In other words, the thrust was probably not to establish a rival deity to the One worshipped in the Jerusalem cult but to establish surrogates for the Ark which represented Yahweh's presence in the Jerusalem temple.

Details from the record about Jeroboam's act shed light on the background of Exod 32. When the people gathered at the (one) calf Aaron had made and said, "These are your gods, O Israel, who brought you up out of the land of Egypt," they are portrayed as anticipating Jeroboam's actions with regard to the (two) calves at Dan and Bethel, here judged as apostasy.

In verses 7-14 of chapter 32, a Deuteronomic writer has added a section which, in effect, anticipates much of the action which ensues. The scene retreats from the community to an exchange between Yahweh and Moses. The Lord informs Moses of the apostasy which is taking place at the base of the mountain and, in doing so, speaks to Moses about Israel as "*your* people, whom *you* brought out of the land of Egypt" (v. 7). God tells Moses to leave aside his role as mediator of the covenant relationship ("now therefore let me alone") for the Divinity's impulsive response to Israel's was to lash out against the people (v. 10a). Using the words of the call to Abraham as recorded in Gen 12:2, Yahweh then resolves to act on that divine passion for relationship by beginning all over again with Moses: "but of you I will make a great nation"(v. 10b). Thereupon Moses gives voice to the first of three intercessions on Israel's behalf. He starts by setting the record straight. In addressing Yahweh he refers to Israel as "*thy* people, whom *thou* hast brought out of the land of Egypt" (v. 11; cf. v. 7). He then undertakes a twofold process of persuasion. He first admonishes Yahweh to turn back from the divine rage because of the satisfaction such a response would give the Egyptians (v. 12). To this he adds the reminder that in the promise made to Abraham, Isaac, and Jacob-Israel, God's great love had bound the Divine Self to be held accountable for the future of their descendants (v. 13). In the final verse of this Deuteronomic insertion, the writer records an awesome reversal; the Divinity "repented" of rage (v. 14). The conclusion to this dialogue anticipates for the reader the resolution of the entire incident at the foot of the mountain.

The older account is resumed in v. 15 with mention of Moses' journey (with tablets intact) back to the community. His anger at coming upon the people's festival seems somewhat out of place in light of the material included in the insertion of vv. 7-14. Nevertheless, in his anger Moses demolished both the tablets and the calf. He then presided over an action which bears similarity to a trial by ordeal described in Num 5:16-28. When Moses confronted Aaron and demanded an explanation, Israel's chief priest attempted to shift blame away from himself: "you know the people, that they are set on evil" (v. 22). He admitted to being pressed into action by the people (v. 24a) but denied any responsibility in the construction of the calf by offering an excuse which can only be described as absurd.

At this point in the narrative many pious Israelites would be tempted to deny Aaron his prestigious place in Israel's priesthood and indeed, one circle of tradition which was probably at odds with members of the Aaronic priestly group took this opportunity to insert a piece which explains why the priesthood was given to the sons of Levi (vv. 25-29). The action which won their ordination, while excessively violent by contemporary standards, was understood by their supporters as proof of their limitless zeal.

The closing section of the chapter (vv. 30-35), like vv. 19-20, reflects no awareness of the material contained in the insertion of vv. 7-14. Moses returns to God, confesses Israel's sin, and begs forgiveness even if it requires his own life. In response to this intercession, Yahweh commissions Moses to lead Israel forward "to the place of which I have spoken to you" in the company of an angel, but adds the ominous announcement that the sinful must be punished. The closing verse of the chapter then briefly records a divine punishment.

CONCERNS ABOUT GOD'S PRESENCE
33:1-23

33 The Lord said to Moses, "Depart, go up hence, you and the people whom you have brought up out of the land of Egypt, to the land of which I swore to Abraham, Isaac, and Jacob, saying, 'To your descendants I will give it.' 2And I will send an angel before you, and I will drive out the Canaanites, the Amorites, the Hittites, the Perizzites, the Hivites, and the Jebusites. 3Go up to a land flowing with milk and honey; but I will not go up among you, lest I consume you in the way, for you are a stiff-necked people."

4When the people heard these evil tidings, they mourned; and no man put on his ornaments. 5For the Lord had said to Moses, "Say to the people of Israel, 'You are a stiff-necked people; if for a single moment I should go up among you, I would consume you. So now put off your ornaments from you, that I may know what to do with you.'" 6Therefore the people of Israel stripped themselves of their ornaments, from Mount Horeb onward.

⁷Now Moses used to take the tent and pitch it outside the camp, far off from the camp; and he called it the tent of meeting. And every one who sought the Lord would go out to the tent of meeting, which was outside the camp. ⁸Whenever Moses went out to the tent, all the people rose up, and every man stood at his tent door, and looked after Moses, until he had gone into the tent. ⁹When Moses entered the tent, the pillar of cloud would descend and stand at the door of the tent, and the Lord would speak with Moses. ¹⁰And when all the people saw the pillar of cloud standing at the door of the tent, all the people would rise up and worship, every man at his tent door. ¹¹Thus the Lord used to speak to Moses face to face, as a man speaks to his friend. When Moses turned again into the camp, his servant Joshua the son of Nun, a young man, did not depart from the tent.

¹²Moses said to the Lord, "See, thou sayest to me, 'Bring up this people'; but thou hast not let me know whom thou wilt send with me. Yet thou hast said, 'I know you by name, and you have also found favor in my sight.' ¹³Now therefore, I pray thee, if I have found favor in thy sight, show me now thy ways, that I may know thee and find favor in thy sight. Consider too that this nation is thy people." ¹⁴And he said, "My presence will go with you, and I will give you rest." ¹⁵And he said to him, "If thy presence will not go with me, do not carry us up from here. ¹⁶For how shall it be known that I have found favor in thy sight, I and thy people? Is it not in thy going with us, so that we are distinct, I and thy people, from all other people that are upon the face of the earth?"

¹⁷And the Lord said to Moses, "This very thing that you have spoken I will do; for you have found favor in my sight, and I know you by name." ¹⁸Moses said, "I pray thee, show me thy glory." ¹⁹And he said, "I will make all my goodness pass before you, and will proclaim before you my name 'The Lord'; and I will be gracious to whom I will be gracious, and will show mercy on whom I will show mercy. ²⁰But," he said, "you cannot see my face; for man shall not see me and live." ²¹And the Lord said,

"Behold, there is a place by me where you shall stand upon the rock; [22]and while my glory passes by I will put you in a cleft of the rock, and I will cover you with my hand until I have passed by; [23]then I will take away my hand, and you shall see my back; but my face shall not be seen."

Chapter 33 is a composite of units some of which continue notions introduced in Exod 32 while others point forward to Exod 34. As such, the material here forms a transition in the movement from Israel's sin to God's forgiveness, from broken relationship to restored covenant. The four units of material in the chapter (vv. 1-6, 7-11, 12-17, 18-23) are loosely linked with one another through an overriding concern about God's presence.

The chapter commences with an order that Moses and the community leave Sinai and resume the journey which from now on will take direction from its end, the fulfillment of God's promise of the inheritance of the land. As in Exod 32:34 so here in Exod 33:1-6 the motif of Israel's departure from Sinai is closely associated with a prominent concern about God's continuing presence along the way. Verses 3 and 5 explain God's decision to be present through an intermediary (the angel) as an attempt to rescue Israel from the divine rage which apparently has not yet forgotten Israel's apostasy at the foot of the mountain. Reminders of divine anger in these verses are intertwined with notices of Israel's mourning. An unresolved tension in this regard can be seen between the witness of Exod 33:4, which suggests that the "putting off of ornaments" arose spontaneously from the people, and the witness of verses 5 and 6 which suggests that this gesture of mourning came about as a result of Israel's obedience to God's directive. Whatever the case, the biblical tradition about Israel's mourning in this context provides a legitimate background out of which Moses can once again intercede for God's favor (vv. 12-17).

Verses 7-11 at first glance have the appearance of a detour from the motif introduced in vv. 1-6 and resumed in vv. 12-17. It is probable that this unit represents an old tradition which was secondarily placed in its present context because of its focus on God's ongoing presence with Israel at the tent of meeting. The verb which governs v. 7 denotes continuous action. As such it suggests that the tent of meeting was an institution in which Israel could depend on God's ongoing presence, especially with regard to matters which required knowledge of God's judgment and will (v. 7b). The tent, then, was an institution wherein Israel had access to God's word when God chose to be present at the tent, a free and transcendent presence symbolized by the descent of the cloud. The distance between Israel and the Divinity is emphasized by the fact that the tent is described as standing outside the camp, indeed, "far off from the camp" (v. 7a). The singularity of Moses' role is clear in his function at the tent. Only with Moses does Yahweh speak "face to face," i.e., directly (cf. Deut 34:10; Num 12:6-8). The community has access to divine guidance only through Moses. In Exod 33, then, the trauma of the command to leave Sinai, a special locus for divine presence and for the communication of the divine will, is soothed by the institution of the tent of meeting wherein Israel had continuous access to divine revelation.

Similarities in the opening and closing lines of the next unit of Exod 33, vv. 12-17, knit it into a literary whole. The content of this unit returns to a concern over God's presence along Israel's journey, a motif which at this point in the narrative has been expressed several times in different ways. Moses reflects no knowledge of the witness of Exod 32:34 and Exod 33:2 when he tells God "Thou hast not let me know whom thou wilt send with me" (Exod 33:12). Moreover, even the Divinity appears not to recall the conversations narrated earlier, for in v. 14 God tells Moses: "My presence will go with you." Complications are further compounded by Moses' response to this: "If thy presence will not go with me..." (v. 15). It is obvious that different traditions have been joined here without being harmonized with one another. The final editors were content to allow these textual inconsistencies. Indeed, the textual difficulties enhance the tension and sense of desperation over the matter at hand, i.e., the question of God's presence. Moses' dealings with Yahweh reach a climax and resolution in verse 17 where we hear God's commitment to be in relation to Israel in accord with Moses' repeated and insistent intercessions. Thus the stage is set for the renewal of the covenant which is narrated in Exod 34.

The closing unit of Exod 33 (vv. 18-23) anticipates the theophany which is narrated in chapter 34. As in Exod 19-24, once again the gift of the revelation of the divine will which binds Israel to Yahweh is preceded by the gift of God's presence. The scene here, however, does not include the entire community. Having secured God's presence for Israel, Moses now asks a similar favor for himself. Our thoughts return to the first theophany at the mountain of God, the encounter between Moses and Yahweh at the burning bush, that meeting which was the foundation of the exodus-Sinai journey (Exod 3). There Moses sought access to the Divinity through knowledge of the divine name (Exod 3:13-15). Now Moses pleads: "I pray thee, show me thy glory" (Exod 34:18). In the wake of the golden calf apostasy Moses' request has the appearance of a poignant plea for reassurance: let me see again who you are now that you know who we are, a sinful people.

Chapter 33 of Exodus comes to a conclusion in full anticipation of the restoration of the relationship between God and Israel which now will be formalized in a covenant-making event. The chapter is permeated with concerns about God's presence. So here, at chapter's end, the text speaks in human-like descriptions of Moses' direct experience of the Divinity even as it secures Yahweh's mystery and freedom in the shielding of the divine face (cf. Exod 24:10-11).

COVENANT RESTORED
34:1-35

34 The Lord said to Moses, "Cut two tables of stone like the first; and I will write upon the tables the words that were on the first tables, which you broke. ²Be ready in the morning, and come up in the morning to Mount Sinai, and present yourself there to me on the top of the mountain. ³No man shall come up with you, and let no man be seen throughout all the mountain; let no flocks or herds feed before that mountain." ⁴So Moses cut two tables of stone like the first; and he rose early in the morning and went up on Mount Sinai, as the Lord had commanded him, and took in his hand two tables of stone. ⁵And the Lord descended in the cloud and stood with him there, and proclaimed the name of the Lord. ⁶The Lord passed before him, and proclaimed, "The Lord, the Lord, a God merciful and gracious, slow to anger, and abounding in steadfast love and faithfulness, ⁷keeping steadfast love for thousands, forgiving iniquity and transgression and sin, but who will by no means clear the guilty, visiting the iniquity of the fathers upon the children and the children's children, to the third and the fourth generation." ⁸And Moses made haste to bow his head toward the earth, and worshiped. ⁹And he said, "If now I have found favor in thy sight, O Lord, let the Lord, I pray thee, go in the midst of us, although it is a stiff-necked people; and pardon our iniquity and our sin, and take us for thy inheritance."

¹⁰And he said, "Behold, I make a covenant. Before all your people I will do marvels, such as have not been wrought in all the earth or in any nation; and all the people among whom you are shall see the work of the Lord; for it is a terrible thing that I will do with you.

¹¹"Observe what I command you this day. Behold, I will drive out before you the Amorites, the Canaanites, the Hittites, the Perizzites, the Hivites, and the Jebusites. ¹²Take heed to yourself, lest you make a covenant with the inhabitants of the land whither you go, lest it become a snare in the midst of you. ¹³You shall tear down their altars, and break their pillars, and cut down their Asherim ¹⁴(for you shall worship no other god, for the Lord, whose name is Jealous, is a jealous God), ¹⁵lest you make a covenant with the inhabitants of the land, and when

they play the harlot after their gods and sacrifice to their gods and one invites you, you eat of his sacrifice, [16]and you take of their daughters for your sons, and their daughters play the harlot after their gods and make your sons play the harlot after their gods.

[17]"You shall make for yourself no molten gods.

[18]"The feast of unleavened bread you shall keep. Seven days you shall eat unleavened bread, as I commanded you, at the time appointed in the month Abib; for in the month Abib you came out from Egypt. [19]All that opens the womb is mine, all your male cattle, the firstlings of cow and sheep. [20]The firstling of an ass you shall redeem with a lamb, or if you will not redeem it you shall break its neck. All the first-born of your sons you shall redeem. And none shall appear before me empty.

[21]"Six days you shall work, but on the seventh day you shall rest; in plowing time and in harvest you shall rest. [22]And you shall observe the feast of weeks, the first fruits of wheat harvest, and the feast of ingathering at the year's end. [23]Three times in the year shall all your males appear before the Lord God, the God of Israel. [24]For I will cast out nations before you, and enlarge your borders; neither shall any man desire your land, when you go up to appear before the Lord your God three times in the year.

[25]"You shall not offer the blood of my sacrifice with leaven; neither shall the sacrifice of the feast of the pass-over be left until the morning. [26]The first of the first fruits of your ground you shall bring to the house of the Lord your God. You shall not boil a kid in its mother's milk."

[27]And the Lord said to Moses, "Write these words; in accordance with these words I have made a covenant with you and with Israel." [28]And he was there with the Lord forty days and forty nights; he neither ate bread nor drank water. And he wrote upon the tables the words of the covenant, the ten commandments.

[29]When Moses came down from Mount Sinai, with the two tables of the testimony in his hand as he came down from the mountain, Moses did not know that the skin of his face shone because he had been talking with God.

30And when Aaron and all the people of Israel saw Moses, behold, the skin of his face shone, and they were afraid to come near him. 31But Moses called to them; and Aaron and all the leaders of the congregation returned to him, and Moses talked with them. 32And afterward all the people of Israel came near, and he gave them in commandment all that the Lord had spoken with him in Mount Sinai. 33And when Moses had finished speaking with them, he put a veil on his face; 34 but whenever Moses went in before the Lord to speak with him, he took the veil off, until he came out; and when he came out, and told the people of Israel what he was commanded, 35the people of Israel saw the face of Moses, that the skin of Moses' face shone; and Moses would put the veil upon his face again, until he went in to speak with him.

The order of events which governed earlier parts of the Sinai narrative is repeated in chapter 34. Thus, theophany (vv. 1-9) is followed by invitation to covenant and by the gift of the law (vv. 10-26) which in turn are followed by a tradition about the tablets of stone on which God's *torah*-instruction was recorded (vv. 27-28). Special concern for the stone tablets (34:1, 4) provide the literary clue that readers have now come full circle in the covenant story. The directive to cut new tablets is at the same time an invitation to begin all over again the relationship which had been broken by Israel's infidelity.

The theophany described in this text features not the smoke and thunder of Exod 19 but the pronouncement of the divine name as anticipated in chapter 33. Verses 6-8 probably have their starting point in a liturgical formula repeated by generations of Israelite believers (cf. Num 14:18; Neh 9:17; Joel 2:13; Jonah 4:2; Pss 86:15; 103:8). The name is the same as on the two other occasions it had been pronounced on this mountain, i.e., in the fire from the bush (Exod 3) and in the smoke at the top of the mountain (Exod 20:2). Over the course of those other name-giving events Israel had changed. A people enslaved had been redeemed, covenanted with its redeemer, and then been unfaithful. All the while the name was constant. Through this theophany Israel learned implications of the meaning of the name which heretofore were not known. On the one hand, in the face of its sinfulness Israel learned of God's fidelity as represented in the name. Generations of worshippers, repeating the chant recorded here, sought life in Yahweh's presence symbolized not by a tangible image but by the name. On the other hand, the theophany featuring the name also attests to the demands of divine justice. Yahweh is the One "who will by no means clear the guilty." The divine name thus holds in dynamic tension the mysterious balance of God's mercy and justice.

The theophany scene includes a hearkening back to the concern expressed in chapters 32 and 33 for God's continuing presence along the way (v. 9) and then evolves into the covenant-making event (vv. 10-28). It is likely that this account represents not so much a restoration of the original covenant concluded at Sinai as an independent, second account of the story which now appears in Exod 19-24. Scholars have suggested that the bulk of Exod 19-24 represents the Sinai covenant-making event as transmitted by the Elohist while Exod 34 represents the Sinai covenant-making event as recorded by the Yahwist. Thus, the two accounts (Exod 19-24 and Exod 34) represent not two events but a single event viewed from two different perspectives. Whatever the case with the traditions behind these chapters, it is clear that the editors who arranged and handed down the traditions felt it valuable to retain both accounts so they arranged them sequentially and placed the story of Israel's sin between the two.

The *torah* which is given in vv. 17-26 is viewed by the writer of v. 28 as an alternate decalogue. Unlike the decalogue of Exod 20, concern here is exclusively fixed on Israel's cult, with particular attention to the three annual pilgrimage festivals. A Deuteronomic hand used this focus on cultic observance as a context in which to add further instructions that Israel take care that its bond with Yahweh remain exclusive (vv. 11-16). For the Deuteronomic writer pagan rituals were particularly dangerous and thus had to be abolished from the land lest they ensnare Israel.

This account of the *torah*-gift concludes, as had the first, with reference to the writing down of the law. Unlike the first instance, Moses, not God, is said to have recorded the law (Exod 34:27-28; cf. Exod 31:18).

The narrative account of the event at Sinai fittingly concludes with the man who was remembered as mediating the profound encounter between Israel and God at this holy place in the wilderness. The man who alone had seen the fire in the bush and with whom God had spoken "as a man speaks to his friend" (Exod 33:11) is now described as leaving the mountain top with skin which shone "because he had been talking with God" (Exod 34:29). Some have pointed out similarities between this biblical witness and the use of masks by religious figures from other traditions. Verse 34 ("whenever Moses went in before the Lord...") suggests that the mask or veil was used continuously and might have been associated with the Mosaic office. At any rate, by the end of Moses' final journey to this mountain of God, his unique encounters with the Mystery had set him apart from members of his community to the point that he was required to wear a veil in their presence. He was "face to face" only with Yahweh.

The story of sin and forgiveness which appears in Exod 32-34 is followed by several chapters which return to the topic of the tabernacle. Exod 35-39 describe how commands regarding the construction of the tabernacle, instructions which God had given to Moses on Mount Sinai (Exod 25-31), were carried out. Moses called the people of Israel to bring materials with which the tabernacle would be built and furnished. Exod 35:29 says: "All the men and women, the people of Israel, whose heart moved them to bring anything for the work which the Lord had commanded by Moses to be done, brought it as their freewill offering to the Lord." The tabernacle was constructed together with all its furnishings (curtains, veil, screen, ark, altars, lampstand, vessels). Likewise, anointing oil and priestly garments were prepared through the gifts and talents of the community. By the end of Exod 39, the work on the tabernacle of the tent of meeting was complete and presented to Moses. All had been done in accord with the Lord's instruction and Moses blessed the people (Exod 39:32-43). Thus, the stage is set for the conclusion of the Book of Exodus, chapter 40.

THE COMPLETION OF THE TABERNACLE
40:1-38

40   The Lord said to Moses, [2]"On the first day of the first month you shall erect the tabernacle of the tent of meeting. [3]And you shall put in it the ark of the testimony, and you shall screen the ark with the veil. [4]And you shall bring in the table, and set its arrangements in order; and you shall bring in the lampstand, and set up its lamps. [5]And you shall put the golden altar for incense before the ark of the testimony, and set up the screen for the door of the tabernacle. [6]You shall set the altar of burnt offering before the door of the tabernacle of the tent of meeting, [7]and place the laver between the tent of meeting and the altar, and put water in it. [8]And you shall set up the court round about, and hang up the screen for the gate of the court. [9]Then you shall take the anointing oil, and anoint the tabernacle and all that is in it, and consecrate it and all its furniture; and it shall become holy. [10]You shall also anoint the altar of burnt offering and all its utensils, and consecrate the altar; and the altar shall be most holy. [11]You shall also anoint the laver and its base, and consecrate it. [12]Then you shall bring Aaron and his sons to the door of the tent of meeting, and shall wash them with water, [13]and put upon Aaron the holy garments, and you shall anoint him and consecrate him, that he may serve me as priest. [14]You shall bring his sons also and put coats on them, [15]and anoint them, as you anointed their father, that they may serve me as priests: and their anointing shall admit them to a perpetual priesthood throughout their generations."

[16]Thus did Moses; according to all that the Lord commanded him, so he did. [17]And in the first month in the second year, on the first day of the month, the tabernacle was erected. [18]Moses erected the tabernacle; he laid its bases, and set up its frames, and put in its poles, and raised up its pillars; [19]and he spread the tent over the tabernacle, and put the covering of the tent over it, as the Lord has commanded Moses. [20]And he took the testimony and put it into the ark, and put the poles on the ark, and set the mercy seat above on the ark; [21]and he brought the ark into the tabernacle, and set up the veil of the screen, and screened the ark of the testimony; as the Lord had commanded Moses. [22]And he put the table in the tent of meeting, on the north side of the tabernacle, outside the veil, [23]and set the bread in order on it before the Lord; as the Lord had commanded Moses. [24]And he put the lampstand in the tent of meeting, opposite the table on the south side of the tabernacle, [25]and set up the lamps before the Lord; as the Lord had commanded Moses. [26]And he put the golden altar in the tent of meeting before the veil, [27]and burnt fragrant incense upon it; as the Lord had commanded Moses. [28]And he put in place the screen for the door of the tabernacle. [29]And he set the altar of burnt offering at the door of the tabernacle of the tent of meeting, and offered upon it the burnt offering and the cereal offering; as the Lord had commanded Moses. [30]And he set the laver between the tent of meeting and the altar, and put water in it for washing, [31]with which Moses and Aaron and his sons washed their hands and their feet; [32]when they went into the tent of meeting, and when they approached the altar, they washed; as the Lord commanded Moses. [33]And he erected the court round the tabernacle and the altar, and set up the screen of the gate of the court. So Moses finished the work.

[34]Then the cloud covered the tent of meeting, and the glory of the Lord filled the tabernacle. [35]And Moses was not able to enter the tent of meeting, because the cloud abode upon it, and the glory of the Lord filled the tabernacle. [36]Throughout all their journeys, whenever the

cloud was taken up from over the tabernacle, the people of Israel would go onward; [37]but if the cloud was not taken up, then they did not go onward till the day that it was taken up. [38]For throughout all their journeys the cloud of the Lord was upon the tabernacle by day, and fire was in it by night, in the sight of all the house of Israel.

In this chapter Israel's Priestly tradition describes the twofold process whereby the community's efforts in the construction of the tabernacle reach their goal.

In the first place, Israel's representative before God, Moses, erects the tabernacle and, through the application of holy oil, consecrates its furnishings and priestly personnel (vv. 1-33). This section contains both a record of Yahweh's instructions to Moses (vv. 1-15) and a careful account of how Moses carried out these instructions (vv. 16-33). Eight times in these verses we are told that Moses did everything in accord with Yahweh's instructions. The Priestly writers thus underscore the legitimacy of the tabernacle as an institution which had its beginnings in the divine will. Everything connected with the construction of the tabernacle was carried out in obedience to God's word.

Fully prepared, the community awaits the second stage of the process without which the tabernacle would remain simply the work of human hands. Exod 40:34-38 narrate the coming of Yahweh's presence to the tent and to the tabernacle. This is the true goal of the Priestly corpus of Exod 25-31 and Exod 35-40 for at the beginning of the effort Yahweh had said: "And let them make me a sanctuary, that I may dwell in their midst" (Exod 25:8). The divine presence is described in ways which by now are familiar, the coming of the fire and the cloud. Throughout the chapters of Exodus we have seen how important moments in Israel's passage were graced by these manifestations of Yahweh's presence (Exod 3:2; 13:21-22; 14:24; 19:9, 16-18; 24:15-18; 33:9; 34:5). Now that same presence abides in the institution of the tabernacle to direct Israel's further journeys. The exercise of divine freedom continues. Israel had to be prepared to move its tabernacle whenever and wherever the cloud moved (cf.

Num 9:15-23) until the Mystery would find a more permanent resting place in Solomon's Temple (1 Kgs 8).

Taken together Exod 25-31 and 35-40 represent Priestly tradition and theology regarding God's ongoing presence with Israel. Written in a late period, the texts reflect familiarity with the Temple of Jerusalem. It is from that perspective that the Priestly writers project back into this early period their vision regarding the primary locus of God's presence and guidance. At the same time they express their conviction about God's gift and commitment to abide with Israel. According to their view, this was the goal of the entire exodus story:

> And I will dwell among the people of Israel, and will be their God. And they shall know that I am the Lord their God, who brought them forth out of the land of Egypt that I might dwell with them; I am the Lord their God.
>
> (Exod 29:45-46)

THE BOOK OF LEVITICUS

THE BOOK OF LEVITICUS

As with other books of the Pentateuch, Jews entitle the third of the Five Books of Moses according to the word which stands at the beginning of the Hebrew text of the book. Thus, in Hebrew Bibles the Book of Leviticus is known as *wayyiqra'*, "and he called." Christians, however, have adopted a latinized form of the title which appears in the Greek Septuagint, *Leveitikon*, "the Levitical (book)." Because most of the book has to do with worship, Greek and Latin versions associated it with the Levites, a group of religious leaders who served in varying cultic capacities in different stages of Israelite religion. It should be noted that, as a matter of fact, the book gives very little attention to the Levites.

Dealing as it does almost exclusively with legislation for ordering proper cultic practice, the Book of Leviticus is more unified in its content than the books which surround it in the biblical canon. Its laws are well organized and carefully grouped according to category. The contents of the book can be summarized as follows.

Chapters 1-7 contain a detailed description of various types of sacrifices and a definition of occasions on which they were to be offered. It includes guidelines for those who bring the offerings as well as instructions for the priests who receive the offerings and conduct the cultic ritual.

Chapters 8-10 contain the heaviest concentration of narrative in the Book of Leviticus. The section begins (chapter 8) with an account of the ordination of Aaron and his sons to the priesthood, a ceremony which unfolds in accord with the directives which appear in Exod 29. In chapter 9 we read an account of the inauguration of Aaron's priestly ministry as he leads the worshipping assembly at Mount Sinai. This is followed in chapter 10 with a story about wrongful exercise of priesthood which proves to be fatal for Aaron's sons, Nadab and Abihu, an event which served as an instruction for the rest of the Levites.

Chapters 11-15 contain laws dealing with religious cleanness and uncleanness. It includes designation of clean and unclean animals, definition of conditions which render people and objects unclean, and instructions for rites of purification whereby people and things in a temporary state of uncleanness might be made clean again.

Chapter 16 begins where chapter 10 ends, with reference to the deaths of Aaron's sons. It then focuses on instructions for the rituals of the annual Day of Atonement (see Excursus on Feasts and Ritual).

Chapters 17-26 constitute an originally independent code of law which is only loosely connected with the framework in which it is now found. While it resembles the foregoing chapters in Leviticus by including much cultic legislation, it reaches beyond an exclusive concern with worship to include ethical directives as well. As such the range of its interest is more comprehensive than other sections of the book. In accord with the general format of ancient Near Eastern law codes, it ends with a series of blessings which await those who obey its instructions and a list of curses for those who disregard them (chapter 26). Chapters 17-26 have come to be designated as the Holiness Code because their chief concern is that Israel be holy as its God is holy.

Chapter 27 forms the conclusion of the book. It is a unit containing instructions about religious vows and tithes. It is commonly regarded by contemporary scholars as an appendix which was attached some time after the rest of the sections of the book had been organized and put together.

Those who undertake to read the Book of Leviticus from beginning to end should be prepared to encounter a low level of vividness and drama, as one would expect from any collection of rubrics and regulations governing cultic life. Its attention to the fine details of ritual make this book particularly tedious reading for many.

Scholars are virtually unanimous in acknowledging the complexity which must have marked the origin and development of this book. Since the exact processes of its composition are unknown, we can only offer a description of its formation which is probable at best.

It is thought that the various sections of the Book of Leviticus which are outlined above represent originally independent traditions which echo the lived observance of faithful worshippers in different generations of Israelite religion. Cultic practices were not uniform in all sanctuaries nor throughout all of Israel's history. Traditions grew and developed in accord with changing circumstances and the particular decisions and directives of cultic specialists (priests or Levites) who officiated at different shrines. It is likely that cultic custom became more uniform and stable with the centralization of Israel's worship in Jerusalem. Although some of the material in Leviticus might have roots in very ancient practice, most of what we read there probably stems from the more or less standardized practices of the Temple. Almost all scholars agree that the final form of the Book of Leviticus dates from the post-exilic period when representatives from the circles of Israel's priests collected and organized these already-existing materials. The Priestly transmitters of tradition intended that this book be a manual for the reorganized cultic life which they hoped to be realized in Israel's return to the land and in the construction of the Second Temple.

This collection of cultic regulations, however, was not designed exclusively as a handbook for worship. The Priestly redactors repeatedly framed their regulations with these words: "The Lord said to Moses" or "The Lord said to Moses, 'Say to the people of Israel'." In doing this, and in placing the Book of Leviticus in the middle of the great exodus-Sinai story, these editors-theologians set Israel's cult within the broader context of Yahweh's covenanted life with Israel. They removed Israel's cult from possible associations with religious practices based in the rhythms of nature or in superstition and taboo and instead firmly rooted it in the movement of God's relationship with Israel in history. They presented Israel's worship as having its origin in the foundational event wherein God redeemed and shaped Israel for the Divine Self in the exodus and Sinai events. Thus did Israel's post-exilic priests fashion a liturgical theology which did not allow believers to divorce their ritual observance in the sanctuary from their covenanted life with God in the historical arena.

Further exploration leads us into a rich theology which breathes in this somewhat arid collection of regulations for external observance. Leviticus forms the second of a three-fold legislative arrangement formulated by representatives from the priesthood. The first stage is marked by concern for the provision of God's ongoing presence with Israel. Accordingly, the tabernacle is constructed (Exod 35-40) in conscientious obedience to instructions which are said to have been given by God to Moses (Exod 25-31). The end of this first segment of Priestly legislation coincides with the end of the Book of Exodus (Exod 40:34-38), where we are told that "the glory of the Lord filled the tabernacle." This "tabernacling" presence of Yahweh serves as the basis for stage two of the Priestly corpus of law. This stage consists of the Book of Leviticus and, as we have seen, addresses itself almost exclusively to regulating Israel's cultic life. According to the Priestly view, proper ritual observance was a key element in the design of how Israel was to live appropriately in God's "tabernacling" presence. Finally, the Priestly theologians present stage three of their legislation. In Num 1-10 they provide for the ongoing organization of Israel in its pilgrimage through time and space. This is offered in terms of Israel's preparations for departure from the mountain in the Sinai wilderness.

Viewed within the context of this larger bulk of Priestly tradition, we see that the instructions which constitute the

Book of Leviticus rise out of Israel's conviction about God's "tabernacling" presence in its midst. For Israel's priests the cult was a gift through which God gave Israel appropriate means for responding to the divine presence. To live appropriately in the divine presence was to abide by the requirements of ritual purity and to undertake measures to restore it in cases where it was lost. Likewise, the priesthood and ritual sacrifices were necessary points of mediation between Israel and the Holy One in its midst. By including the Holiness Code, the Priestly circle demonstrated its conviction that the implications of being in God's presence extended as well to areas of life beyond the cult. When viewed within this perspective, it is clear that the Priestly writers' theology is theocentric through and through. Israel is beckoned to careful observance of all this legislation not so much to secure any merit or gain for itself but because such behavior is appropriate to a people which is holy by association with the Holy One who "tabernacles" in its midst.

In this connection Lev 17-26 warrant special attention. This Holiness Code shares elements in common with the predominantly priestly perspectives of the prophet Ezekiel, although the direction of influence is uncertain. Both works offer a basis on which Israel might reorganize itself after the chaotic experience of exile in Babylon. The legislation contained in the Holiness Code extends to such matters as sexual relations, economic justice, and other requirements of an ethical lifestyle (see especially Lev 19). The treatment of other people is encapsulated in the well-known directive of Lev 19:17-18:

> You shall not hate your brother in your heart, but you shall reason with your neighbor, lest you bear sin because of him. You shall not take vengeance or bear any grudge against the sons of your own people, but you shall love your neighbor as yourself: I am the Lord.

The Code received its name in post-biblical tradition because its directives are based in the frequently-repeated "I am the Lord (your God)" and sometimes "I am the Lord who sanctifies." In other words, the directives of the Code are grounded in the very person of Israel's God, the One who is Holy. Israel is told:

> You shall be holy; for I the Lord your God am holy.
> (Lev 19:2)

and again,

> You shall be holy to me; for I the Lord am holy, and have separated you from the peoples, that you should be mine.
> (Lev 20:26)

Through the Exodus event Israel had become Yahweh's. The Code delineates the consequences of Yahweh's claim not only in cultic requirements but also in terms of one's association with other members of the community.

The Holiness Code is easily at home in the Priestly writers' concern for the requirements which stemmed from God's "tabernacling" presence in Israel's midst. In their presentation of the notion of God's presence in the tabernacle (Exod 40:34-38) the Priestly writers expressed their convictions about the holiness which resided at the center of the Israelite community. They had a profound sense of Israel's being centered in the One who is Holy. This realization occasioned the need for mediatorial persons and rituals. At the same time, its center was also the Holy with whom Israel had become one in the covenant bond. This center unified, gave direction to and ordered Israel's existence. Thus, to be most completely and most truthfully who it was at its core, Israel had to separate itself from what did not belong to the realm of the Holy. Israel itself was set apart from the nations; holy times and places were set apart; holy things (objects, food) were set apart. The rubrics of ritual performance guided Israel's response to the "tabernacling" presence of the Holy One in its midst.

In the minute directives of Leviticus, then, Israel's priests offered a program to foster the community's recovery of identity following the chaos of the Exile. As the remnant from the exiled community readied itself to undertake a restored life in the land, this circle of theologians drew together its liturgical traditions and cast them in terms which blurred the distance between the post-exilic community and those who once had sojourned through the wilderness of Sinai. They instructed Israel in who it was to be from its very beginnings and they offered an orderly way in which Israel might express who it is: the people set apart and hallowed by virtue of its covenant with the Holy One. The directives of Leviticus orient Israel, bringing it into one with its center. In doing so they invite wholeness, holiness.

EXCURSUS ON FEASTS AND RITUAL

Feasts

The life of worship which permeates the Book of Leviticus flowed according to a rhythm measured by the regular celebration of annual festivals. The major feasts of ancient Israel's liturgical year are listed in five different texts of the Hebrew canon. The earliest lists are found in Exod 23:14-17, part of the Covenant Code, and in Exod 34:18-24, part of the second account of the formalization of the covenant at Sinai. These texts refer to three annual feasts which all covenant members observed in common by making pilgrimage to a central sanctuary. The three feasts were Unleavened Bread, the Feast of Weeks, and the Feast of Booths. The same three feasts are grouped in a later list which appears in Deut 16:1-8. By the time this was written the Feast of Unleavened Bread had been joined to Passover. Yet another list is found in Lev 23, part of the Holiness Code. Lev 23 is a liturgical calendar which lists the feasts in the order in which they were celebrated during the post-exilic period. Finally, the order of the feasts in Lev 23 corresponds closely to the sequence in which they appear in Num 28-29, a unit containing detailed instructions for the rituals to be conducted at each of the feasts.

While the three pilgrimage feasts seem to have consistently enjoyed prominent status in ancient Israel's liturgical life, it is probable that other feasts were commemorated as well. In referring to the feast which was held on the first day of the seventh month, Lev 23:23-25 (cf. Num 29:1-6) may bear a trace of an ancient New Year's festival. Likewise, the addition of the Day of Atonement in the late lists (Lev 23:26-32 and Num 29:7-11) suggests that this feast had come to hold a prominent place in the post-exilic community's life of worship.

Israel's three pilgrimage feasts probably had their beginnings in the processes of nature. In a very real way the lives of agricultural people in the ancient world were connected with the rhythmic life-cycle of the earth itself. Because the earth's productivity largely determined its peoples' well-being and prosperity, it was naturally associated with sacred bearers and nurturers of life. Harvest times were not only occasions for social gatherings and festivity; they were also opportunities for marking the sacred dimension of the earth's life. Thus, community harvest festivals were at the same time religious festivals.

When Israel came into the land and settled there, it is likely that it borrowed agricultural notions and customs from Canaanite farmers. The three pilgrimage festivals (Unleavened Bread, Weeks, Booths) coincided with the beginning and end of the grain harvest in the spring and with the harvest of grapes and olives in the fall. Traditions from an early period (Exod 23:16, Exod 34:22) indicate that Israel adopted the calendar of the Canaanites so that the year had its beginning in autumn (September-October) although during the Exile this was replaced by a calendar which imitated the Babylonian reckoning of time according to which the year's beginning was marked in the spring (March-April). The calendar in Lev 23 which legislates for cultic practice in the post-exilic period reflects this change.

Israel's stance with regard to Canaanite practices was not one of wholesale borrowing, however. It wove into the agricultural festivals its own experience of the Holy, an experience based in history. Ultimately the three agricultural festivals were all reinterpreted in terms of Israel's unique experience as a people chosen and covenanted by Yahweh. This will be clear as we proceed with a brief examination of each of the major festivals of Israel's liturgical year.

Passover and Unleavened Bread. The Bible's most comprehensive presentation of the feasts of Passover and Unleavened Bread appears, not in one of the five lists mentioned above, but in the text of Exod 12:1—13:16. There the Priestly redactors of the Pentateuch wove a treatment of the two feasts into the story of the exodus event. For information regarding the origin and development of the Feasts of Passover and Unleavened Bread, the reader is referred to our commentary on Exod 12:1—13:16. A few additional remarks, however, are offered here.

Passover was an ancient festival with roots in a semi-nomadic civilization. It appears to have been commemorated in the home whereas Unleavened Bread, together with Weeks and Booths, were occasions on which members of the community came together at a central shrine. With the Deuteronomic reform and its insistence upon the centralization of worship, the slaughter of the Passover lamb was transferred from the home to Jerusalem. Although Passover is mentioned in the earliest lists of religious feasts in ancient Israel (Exod 34:25; cf. Exod 23:18), it is not included there as one of the three major pilgrimage feasts (cf. Exod 23:14-17; Exod 34:18-23). The one-day Feast of Passover is connected with the seven-day Feast of Unleavened Bread for the first time in the list of Deut 16:1-17 and subsequently in the Priestly records (Exod 12-13; Lev 23; Num 28). Whereas the original date for the Feast of Unleavened Bread probably depended upon the ripening of the grain and was therefore somewhat flexible, Passover seems to have been celebrated from ancient times at the full moon (the fourteenth day) of a fixed month in spring. When the Feasts of Passover and Unleavened Bread were combined, the observance of Unleavened Bread was simply attached to the already-established date for the celebration of Passover. Thus, according to Lev 23, the combined festival began with the observance of Passover on the fourteenth day of the first month (of the post-exilic calendar, i.e., of a year beginning in the spring) and the following day, the fifteenth, marked the initiation of the celebration of Unleavened Bread. Together they constituted an eight-day festival characterized by the eating of unleavened bread or cakes prepared from newly-harvested grain. The first and eighth days of the festival were special in that they were observed with "a holy convocation," i.e., a solemn assembly of the community, and by the abstention from "laborious work," probably a technical reference the exact intent of which is no longer clear (Lev 23:5-8).

Feast of Weeks. The second of the three major feasts in Israel was the Feast of Weeks. It was celebrated seven weeks after the Feast of Unleavened Bread, that is, seven weeks after the beginning of the grain harvest. Deut 16:9-10a says:

> You shall count seven weeks; begin to count the seven weeks from the time you first put the sickle to the standing grain. Then you shall keep the feast of weeks to the Lord your God...

Both the first and the last days of the seven-week period were counted so that the Feast of Weeks actually fell on the fiftieth day after the beginning of the Feast of Unleavened Bread. For this reason, it is also referred to as Pentecost, from the Greek word *pentekostos*, "fiftieth."

Like the Feast of Unleavened Bread, the Feast of Weeks is intricately connected with the life-cycle of the earth. It marked the end of the grain harvest and is referred to simply as the "feast of harvest" in Exod 23:16. Num 28:26 calls it "the day of the first fruits," a reference to the offering of two loaves made with grain from the new harvest. Exod 34:22 names it "the feast of weeks, the first fruits of wheat harvest." The feast presupposes that those who celebrate it are an agricultural people so its occurrence in Israel must date from sometime after Israel's inheritance of the land. Like the Feast of Unleavened Bread, it is likely that originally the date for the Feast of Weeks fluctuated with the actual time of the grain harvest in any given year. After Unleavened

Bread was attached to the fixed date of Passover, the Feast of Weeks assumed a fixed date measured in relation to the observance of Unleavened Bread. Apparently the ripening of grains (barley, wheat) was estimated to span a period of seven weeks.

Like Unleavened Bread and Booths, the Feast of Weeks was a pilgrimage festival. However, unlike the others which lasted several days, Weeks appears to have been celebrated for only one day. Deut 16:10 instructs that all who make pilgrimage are to bring a freewill offering. Lev 23:15-21 and Num 28:26-31 contain much more detailed instructions regarding the elaborate offerings which were to be made on the Feast of Weeks. The two loaves of bread brought to this feast were to be leavened. To eat leavened bread was the ordinary custom for Israelite farmers. The offering of the leavened loaves at the Feast of Weeks thus signalled the beginning of ordinary time in the sacred cycle of the year, just as the unleavened bread associated with the spring feast heralded a new beginning, a new departure from the leavened grain of the former year's harvest. In addition to offerings from the new grain and drink offerings, the pilgrims were to offer animal sacrifices (see below our discussion of sacrificial ritual). Like the Feast of Unleavened Bread, the Feast of Weeks was marked by "a holy convocation" and by abstention from "laborious work."

In Lev 23:22 (cf. Lev 19:9-10) a non-cultic directive is attached to the legislation for the ritual celebration of the end of the harvest:

> And when you reap the harvest of your land, you shall not reap your field to its very border, nor shall you gather the gleanings after your harvest, you shall leave them for the poor and for the stranger: I am the Lord your God.

This instruction presupposes a regard for the poor which is characteristically present in the Deuteronomic corpus but which appears in earlier traditions as well (see Exod 22:25-27 and 23:6-7).

Of the three annual pilgrimage festivals from ancient Israel, the Feast of Weeks is the one least explicitly associated with an event from Israel's unique history. Whereas the biblical tradition associated the Feast of Unleavened Bread with the coming out of Egypt and the Feast of Booths with Israel's time in the wilderness, little effort is made in the texts to connect the Feast of Weeks with a specific event in salvation history. Post-biblical Jewish tradition included in its observance of the Feast of Weeks a celebration of the gift of the law on Mount Sinai; it is difficult to know with certainty whether or not this reflects the practice of believers from biblical times.

Feast of Booths. For most of the biblical period the feast which enjoyed greatest prominence in Israel's liturgical year was the Feast of Booths. The feast is known by several names. Exod 23:16 and Exod 34:22 refer to it as the Feast of Ingathering while Deut 16:13 and Lev 23:34 designate it the Feast of Booths. The Hebrew *sukkot* ("booths" or "huts") is rendered in Latin as *tabernacula*, hence the name in some English works, the Feast of Tabernacles. In some biblical texts (1 Kgs 8:2, 65) it is also referred to simply as "the feast" and as "the feast of the Lord" (Lev 23:39; cf. Judg 21:19), designations which reflect the prominence of this feast in Israel's religious life.

The Feast of Booths was celebrated in the fall, the seventh month (September-October) during the post-exilic period which reckoned the beginning of the year in spring. Like the other pilgrimage festivals in ancient Israel, it was related to the agricultural cycle. Whereas the Feast of Weeks marked the end of the grain harvest, the Feast of Booths marked the end of the harvest of grapes and olives. Originally the name Booths may have derived from the custom of harvesters' dwelling in temporary quarters of branches and leafy boughs constructed in the orchards and vineyards during the harvest period. Whatever the case, the dwelling in huts or booths characterized the observance of this feast. Lev 23:42-43 offers an interpretation of this practice which anchors it in Israel's salvation history:

> You shall dwell in booths, that your generations may
> know that I made the people of Israel dwell in booths
> when I brought them out of the land of Egypt: I am the
> Lord your God.

Thus for generations of worshippers in Israel this great
pilgrimage feast recalled the experience of their ancestors
who did not yet enjoy the bounty of the land as they made
their way through the wilderness as a caravan of tent-
dwellers.

The Feast of Booths, like the Feast of Unleavened Bread,
was originally a seven-day festival to which an eighth day
was attached. Lev 23:33-36 and Num 29:12-38 agree in
legislating for the special observances of solemn assembly
and abstention from "laborious work" on the first and last
days of the feast. In addition, during the post-exilic period
elaborate offerings were made throughout the course of the
week (Num 29:12-38). Deut 16:14-15 and Lev 23:40 under-
line the spirit of great rejoicing and thanksgiving which
marked the feast. It is likely that the celebration included
dances and processions by the harvesters as well as other
forms of merriment appropriate to a vintage feast (cf. Judg
9:27 and 21:19-21). According to the witness of Deut 31:9-
13, when the law was solemnly proclaimed once every seven
years, it was to take place during the Feast of Booths.

Day of Atonement. The late liturgical calendars (Lev 23
and Num 28-29) refer to a Day of Atonement which was
celebrated during the seventh month, just prior to the Feast
of Booths which began on the fifteenth day. Although a
spirit of repentance was present from ancient times in
Israel's tradition, the fact that an official Day of Atonement
is mentioned only in late strata of the biblical record suggests that this particular penitential observance arose only
during a relatively late date. Lev 16:29, 23:27 and Num 29:7
agree with one another in designating the tenth day of the
seventh month as the Day of Atonement. The Hebrew text
of Ezek 45:20 appears to refer to the same feast but links it to
the seventh day of the seventh month while the Greek
Septuagint of Ezekiel understood the day of penitence as

falling on the first day of the seventh month. Finally, Neh 9:1 designates the twenty-fourth day of the seventh month as a day of fasting and penitence. These variations suggest that the feast was still in a state of evolution while the biblical texts were being written.

More is known of the rituals for observing the Day of Atonement than of its origin and development. In addition to the witness of Lev 23 and Num 29, prescriptions for the observance of the Day of Atonement appear in Lev 16. It was a day (measured from evening to evening according to Lev 23:32) on which community members rested from their ordinary labors and gathered for "a holy convocation." All three texts (Lev 16 and 23; Num 29) describe the community's participation in this feast: the people are to "afflict themselves," an expression which is believed to be technical terminology but the exact content of which is no longer known. It probably included fasting and perhaps other penitential exercises as well.

The texts (especially Lev 16) offer considerable information on the priest's duties for the Day of Atonement. This was the one day of the year on which he was allowed to enter "the holy place within the veil" (Lev 16:2), that is, the Holy of Holies. The priest entered the Temple's most sacred space and conducted there rituals which featured the smearing of blood, an expression of the oneness of life which worshippers sought with God. The day was also marked by elaborate sacrificial offerings designed to abolish uncleanness from the sanctuary, the tent of meeting, the altar, the priests, and the people (see below on rituals).

A second feature of the service for the Day of Atonement has to do with the scapegoat. Lev 16:6-10 and Lev 16:20-22 are the two texts which specifically describe the ritual with the scapegoat. They may represent two originally independent traditions. However, in the present arrangement of the chapter, they appear to be successive stages of the ceremony centering on the goat. Lev 16:6-10 says that two goats were presented to the priest who cast lots upon them: a lot assigned one of the goats "for Yahweh" while the other designated the second goat "for Azazel," thought to be a demon or evil spirit which lived in the desert wilderness. The goat "for Yahweh" was sacrificed as a sin offering. Thereupon the priest undertook the rite for the scapegoat:

> And when he has made an end of atoning for the holy place and the tent of meeting and the altar, he shall present the live goat; and Aaron shall lay both his hands upon the head of the live goat, and confess over him all the iniquities of the people of Israel, and all their transgressions, all their sins; and he shall put them upon the head of the goat, and send him away into the wilderness by the hand of a man who is in readiness. The goat shall bear all their iniquities upon him to a solitary land; and he shall let the goat go in the wilderness.   (Lev 16:20-22)

The rite appears to symbolize and effect the transfer of the people's sins onto the goat. Because such a transfer rendered the goat unclean, it could not be sacrificed. It was taken to the edge of the wilderness and driven into the desert. The origin of this practice is unknown, although other ancient Near Eastern peoples are known to have conducted similar rites designed to transfer impurity or guilt onto an animal which was then in some way removed from the midst of the community. It is possible that a scapegoat ceremony used in non-Yahwist circles appealed to and was meaningful for Israelite believers. Because of its popularity the scapegoat ritual was adopted by Israel's liturgical officials who adapted and monitored the rite for use in the worship of Yahweh.

The Day of the Trumpets. Lev 23:23-25 and its corresponding text in Num 29:1-6 both refer to an annual religious feast which was to take place on the first day of the seventh month. Like the other major feasts in Israel, it was a day of solemn rest when the community gathered for a "holy convocation." Like the other feasts, it was also marked by the offering of sacrifice. What was distinctive in these Priestly prescriptions for the observances of this feast was the prominence of the blasting of trumpets.

Several scholars see in these brief texts the remains of what had been a New Year's festival in pre-exilic Israel, prior to the adoption of the Babylonian calendar which transferred the beginning of the year from the autumn to the spring. Like Lev 23 and Num 29, the late witness of Neh 8:1-12 attests to the celebration of a feast on this day but none of these texts refer to the feast as New Year's. According to the passage in the Book of Nehemiah, the law was read before the assembly on this feast (cf. Deut 31:9-13).

Scholars are in widespread agreement that these brief texts contain only a mere trace of what was in an earlier period a much more prominent religious festival. Unfortunately, scholarly consensus does not include a common view regarding the exact nature of the festival in question. One position is that the old autumnal New Year featured the celebration of the enthronement of Yahweh as universal king. The enthronement festival is thought to have included themes borrowed from ancient Near Eastern New Year's celebrations such as creation, divine victory over enemies, and the judgment of the nations.

A second opinion views the festival in question as a prominent occasion for covenant renewal in pre-exilic Israel. As such it is thought to have included some cultic representation of theophany, a recital of Yahweh's saving deeds on Israel's behalf, a reading of the law, and the solemn pronouncement of blessings and curses. Through this rite it is thought that the covenant between Yahweh and Israel was renewed annually.

Another perspective on this feast regards it as having focused upon God's choice of the Davidic line for the royal throne and of Zion as the special place of divine presence. Still others see it merely as a solemn beginning to a month which features the prominent feasts of Atonement (on the tenth day) and Booths (beginning on the fifteenth day).

The broad range of opinions which have been advanced regarding the feast held on the first day of the seventh month demonstrates the ambiguity of the textual evidence. In the face of this, it is best to reserve hypothetical reconstructions and simply acknowledge that the calendars of Lev 23 and Num 29 include the first day of the seventh month as a special day in post-exilic Israel's liturgical year.

Israelite Feasts and the Megillot. In post-biblical times
the reading of short books of the Bible was added to the
liturgy of the three ancient pilgrimage festivals, the feasts of
Passover/Unleavened Bread, Weeks, and Booths. Two
other short biblical books were read at two additional
feasts. Because of this liturgical custom the Books of the
Song of Songs, Ruth, Ecclesiastes, Esther and Lamentations are grouped together in some Hebrew Bibles. The five
are sometimes referred to as the *megillot* ("scrolls").

The Song of Songs is read during the celebration of
Passover. The rabbis interpreted the love poetry of the Song
of Songs as an allegorical expression of the love between
God and Israel. The common association between love and
springtime and the reference to spring in one of the love
poems (Songs 2:11-13) were points which linked the biblical
book and the springtime festival of Passover. Other points
of connection may be found in the Song's reference to
Pharaoh's chariots (Songs 1:9) and the biblical view that the
exodus-wilderness experience formed the honeymoon
period in the relationship between God and Israel (Jer 2:2;
Hosea 2:14-15).

The Book of Ruth is read during the celebration of the
Feast of Weeks, i.e., Pentecost. Since the biblical writer
casts much of the story of Ruth within the context of the
barley harvest (Ruth 1:22 and 2:23), the association between
Ruth and the celebration rooted in the harvest of grain was
natural. The rabbis offered further explanations for the
association of the two. They pointed to the genealogy of
David which appears at the conclusion of the Book of Ruth
(Ruth 4:17-22) and to the post-biblical tradition that David
was born and died on the Feast of Weeks. Moreover, after
the Feast of Weeks came to include a celebration of the gift
of the Law on Mount Sinai, they pointed to the parallel
between Israel's acceptance of the Law and the embrace of
the Jewish faith by the Moabite woman Ruth.

The Book of Ecclesiastes is read during the celebration of
the Feast of Booths, i.e., Tabernacles. The rabbis explained
the practice by referring to the traditional view that
Solomon wrote the Book of Ecclesiastes in his old age and

that the somber, pessimistic tone of the book is appropriate for the autumn of the year during which the Feast of Booths is celebrated.

The Books of Esther and Lamentations are read during the Jewish observance of the Feasts of Purim and the Ninth of Av respectively. The Bible itself links the story of Esther with the Feast of Purim (Esther chapter 9). The Ninth of Av is a day in which Jews mourn a series of disasters which have occurred during their history, including the destruction of the first and second Temples. The spirit of the day makes it a fitting occasion for the believing community to hear the laments over Jerusalem which constitute the Book of Lamentations.

Ritual

Just as the flow of Israel's liturgical year was given order and orientation by the regular recurrence of major feasts, so the movement of cultic activity itself was carefully ordered by specific rituals. In Israel worship was not a performance undertaken before the throne of a passive, albeit divine, spectator. To come into God's presence at a holy place was to enter a sphere of sacred activity, to encounter a dynamic presence-in-power. The process of engaging such a presence required safe and approved ways of acting. In its established rituals Israel gave order to and regularized its movement within God's continuing presence in the cult.

Sacrificial Ritual

The offering of sacrifice was one of many ritual activities in ancient Israelite worship. Indeed, it was often the focal point of worship services. Its custodians were the priests who not only guided the design, development and observance of approved sacrificial rituals but also functioned as mediators between Yahweh and worshippers who brought offerings to the altar.

The Bible's most extended treatment of Israelite ritual is

the catalogue of sacrifices and their rubrics which appear in the Priestly tradition of Leviticus 1-7. Presumably this collection served as a manual for services conducted in the post-exilic Temple. Even though these chapters were formulated in a relatively late period, it is probable that the practices which they describe had grown and developed over the course of centuries of religious observance.

The manual offers guidance for those worshippers who came into God's presence with sacrificial offerings. It contains no rationale or theology of sacrifice. Neither does it discuss motivation on the part of the offerer nor of God's response to the offering (cf. Amos 5:21-24; Isa 1:12-17; Mic 6:6-8; etc.). The focus is on proper procedure.

In the absence of explicitly stated explanations, we search between the lines of the rubrics of Lev 1-7 for clues to the meaning of Israel's sacrificial ritual. The manual indicates that when worshippers approached the altar, they presented prized animals from their own flocks and herds or grain which they themselves had sown and harvested. In bringing sacrifice, therefore, worshippers set apart something significant from their lives, something precious which they offered as an extension of themselves. Thus, sacrifice had the character of gift, although Israelites always recognized that what they presented for Yahweh was but a token of the bountiful gifts God had first given them. When the sacrifice was offered, all or part of it was destroyed. This ritual action suggests the irrevocability of the gift. In being destroyed the offering could not revert back to the offerer. It truly was given over to God.

The prominence given to the ritual use of blood in Israel's sacrifices bears strong connotations of life, life poured out before Yahweh's saving presence-in-power, life brought in touch with the Sacred represented by the altar. Thus, in rituals undertaken with the blood of sacrificial victims (and also in the meals which frequently were associated with sacrifice), worshippers symbolically shared life with God and with one another (cf. Exod 24).

Finally, although the notion of atonement seems to have come to prominence only in post-exilic sacrificial tradition, it is likely that the pouring out of blood also bore connotations of expiation or reparation in earlier times as well. The association is clearly stated in the Holiness Code:

> For the life of the flesh is in the blood; and I have given it for you upon the altar to make atonement for your souls; for it is the blood that makes atonement, by reason of the life.   (Lev 17:11).

Atonement, communion, self-gift: the three are not mutually exclusive notions. Sometimes together, sometimes apart, they weave through and between the ritual activities of those believers who drew near to offer sacrifice for Yahweh.

Leviticus 1-7 describes the main types of sacrifices in the post-exilic worshipping community. We turn now to survey them briefly.

Burnt Offerings. The most common Hebrew term for the burnt offering comes from a root, *'alah*, which means "to go up." The distinguishing feature of this kind of sacrifice was that all of it was given over to God, that is to say, all of it "went up" to God by being burned. It was a holocaust.

Late Priestly regulations for the burnt offering appear in Leviticus chapter 1. The sacrificial victim was to be taken from the best of what the offerer could afford. Thus, those who could offered bulls while others presented sheep and goats. The poor were allowed to bring doves or pigeons. The sacrificial victim was brought to the Temple by the offerer who laid hands on it, a gesture which probably intended to express that the offering truly represented the one who brought it. The slaughter of the animal was necessary for the ritual to proceed, but it was not in itself a ritual act. It was done by the lay person, not the priest. The lay person also separated the blood from the rest of the animal, washed the animal and cut the flesh into pieces. The priest poured the blood at the base of the altar and laid the flesh upon the altar to be burned in holocaust.

Although Leviticus 1 does not specify the occasions on which burnt offerings were made, Exod 29:38-42 directs that two lambs were to be sacrificed as burnt offerings on a daily basis, one in the morning and the other in the evening. A reference to burnt offerings in the ancient Covenant Code (Exod 20:24-26) suggests that they were offered in early stages of Israelite worship. Late Priestly legislation characteristically attributed to them an atoning function (Lev 1:4). In the Priestly work, burnt offerings constituted one of several kinds of offerings presented in conjunction with one another (see Lev 23:18; Exod 29:38-42; Num 15:1-16).

Peace Offerings. A second type of sacrifice in Israel was the peace offering. It was also known as the communion sacrifice because its purpose was to bring about union, wholeness. The ritual for the peace offering closely resembled that of the burnt offering described above. A notable difference was that in the peace offering only the fat of the animal was burned while its flesh was reserved and shared in the form of a sacred meal. God's participation was symbolized by the burning of the animal's fat as well as by the pouring out of the victim's blood at the base of the altar. The priest, the offerer and guests shared the rest of the offering in the form of a ritual meal in God's presence. This symbolized their oneness in and with the Divinity. The sacred meal was the high point of the peace offering and was a joy-filled social occasion as well as a religious ritual.

Although the peace offering was probably a prominent part of pre-exilic Israel's cultic observance, it is not given extensive treatment in Priestly legislation. Prescriptions for the peace offering appear in Leviticus chapter 3 and in Lev 7:11-36. The latter text specified three different occasions on which peace offerings were made. Sometimes they were presented as acts of thanksgiving; at other times they served as freewill offerings, i.e., offerings made at the discretion of the worshipper. They also served as votive offerings for those worshippers who had bound themselves by vow to offer sacrifice.

Cereal Offerings. In the Priestly legislation the animal sacrifices of the burnt offering and the peace offering are almost always accompanied by a cereal offering (see Lev 7:11-14; Num 15:1-10). The Hebrew word for this type of offering simply means "gift." It consisted of an offering of flour (baked or unbaked) which, together with oil and incense, was presented at the altar. A portion of the offering (part of the flour and oil and all of the incense) was burned on the altar and this was said to be a "memorial." It was to remind God of the worshipper or perhaps to call God's attention to the totality of what the worshipper brought, i.e., not only the part which was burned but also the part which was reserved for the priest's use. Legislation governing the cereal offering appears in Leviticus chapter 2.

Sin Offerings and Guilt Offerings. Whereas holocausts, peace offerings, and cereal offerings seem to have been prominent parts of pre-exilic Israel's worship life, the post-exilic Priestly circle focused attention on sacrifices which addressed Israel's need to restore its covenant life with God after the experience and acknowledgment of sin. The sin offering and the guilt offering thus became prominent expressions of the community's desire for reparation. While the two appear to be separate sacrifices, they lack features which clearly distinguish them from one another and in some instances appear to be mentioned interchangeably in the biblical texts.

Directives for the sin offering appear in Lev 4:1—5:13. This sacrifice was designed to secure reparation for the one who sinned "unwittingly," a probable reference to unintentional violations of ritual cleanness or other cultic infractions. The rite of the sin offering resembled that of the burnt offering, with the exception that the blood of the sacrificial victim was smeared on the horns of the altar in addition to being poured at its base and the flesh of the victim was burned outside the Temple (presumably because of this offering's association with sin). The victims which were sacrificed as sin offerings ranged from bulls to doves and pigeons depending on the status of the offerer. The main features of the sacrifices were the rites performed with the blood of the victim.

Prescriptions for guilt offerings appear in Lev 5:14—6:7 and in Lev 7:1-10. Like sin offerings, guilt offerings sought expiation for sins committed "unwittingly." Lev 5:15 associates this situation with a "breach of faith," an expression which is not further specified. Lev 6:2, however, associates the "breach of faith" with deliberate acts of injustice. In those cases worshippers were required to make full restitution with those people against whom they had sinned (cf. Num 5:5-10). Only then were guilt offerings to be presented for Yahweh (Lev 6:1-7). The sacrificial victim for the guilt offering was the ram.

Non-Sacrificial Ritual

While the offering of sacrifice was a prominent part of ritual in Israelite circles, it would be erroneous to think that all of Israel's ritual was sacrificial in nature. Unfortunately, however, the Bible does not contain a systematic compendium of non-sacrificial rituals. To learn of these one must be attentive to scattered references throughout the biblical canon. Once discovered, texts which witness to non-sacrificial ritual yield little information about their rubrics and rationale. Because of the elusiveness of the biblical tradition on this, perhaps it is best for readers to leave aside attempts at analytic investigation and simply stretch to hear the sound and strain to see the movement of Israel's non-sacrificial rituals.

To speak of ritual is to speak of bodily expressions, indeed, embodiments of the dynamics of entering into the presence of Yahweh. Ancient Israelite worshippers raised and lowered their eyes, their arms, their entire bodies and in doing so they brought themselves into harmony with the movement of the Sacred in their midst. They moved to the beat of clapping hands and pulsating tambourines. Their bodies absorbed rhythm and became dance and dance extended itself into procession.

Words spoken in ritual named and interpreted both symbolic movement and religious experience. In Israel's worship word took many diverse forms: confession and commitment, invocation and reassurance, lament and praise, blessing and curse. Spontaneous shouts formed a chorus with measured chants and songs laden with poetry.

They harmonized with the melodic movement of harps, lyres, flutes, horns, and trumpets (cf. Ps 150).

At the major feasts, movement and sound came together to create symbolic drama which coaxed and unleashed the power of past saving events as they were acted out in some form of ritual rehearsal. Yahweh's dynamic and saving presence in Israel's history was not simply remembered but re-presented (made present again) in the lives and movements of worshippers. In trying to picture for ourselves these festival celebrations, we do well to leave aside notions of the relatively muted, restrained decorum with which worship services occur in many assemblies today in the Western world. Instead, we might imagine gatherings marked by varied sensory stimulations: vivid color, intense sound and movement, pronounced fragrances, and a spirit of participation which gave due expression to what Israel experienced as God's dynamic presence with the worshipping assembly.

THE BOOK OF NUMBERS

INTRODUCTION TO THE BOOK OF NUMBERS

Title

In the Hebrew Bible, this fourth book of the Pentateuch takes its title from a key word of the opening verse, *bemidbar*, "in the wilderness." The Greek Septuagint, however, called the book *Arithmoi* ("Numbers") and the Latin Vulgate followed with *Numeri*, presumably because the people of God are numbered in the book (see chapters 1 and 26). However, since the actual numbering of the tribes of Israel constitutes such a small portion of the book, it is clear that the Greek, Latin and English titles do not fully describe the overall content of the book.

Character

Scholars agree that the Book of Numbers is one of the least unified works in the Bible. In it lists and legal materials covering a broad range of topics are juxtaposed and mixed with narratives about Israel's wilderness sojourn. Poetry and liturgical materials likewise appear from time to time in the pages of the book. Thus, contributions from storytellers and lawyers, poets and cultic officials have come together to form the composite witness of the Book of Numbers. The complexity of the book is enhanced further with the recog-

nition that its disparate pieces of tradition probably have
origins in very different periods of Israel's long history.

Contents and Their Arrangement

Although the final editors of the composite traditions of
the Book of Numbers did not leave us clear indications
regarding how to subdivide the material which now appears
in thirty-six chapters, biblical scholarship is in wide agreement in viewing the book as consisting of three sections.

The initial section consists of Num 1:1—10:10. It is a
continuation of the Priestly corpus which appears in the
final chapters of the Book of Exodus and in the entire Book
of Leviticus. Like the rest of the Priestly corpus this section
of the Book of Numbers has its setting at Mount Sinai where
Israel receives divine directives regarding proper conduct
for a people whose God tabernacles in its center. Numbers
1-10 function as preparation for the departure from Sinai by
providing directives according to which God's holy people
might arrange and conduct themselves in a continuing posture of worship along the way. Chapters 1-4 include a census
of the tribes as well as their proper arrangement within the
camp, the sacred personnel (the Levites) closest to its center,
the tabernacle. The remaining chapters of the section form a
composite of various laws designed to regulate life within
the sacred community. These include directives regarding
vows, sacred offerings, religious leaders, liturgical instru-
ments such as the sanctuary lamp and trumpets, and other
topics as well. This first section of the Book of Numbers
includes the blessing familiar to ancient and contemporary
believers alike:

> The Lord bless you and keep you:
> The Lord make his face to shine upon you,
>   and be gracious to you:
> The Lord lift up his countenance upon you,
>   and give you peace (Num 6:24-26).

These lines feature the threefold pronouncement of the divine name out of which blessing unfolds. They begin in beautiful simplicity and spiral through widening lines which reach toward peace, that human yearning and divine blessing which mean not just the absence of war but total wholeness wherein all things connect in harmonious ways.

The second section of the Book of Numbers begins in Num 10:11 with the notice of Israel's departure from Mount Sinai. It is more difficult to pinpoint the end of this section. In the commentary which follows, we regard Num 20:13 as the conclusion of the section because attention thereafter is primarily (though not exclusively) turned away from the prevailing theme of chapters 10-20, life in the wilderness, and turns instead to the theme of the inheritance of the Promised Land. It should be noted that some scholars mark the end of this section at Num 21:9 after which materials focus even more exclusively on Israel's approach of the land. Still others cite Num 22:1 as the end of the section and thereby view this second section of the Book of Numbers as marking the span between Israel's encampment at Sinai and its encampment in the plains of Moab east of the Jordan River.

Except for isolated appearances of legal material (Num 15, 18, 19), this section consists of narratives about Israel's time in the wilderness, especially the stay at the oasis at Kadesh. Some of the incidents recorded here are similar to stories told about the wilderness journey from the sea to Sinai (Exod 15-18). Thus the traditions feature Israel's problems with food and water in the wilderness as well as leadership controversies. Although some of these stories resemble those already narrated in the Book of Exodus, the wilderness traditions of Numbers are marked by a pronounced infidelity on Israel's part and by Yahweh's judgment. Another difference between the two complexes of wilderness traditions is the inclusion in Num 13-14 of an account of Israel's reconnaissance of the Promised Land, the people's failure in courage, and a faithless attempt to enter the land. It is this last incident which accounts for the tradition that the rebellious exodus generation would die in the wilderness before Yahweh would bring the "little ones" into the land.

In the third and final section of the Book of Numbers, Num 20:14—36:13, Israel moves from the wilderness of Kadesh to the land east of the Jordan River opposite Jericho. In this section legal and narrative materials alike focus on the inheritance of the Promised Land. The chapters include stories of victory whereby Israel won footholds in the Transjordan territory, blessings pronounced over Israel there, information regarding Moses' imminent death along with the commissioning of Joshua as his successor, and the apportioning of the land east of the Jordan to some of the tribes. The rest of the material in these chapters is exceedingly disparate in character, content, and probably in age: a census, genealogies, itineraries, inheritance laws, directives for offerings to be made on liturgical feasts, regulations for the taking of vows by women, instructions about the allotment of the land. In spite of the variety in subject matter, the topics treated in these chapters are generally concerned in one way or another with preparations for life in the land. The order of their presentation, however, more closely resembles a miscellaneous collection than a carefully organized progression of thought.

Literary Sources

The heterogeneous materials which have come together in the Book of Numbers no doubt date from different periods of Israel's history. Some of the poetry in these chapters comes from very early times. Some of the lists and legal materials, on the other hand, stem from the post-exilic period although it is possible that they contain remnants of earlier views and customs. Regarding the composition of the materials, it is generally believed that the first section of the Book of Numbers comes entirely from the Priestly tradition as was mentioned above. In the second and third sections we see the first appearance of the old literary sources (the Yahwist and Elohist) since the account of the apostasy around the calf and the renewal of the covenant as narrated in Exod 32-34. While the early sources probably form the base of these sections, one must also note that they have been supplemented by Priestly narratives. At some time the three narrative strands (J, E, and P) were given final shape alongside later interpolations of legal material. It is likely that this editorial process took place in post-exilic Priestly circles.

Significance

The Book of Numbers is not a work to be viewed by itself. Its context and significance are fundamentally rooted in the great Pentateuchal story of God's promise to the ancestors working itself through considerable delays to fulfillment in the inheritance of the land. Between the promise and its fulfillment lay traditions about the bondage in Egypt and the exodus, the encounter with God at Sinai, and stories about life in the wilderness. Viewed against this framework it is clear that the Book of Numbers touches upon three of the major Pentateuchal themes: Sinai, wilderness, and land.

At the beginning of the book the tribes of Israel are poised to receive guidance regarding the implications of God's tabernacling presence in their midst as they prepare to leave the holy mountain. At the end of the book they are poised to receive blessing and guidance for the conduct of their life in the land. In between the beginning and the end of Numbers Israel records its story of life along the way. There we see a community needy and rebellious, not yet fully formed. They struggle to continue the journey they had undertaken even as they struggle to live faithfully within the bond they had already entered with Yahweh. Their way is surely that of trial and error. The biblical writers set before us people being shaped by their own failures in fidelity and courage and by the Mystery at their center who was zealous for holiness and for relationship.

Some materials in the Book of Numbers were utilized by early Christian writers in their efforts to express God's saving presence and action in their own day. The Priestly writers' notion of God's "tabernacling" presence was applied to Jesus by the writer of the Fourth Gospel: "the Word became flesh and dwelt ('tabernacled') among us" (John 1:14). Likewise, in John 3:14-15 the death of the Son of Man is likened to Moses' lifting up of the bronze serpent in the wilderness (Num 21:4-9). The gift of manna in the wilderness served as a basic point of comparison for the Christian understanding of the gift of Christ's body (John 6:25-59). The wilderness traditions about God's grace and Israel's rebellion also surface as a point of comparison in 1 Cor 10:1-13 (see our Excursus on Typology) and in Hebrews 3:7—4:13. Thus did the story of the Book of Numbers offer later generations of believers ways in which to interpret their own encounters with the Sacred.

Our Commentary on Numbers

Since we are unable to treat the whole of the Book of Numbers in this commentary, it is necessary that we set aside certain portions of the biblical text. We have chosen to focus on those traditions connected with Israel's life in the wilderness between Sinai and Moab and with some of the traditions which narrate Israel's approach toward the full inheritance of the land. We have omitted the Priestly lists and regulations which constitute the first section of the book (Num 1:1—10:10). Moreover, we have omitted isolated chapters of legal material (namely, chapters 15, 18, and 19) which appear in the second section of the book. Finally, we have not included in the text or commentary the miscellaneous materials which have come together in the final chapters of the book (namely, chapters 25 to 36). For more complete treatments readers are directed to those commentaries on the Book of Numbers which are listed under "Suggestions for Further Reading" at the end of this volume.

RETURN TO THE WILDERNESS
10:11—20:13

The huge corpus of material associated with Mount Sinai (Exod 19-40, the Book of Leviticus, Num 1-10) comes to an end in the tenth chapter of the Book of Numbers. The monumental Sinai tradition concludes with the Priestly writer's description of Israel's departure from the mountain of God (Num 10:11-28). With this account we turn once more to narratives about Israel's life in the wilderness. In this case the wilderness is that desert region which stretches between Mount Sinai and the borders of habitable land which lay to the east of the Jordan River.

In several ways the wilderness traditions recorded in Num 10:11—20:13 resemble some of the traditions of the first stage of Israel's life in the wilderness as recorded in Exod 15-18. Like Exod 15-18, the wilderness traditions in the Book of Numbers are of varied content and origin. Like Exod 15-18, originally independent materials have been joined to one another by means of an editorial itinerary which creates the impression that these stories recount incidents which took place at different stopping places along the way between Sinai and the land east of the Jordan. Like Exod 15-18, recurring and unifying devices are present in the motifs of Israel's murmuring and Yahweh's gracious care. Like Exod 15-18, the wilderness stories in Numbers were recorded by Yahwist and/or Elohist sources and in many cases these early traditions were later supplemented and reshaped by the Priestly writer. Like Exod 15-18, these writers and theologians projected their own concerns and views into the wilderness period which they considered to be foundational for their own lives.

Although the wilderness narratives in the Book of Numbers share much with the material found in Exod 15-18, the motifs of Israel's murmuring and Yahweh's gracious aid appear in a different pattern than in the Book of Exodus. Whereas in the wilderness between the sea and Sinai, Israel's murmuring rose out of some legitimate need like thirst or hunger, the wilderness traditions in the Book of Numbers typically portray Israel's murmuring as based in general dissatisfaction rather than in need (cf. Num 20:2-13). Just as the starting point or basis for murmuring is different, so is God's response. In these narratives God responds to Israel's ill-based murmuring with anger and punishment. This occasions the need for Moses' intercession. Finally, God's gracious response in this pattern consists in curbing divine punishment. In general, then, the Book of Numbers presents a more tragic version of Israel's life in the wilderness than the witness of Exod 15-18.

The exact theological message of the above-mentioned change in tone of the wilderness narratives is difficult to pinpoint. Between the first and second wilderness journeys, of course, had come Sinai. There the people of Israel had formally committed themselves to a covenantal relationship with the One who had brought them out of Egypt. There they had agreed to a future with Yahweh based on the past. They undertook a life of trust bound to the One whose signs and wonders had proven trustworthy. After the formalization of such a relationship, murmuring which has no real basis smacks of fundamental infidelity. The breadth and depth of the infidelity are expressed in the persistent regret at ever having left Egypt in the first place and in the increasing hostility directed at Moses, Yahweh's representative.

Whereas several of the Exodus stories featured life and the nurturing presence of the One who sustained Israel's life in the harshness of the desert, the wilderness journey between Sinai and the land east of the Jordan is marked by recurring instances of death. Tragically, the whole adult community forfeits its life in the land when they choose fear over trust (Num 13-14). In the end, even the wilderness leaders fail in a matter of grace thereby exchanging life in the promised land for a freedom journey which must end along the way.

DEPARTURE FROM SINAI
10:11-36

[11]In the second year, in the second month, on the twentieth day of the month, the cloud was taken up from over the tabernacle of the testimony, [12]and the people of Israel set out by stages from the wilderness of Sinai; and the cloud settled down in the wilderness of Paran. [13]They set out for the first time at the command of the Lord by Moses. [14]The standard of the camp of the men of Judah set out first by their companies; and over their host was Nahshon the son of Amminadab. [15]And over the host of the tribe of the men of Issachar was Nethanel the son of Zuar. [16]And over the host of the tribe of the men of Zebulun was Eliab the son of Helon.

[17]And when the tabernacle was taken down, the sons of Gershon and the sons of Merari, who carried the tabernacle, set out. [18]And the standard of the camp of Reuben set out by their companies; and over their host was Elizur the son of Shedeur. [19]And over the host of the tribe of the men of Simeon was Shelumi-el the son of Zurishaddai. [20]And over the host of the tribe of the men of Gad was Eliasaph the son of Deuel.

[21]Then the Kohathites set out, carrying the holy things, and the tabernacle was set up before their arrival. [22]And the standard of the camp of the men of Ephraim set out by their companies; and over their host was Elishama the

son of Ammihud. ²³And over the host of the tribe of the men of Manasseh was Gamaliel the son of Pedahzur. ²⁴And over the host of the tribe of the men of Benjamin was Abidan the son of Gideoni.

²⁵Then the standard of the camp of the men of Dan, acting as the rear guard of all the camps, set out by their companies; and over their host was Ahiezer the son of Ammishaddai. ²⁶And over the host of the tribe of the men of Asher was Pagiel the son of Ochran. ²⁷And over the host of the tribe of the men of Naphtali was Ahira the son of Enan. ²⁸This was the order of march of the people of Israel according to their hosts, when they set out.

²⁹And Moses said to Hobab, the son of Reuel the Midianite, Moses' father-in-law, "We are setting out for the place of which the Lord said, 'I will give it to you'; come with us, and we will do you good; for the Lord has promised good to Israel." ³⁰But he said to him, "I will not go; I will depart to my own land and to my kindred." ³¹And he said, "Do not leave us, I pray you, for you know how we are to encamp in the wilderness, and you will serve as eyes for us. ³²And if you go with us, whatever good the Lord will do to us, the same will we do to you."

³³So they set out from the mount of the Lord three days' journey; and the ark of the covenant of the Lord went before them three days' journey, to seek out a resting place for them. ³⁴And the cloud of the Lord was over them by day, whenever they set out from the camp.

³⁵And whenever the ark set out, Moses said, "Arise, O Lord, and let thy enemies be scattered; and let them that hate thee flee before thee." ³⁶And when it rested, he said, "Return, O Lord, to the ten thousand thousands of Israel."

These verses contain two accounts of Israel's departure from Mount Sinai. Verses 11-28 represent the Priestly writer's view. This late version has been prefixed to an earlier (Yahwist and/or Elohist) account which now appears in verses 29-36. One can see two distinct emphases which characterized these same literary sources in the Book of Exodus.

The Priestly writer's style is almost cultic in character. This writer's view of Israel's departure from Sinai bears likeness to a solemn procession on a sacred feast. The date of departure is carefully marked like on a festal calendar. God's presence is signalled by the cloud which had heretofore been over the "tabernacle of the testimony." The order of the march is arranged with precision. It corresponds closely to the Priestly writer's record of the organization of the camp which is recorded in Num 2.

Num 10:29-36 marks the first appearance of the older literary traditions since the narrative of Exod 32-34. A chief concern of those chapters in Exodus, i.e., concern for guidance along the way, continues in the present text. In verses 29-32 Moses requests the human guidance of his father-in-law for the remainder of the journey toward the land. The Midianite, otherwise known as Jethro (Exod 3:1; 4:18; 18), is here referred to as Hobab (cf. Judg 4:11). The narrator complements Moses' request for human guidance in the wilderness with a description of the divine guidance which was present in the ark (v. 33) and in the cloud (v. 34).

The chapter comes to a close with an ancient chant which probably stems from times in which Israel invoked God's presence in war. At an early period the ark was viewed as a visible throne for the invisible God. When it was borne into battle by cultic personnel alongside Israelite military troops it symbolized God's presence, thus transforming the battle into a Holy War, i.e., war in which God was present in power to save Israel (see Josh 6; 1 Sam 4). The ark which would later signal God's saving presence in battle is here presented as accompanying Israel on its journey through the wilderness from Sinai to the land.

ONCE AGAIN, MURMURING
11:1-3

> **11** And the people complained in the hearing of the Lord about their misfortunes; and when the Lord heard

it, his anger was kindled, and the fire of the Lord burned among them, and consumed some outlying parts of the camp. ²Then the people cried to Moses; and Moses prayed to the Lord, and the fire abated. ³So the name of that place was called Taberah, because the fire of the Lord burned among them.

This first incident in Israel's life upon its departure from Mount Sinai sets the tone for the entire story of the second stage of the wilderness journey, the passage from Sinai to the borders of the land. The structure of this narrative introduces in simplest form a pattern which characterizes other stories in the chapters which follow: Israel's complaint, God's anger and punishment, Moses' intercession with God on behalf of the people, and God's gracious response in abating the divine anger and punishment.

Like some of the other wilderness traditions, the incident described in Num 11:1-3 serves as the basis for the place name with which the incident is associated. When Israel murmured out of infidelity God's anger burned part of the camp. Because of this the place was called Taberah ("burning").

DEMANDS FOR DIVERSITY
11:4-35

⁴Now the rabble that was among them had a strong craving; and the people of Israel also wept again, and said, "O that we had meat to eat! ⁵We remember the fish we ate in Egypt for nothing, the cucumbers, the melons, the leeks, the onions, and the garlic; ⁶but now our strength is dried up, and there is nothing at all but this manna to look at."

⁷Now the manna was like coriander seed, and its appearance like that of bdellium. ⁸The people went about and gathered it, and ground it in mills or beat it in mortars, and boiled it in pots, and made cakes of it; and

the taste of it was like the taste of cakes baked with oil. ⁹When the dew fell upon the camp in the night, the manna fell with it.

¹⁰Moses heard the people weeping throughout their families, every man at the door of his tent; and the anger of the Lord blazed hotly, and Moses was displeased. ¹¹Moses said to the Lord, "Why hast thou dealt ill with thy servant? And why have I not found favor in thy sight, that thou dost lay the burden of all this people upon me? ¹²Did I conceive all this people? Did I bring them forth, that thou shouldst say to me, 'Carry them in your bosom, as a nurse carries the sucking child,' to the land which thou didst swear to give their fathers? ¹³Where am I to get meat to give to all this people? For they weep before me and say, 'Give us meat, that we may eat.' ¹⁴I am not able to carry all this people alone, the burden is too heavy for me. ¹⁵If thou wilt deal thus with me, kill me at once, if I find favor in thy sight, that I may not see my wretchedness."

¹⁶And the Lord said to Moses, "Gather for me seventy men of the elders of Israel, whom you know to be the elders of the people and officers over them; and bring them to the tent of meeting, and let them take their stand there with you. ¹⁷And I will come down and talk with you there; and I will take some of the spirit which is upon you and put it upon them; and they shall bear the burden of the people with you, that you may not bear it yourself alone. ¹⁸And say to the people, 'Consecrate yourselves for tomorrow, and you shall eat meat; for you have wept in the hearing of the Lord, saying "Who will give us meat to eat? For it was well with us in Egypt." Therefore the Lord will give you meat, and you shall eat. ¹⁹You shall not eat one day, or two days, or five days, or ten days, or twenty days, ²⁰but a whole month, until it comes out at your nostrils and becomes loathsome to you, because you have rejected the Lord who is among you, and have wept before him, saying, "Why did we come forth out of Egypt?"'" ²¹But Moses said, "The people among whom I am number six hundred thousand on foot; and thou hast

said, 'I will give them meat, that they may eat a whole month!' ²²Shall flocks and herds be slaughtered for them, to suffice them? Or shall all the fish of the sea be gathered together for them, to suffice them?" ²³And the Lord said to Moses, "Is the Lord's hand shortened? Now you shall see whether my word will come true for you or not."

²⁴So Moses went out and told the people the words of the Lord; and he gathered seventy men of the elders of the people, and placed them round about the tent. ²⁵Then the Lord came down in the cloud and spoke to him, and took some of the spirit that was upon him and put it upon the seventy elders; and when the spirit rested upon them, they prophesied. But they did so no more.

²⁶Now two men remained in the camp, one named Eldad, and the other named Medad, and the spirit rested upon them; they were among those registered, but they had not gone out to the tent, and so they prophesied in the camp. ²⁷And a young man ran and told Moses, "Eldad and Medad are prophesying in the camp." ²⁸And Joshua the son of Nun, the minister of Moses, one of his chosen men, said, "My lord Moses, forbid them." ²⁹But Moses said to him, "Are you jealous for my sake? Would that all the Lord's people were prophets, that the Lord would put his spirit upon them!" ³⁰And Moses and the elders of Israel returned to the camp.

³¹And there went forth a wind from the Lord, and it brought quails from the sea, and let them fall beside the camp, about a day's journey on this side and a day's journey on the other side, round about the camp, and about two cubits above the face of the earth. ³²And the people rose all that day, and all night, and all the next day, and gathered the quails; he who gathered least gathered ten homers; and they spread them out for themselves all around the camp. ³³While the meat was yet between their teeth, before it was consumed, the anger of the Lord was kindled against the people, and the Lord smote the people with a very great plague. ³⁴Therefore the name of that place was called Kibroth-hattaavah, because there they buried the people who had the craving.

35From Kibroth-hattaavah the people journeyed to Hazeroth; and they remained at Hazeroth.

The bulk of Numbers 11 is a complex narrative wherein the writers' interest vacillates between two juxtaposed stories: the Israelites' demand for variety in their diet and the burden of Moses' singular leadership. The crisis over food parallels the story of Exod 16, God's gracious gift of manna in the wilderness between the sea and Mount Sinai, while the narrative about leadership roles bears similarity to the story of the appointment of judges which is recorded in Exod 18.

One strand of the narrative, the demand for meat, is found in Num 11:4-13, 18-24a, and 31-35. This incident of murmuring is said to have been precipitated by a "rabble" who incited the rest of the Israelites to complain about their lot. Unlike the parallel incident in Exod 16 which began in real need, the starting point here is loss of appetite ("our strength is dried up"; v. 6) caused by the monotony of God's gift of manna. The gift which once had satisfied the Israelites' needs now taxed their wants. The community craved meat. As in Exod 16 this growling for food led the community to remember the good old days of Egyptian cuisine which at least provided a tasty variety of foods. Ultimately the complaint about the food reflects Israel's regret at ever having left Pharaoh's table.

Following a brief reminder about the nature of manna (vv. 7-9), the second part of the structure of the murmuring motif is reported: the Lord was angry (v. 10). Moses then intercedes with God although he does not address the divine anger as we might expect of an intercessor. Instead, he voices his own frustration. In the rhetorical questions recorded in verse 12, the writer presents Moses as confronting Yahweh with the divine responsibility to follow through in relationship with this people. The unusual and striking analogy which Moses uses is the role of mother: "Did I conceive all this people? Did I bring them forth. . .?". The questions require a response rather than an answer. The implication is that Yahweh, not Moses, is the mother who brought this people to birth. Thus, it is Yahweh's responsibility to nurse her offspring until they come to the ultimate nourishment which the Promised Land will offer. Against the background of this forthright presentation of the facts and their implications, Moses' concluding question has the air of an ultimatum: "Where am I to get meat to give all this people?"

Moses' "mothering talk" to Yahweh becomes the thread to which was attached the second thematic strand of Num 11. As Moses had challenged Yahweh to take the responsibility for "carrying" this people on to the land as promised, the leader now reflects on the "carrying" involved in his own leadership role. In vv. 14-15 Moses says that his job had become too burdensome. These verses form the transition to the topic of human leadership roles which continues in vv. 16-17 and 24b-30. Verses 16-17 report the divine response to Moses' complaint. Seventy (a number suggesting sufficiency or completeness; cf. Exod 24:1, 9) of the elders will receive some of the charism which Moses has. In other words, they will be given proper credentials for assisting him in community leadership. The official installation is to take place at the tent of meeting where the gift of the spirit will be transferred by God whose presence is symbolized in the cloud. This text legitimates "gifted" roles within the community by portraying them as having been initiated by God's design. The new roles are fitted into the community's already-existing leadership structure in that they are said to derive from the central gift and ministry of Moses.

What is announced and prescribed in vv. 16-17 is reported as taking place in vv. 24b-25. The translation of the end of verse 25 is problematic. The RSV rendering ("But they did so no more") is a literal translation of the Hebrew text. Because its meaning in this context is uncertain, some interpreters have emended the text slightly to read: "And they did so unceasingly."

The gift under consideration in these verses is that of ecstatic prophecy which Israel probably encountered for the first time when it arrived in the land of Canaan (cf. 1 Sam 10:6, 10-13; 1 Kgs 22:6, 10-12). The present text represents

an attempt to legitimate Israel's adaptation of this Canaanite phenomenon by anachronistically projecting its origins
to Mosaic faith and practice as developed prior to Israel's
entrance into the land.

Verses 26-30 constitute an adjunct to the legitimation of
ecstatic prophecy. Eldad and Medad appear to have been
community members in good standing ("they were among
those registered"), and they too received the spirit to proph-
esy although the spirit did not come to them as to the rest
through institutionally recognized channels (i.e., at the tent
of meeting, in the presence of the cloud, from the spirit of
Moses). This text suggests that at some period in Israel's
religion a prophetic group (represented by Eldad and
Medad) became a center of controversy within the community. In the face of efforts to squelch their prophetic
ministry, they were forced to battle for recognition and
community acceptance. The writer of this text renders a
definitive conclusion to the dispute with the poignant words
placed on Moses' lips: "Would that all the Lord's people
were prophets...".

The remaining verses of Num 11 return to the topic of the
peoples' craving for meat and the Lord's response to their
complaint. The narrative description of the quail falling in
the vincinity resembles a contemporary phenomenon wherein migratory birds stop to rest in the desert and are easily
caught there during certain seasons of the year. The text
emphasizes the abundance of quail. Indeed, it borders on
sarcastic exaggeration (the quail fell "... beside the camp,
about a day's journey on this side and a day's journey on the
other side, round about the camp, and about two cubits
above the face of the earth") just as the description of the
people's response suggests grotesque gluttony: "And the
people rose all that day, and all night, and all the next day,
and gathered the quails." Even the one who gathered the
least took up nearly one hundred bushels (ten homers) of
quail. The people got what they had asked for and it became
their punishment. Although this runs counter to the usual
witness to God's graciousness in the wilderness, it functions
as a fitting context for the writer's explanation of how this

particular place on the wilderness itinerary came to receive its name, Kibroth-hattaavah, "graves of craving." Thus the story which had begun with a negative portrait of Israel's craving ends on a sorry note of God's punishment. The writer used a catchword technique ("'Carry them in your bosom, as a nurse carries the suckling child...'", v. 12, and "I am not able to carry all this people alone...," v. 14) to link what may at one time have been separate stories about wilderness food and community leadership.

In the final text of this complex narrative editors have enveloped an originally independent story which positively interprets and legitimates the institution of the office of elders (vv. 16-17, 24b-30) with a negative portrait of Israel's craving for meat in the wilderness (vv. 4-13, 18-24a, 31-35). This has given rise to the suggestion that by placing the official installation of the elders within a context of Israel's rebellion the group responsible for the final text intended to cast a negative light on an exercise of community leadership which had been affirmed by another circle in ancient Israel.

The narrative ends with an itinerary notice which sets the scene for the story which follows.

THE UNIQUENESS OF MOSES
12:1-16

12 Miriam and Aaron spoke against Moses because of the Cushite woman whom he had married, for he had married a Cushite woman; 2and they said, "Has the Lord indeed spoken only through Moses? Has he not spoken through us also?" And the Lord heard it. 3Now the man Moses was very meek, more than all men that were on the face of the earth. 4And suddenly the Lord said to Moses and to Aaron and Miriam, "Come out, you three, to the tent of meeting." And the three of them came out. 5And the Lord came down in a pillar of cloud, and stood at the door of the tent, and called Aaron and Miriam; and they both came forward. 6And he said, "Hear my words: If there is a prophet among you, I the Lord make myself known to him in a vision, I speak with him in a dream. [7]Not so with my servant Moses; he is entrusted with all my house. [8]With him I speak mouth to mouth, clearly, and not in dark speech; and he beholds the form of the Lord. Why then were you not afraid to speak against my servant Moses?"

[9]And the anger of the Lord was kindled against them, and he departed; [10]and when the cloud removed from over the tent, behold, Miriam was leprous, as white as snow. And Aaron turned towards Miriam, and behold, she was leprous. [11]And Aaron said to Moses, "Oh, my lord, do not punish us because we have done foolishly and have sinned. [12]Let her not be as one dead, of whom the flesh is half consumed when he comes out of his mother's womb." [13]And Moses cried to the Lord, "Heal her, O God, I beseech thee." [14]But the Lord said to Moses, "If her father had but spit in her face, should she not be shamed seven days? Let her be shut up outside the camp seven days, and after that she may be brought in again." [15]So Miriam was shut up outside the camp seven days; and the people did not set out on the march till Miriam was brought in again. [16]After that the people set out from Hazeroth, and encamped in the wilderness of Paran.

Num 12 is a leadership controversy which has been placed among the wilderness traditions. It follows the narrative about diversification in prophetic roles which appears in Num 11 and precedes the account of struggles in priestly circles as narrated in Num 16. Unlike the murmuring tradition which has been reported thus far, this story represents the rebellion not of the entire community but of Moses' close associates, Miriam and Aaron. In addition, this story is different from other instances of murmuring in the wilderness in that it does not constitute a rejection of the redemption from Egypt like so many of the other murmurings in the wilderness, but it is limited to the question of the extent of Moses' authority.

Two originally independent stories have been brought together in Num 12. The text has a complex history the precise details of which elude us. However, it appears that at one time there was a tradition which featured a controversy about Moses' wife which was raised by Miriam and for which she alone was punished with leprosy (vv. 1, 9-15). A second controversy, one centering on the extent of Moses' role as mediator of God's word (vv. 2-8), has been inserted into the middle of the first story. Even though the two stories appear as one in the present text, details from the two were not perfectly harmonized in the process of their coming together. For example, when the two stories were brought together Aaron was added alongside Miriam in the controversy over the Cushite wife as recorded in verse 1. However in the Hebrew text the verb governing this first sentence remains the feminine singular, a clear indication that originally this controversy was attributed to Miriam alone. Likewise the account of the punishment (vv. 9-15) is not without difficulty. Whereas in v. 11 Aaron includes himself alongside Miriam as a guilty party, the remainder of the account witnesses only to Miriam's leprosy (cf. Deut 24:9). This suggests that the tradition of Miriam's leprosy was originally part of the earlier story about the controversy over the Cushite wife and that when the two stories were joined, Israel's high priest was spared the embarrassment of sharing the ritual defilement of Miriam's leprosy even though he shared her guilt.

Details about the controversy over the Cushite wife are unknown. Other biblical texts say that Moses' wife was a Midianite woman (Exod 2:21; 18:1-5). It is unknown whether "Cushite" and "Midianite" are to be identified with one another or if the two traditions simply represent two different versions of the community's memory that Moses had a foreign wife. Just as the reference to the "Cushite wife" is mysterious, so is the knowledge of why she would have been the occasion for a controversy. Because other controversy stories which appear in the wilderness traditions deal with matters of community interest and not with private affairs, it is probable that Moses' Cushite wife, for some reason no longer known, was the center of a public issue and that in confronting Moses on this matter Miriam voiced the concerns of at least a segment of the community.

In vv. 2-8 Miriam and Aaron together represent another controversy with Moses, this one over his unique status as one who speaks for God. In their rhetorical questions ("Has the Lord indeed spoken only through Moses? Has he not spoken through us also?"), Aaron and Miriam imply that although they consider themselves spokespersons for the Divinity, Moses' position does not allow for their recognition as such. In verse 3 the writer suggests that this controversy, like the others in the wilderness traditions, is really a rebellion against God, so Moses remains silent while Yahweh summons all three leaders to the tent of meeting where the Divinity will settle the issue. When the cloud descends, Miriam and Aaron are called forward to receive the verdict. The divine judgment expressed in vv. 6-8 distinguished the word of God rendered by Moses from that rendered by prophets. The distinction is that Moses, God's "servant," knows God's will directly ("With him I speak mouth to mouth. . .") whereas the prophets receive God's word indirectly through means which need interpretation (dreams and visions). The pronouncement does not deny that prophets bear God's word. It simply clarifies that Moses does so in a unique and authoritative way. The divine speech ends in a counter-accusation directed to Aaron and Miriam: "Why then were you not afraid to speak against my servant Moses?" (v. 8c).

It is unclear why a speech distinguishing Moses' authority from that of prophets would have been addressed to Aaron and Miriam since neither of them is renowned for prophecy. It seems best to regard verses 6-8 as an independent tradition about prophetic roles which originated outside the present context. Aaron and Miriam probably represent a priestly group which was asserting its authority as caretakers of God's word over against the claims of Levitical priests who viewed themselves as guardians of God's word in the tradition of Moses. The issue is settled, of course, in favor of the group which claimed that its authority was based in Moses.

As mentioned above, the biblical witness about the Lord's

punishment for this act of rebellion (vv. 9-15) is a complex web of traditions. Whatever its background, the biblical writer presents both Aaron and Moses as interceding on Miriam's behalf. Unlike others who were sentenced to die in the wilderness because of their rebellion (cf. Num 11:33-34; 14:20-38; 16), Miriam's life was spared at this juncture by a special declaration of divine clemency (vv. 14-15). Her punishment is made temporary and the rest of the members of the community do not continue their journey until she rejoins them.

This tradition probably has roots in the community's memory of Miriam as a leader in the wilderness community alongside Moses and Aaron (cf. Mic 6:4). In some cases (Num 26:59; 1 Chr 6:3) biblical tradition used kinship terminology to express the affiliation of the three leaders in the wilderness period. As the tradition developed, Moses grew to become the overtowering figure of the Pentateuchal traditions and Aaron became the figurehead for Israel's priests. The portrait of Miriam survived only in slight glimpses such as the present text where she is portrayed as a community leader representing the interests of one group of Israel's priests on the issue of their authority in rendering God's word.

Whatever the background to this complex text, its chief feature within the context of the wilderness story is that it asserts the uniqueness of Moses' access to God's word. Although others may function as legitimate spokespersons for God (cf. Num 11), Moses' authority in this matter is unique.

A STOLEN GLIMPSE OF THE LAND
13:1-33

> **13** The Lord said to Moses, [2]"Send men to spy out the land of Canaan, which I give to the people of Israel; from each tribe of their fathers shall you send a man, every one a leader among them." [3]So Moses sent them from the wilderness of Paran, according to the command of the

Lord, all of them men who were heads of the people of Israel. ⁴And these were their names: From the tribe of Reuben, Shammu-a the son of Zaccur; ⁵from the tribe of Simeon, Shaphat the son of Hori; ⁶from the tribe of Judah, Caleb the son of Jephunneh; ⁷from the tribe of Issachar, Igal the son of Joseph; ⁸from the tribe of Ephraim, Hoshea the son of Nun; ⁹from the tribe of Benjamin, Palti the son of Raphu; ¹⁰from the tribe of Zebulun, Gaddiel the son of Sodi; ¹¹from the tribe of Joseph (that is from the tribe of Manasseh), Gaddi the son of Susi; ¹²from the tribe of Dan, Ammiel the son of Gemalli; ¹³from the tribe of Asher, Sethur the son of Michael; ¹⁴from the tribe of Naphtali, Nahbi the son of Vophsi; ¹⁵from the tribe of Gad, Geuel the son of Machi. ¹⁶These were the names of the men whom Moses sent to spy out the land. And Moses called Hoshea the son of Nun Joshua.

¹⁷Moses sent them to spy out the land of Canaan, and said to them, "Go up into the Negeb yonder, and go up into the hill country, ¹⁸and see what the land is, and whether the people who dwell in it are strong or weak, whether they are few or many, ¹⁹and whether the land that they dwell in is good or bad, and whether the cities that they dwell in are camps or strongholds, ²⁰and whether the land is rich or poor, and whether there is wood in it or not. Be of good courage, and bring some of the fruit of the land." Now the time was the season of the first ripe grapes.

²¹So they went up and spied out the land from the wilderness of Zin to Rehob, near the entrance of Hamath. ²²They went up into the Negeb, and came to Hebron; and Ahiman, Sheshai, and Talmai, the descendants of Anak, were there. (Hebron was built seven years before Zoan in Egypt.) ²³And they came to the Valley of Eshcol, and cut down from there a branch with a single cluster of grapes, and they carried it on a pole between two of them; they brought also some pomegranates and figs. ²⁴That place was called the Valley of Eshcol, because of the cluster which the men of Israel cut down from there.

²⁵At the end of forty days they returned from spying out the land. ²⁶And they came to Moses and Aaron and to all the congregation of the people of Israel in the wilderness of Paran, at Kadesh; they brought back word to them and to all the congregation, and showed them the fruit of the land. ²⁷And they told him, "We came to the land to which you sent us; it flows with milk and honey, and this is its fruit. ²⁸Yet the people who dwell in the land are strong, and the cities are fortified and very large; and besides, we saw the descendants of Anak there. ²⁹The Amalekites dwell in the land of the Negeb; the Hittites, the Jebusites, and the Amorites dwell in the hill country; and the Canaanites dwell by the sea, and along the Jordan."

³⁰But Caleb quieted the people before Moses, and said, "Let us go up at once, and occupy it; for we are well able to overcome it." ³¹Then the men who had gone up with him said, "We are not able to go up against the people; for they are stronger then we." ³²So they brought to the people of Israel an evil report of the land which they had spied out, saying, "The land, through which we have gone to spy it out, is a land that devours its inhabitants; and all the people that we saw in it are men of great stature. ³³And there we saw the Nephilim (the sons of Anak, who come from the Nephilim); and we seemed to ourselves like grasshoppers, and so we seemed to them."

Num 13 is closely bound to the story which follows it in chapter 14 for both are directed to the question of Israel's inheritance of the Promised Land. It is likely that the starting point for this story was a tradition about an attempt to invade the land of Canaan from a southern entrance, an attempt which may have been aborted. The present account is a theological interpretation showing the part this event played in the relationship between God and Israel. The narrative is comprised of both an early tradition (probably a combination of Yahwist and Elohist sources) and a late (Priestly) one. In the combined account two ways of viewing and responding to reality are presented to the reader through the dialogue of the characters involved. As the voices argued, they set in relief the ultimate choice of faith, a decision upon which rests life and death.

The beginning of the story (13:1-17a) comes from the hand of the Priestly writer who says that the spies were sent from the wilderness of Paran. According to this account, Moses was obeying Yahweh's command in sending the spies to reconnoiter the land although Deuteronomic tradition presents the spying as the choice of the people themselves (see Deut 1:22-25). In the Priestly writer's view the spies were twelve men who were leaders in their respective tribes. The list of their names resembles the Priestly writer's list which appears in Num 1:1-16 although the names of the tribal leaders differ. The double-name tradition for Hoshea-Joshua is recorded as a change of name which Moses initiated although no reason for the change is offered.

With Moses' instructions which begin in v. 17b, we encounter the older tradition which continues uninterrupted (except for v. 21) through verse 24. Unlike the Priestly account which concentrated on the identification and tribal affiliation of the spies, this alternate version fixes its interest on the land. Moses commissions the spies to check out both the land and its people. According to this source, the spies ventured only into the Judean hill country around Hebron and the dry, wilderness region (the Negeb) which lies to the south of it. The Priestly writer's addition in v. 21 reflects the view that the spies reached into the northern area of the land as well ("near the entrance of Hamath"). From the Valley of Eshcol ("cluster") in the Hebron region the spies secured fruit which they brought back to the wilderness community as a sign of the bounty of the land.

Next the Priestly writer notes that the spies reconnoitered for forty days (i.e., a sufficient or full period of time) and then returned to the camp (vv. 25-26). The older version is then resumed (vv. 27-31). In it the spies report the idyllic quality of the land: "it flows with milk and honey." And they report that the inhabitants of the land are formidably organized in strong city-states. Those are the facts. Now a decision must be made. Caleb confidently and without hesitation urges an invasion. He stands in sharp contrast to the rest who see no hope for themselves against the inhabitants of the land (vv. 30-31). The Priestly writer attaches what appears to be an addition to the spies' initial report (vv. 32-33). The "evil report" lapses into Semitic hyperbole in connecting the descendants of Anak ("neck"; perhaps a relatively tall population) with the demi-gods (Nephilim) of Gen 6:4. Later tradition (namely, the Greek Septuagint and the Latin Vulgate) regarded these Nephilim as giants, thus capturing the sense of the spies' being overwhelmed by these native inhabitants: "we seemed to ourselves like grasshoppers and so we seemed to them."

Thus the intriguing spy story of Num 13 comes to a dramatic conclusion, setting forth as it does alternative stances regarding the land. As in the cases of hunger and thirst along the way, so here the community is challenged in a life-threatening situation to maintain that trust which is the heart of the covenantal relationship. In this case the challenge to trust assumes the weightiest of proportions. The matter touches upon the reliability of God's ultimate intention in the whole exodus-wilderness journey, for the voice in the burning bush had said: "...I have come down to deliver them out of the hand of the Egyptians, and to bring them up out of that land to a good and broad land, a land flowing with milk and honey..." (Exod 3:8).

LOSS OF COURAGE, LOSS OF LIFE
14:1-45

14 Then all the congregation raised a loud cry; and the people wept that night. ²And all the people of Israel murmured against Moses and Aaron; the whole congregation said to them, "Would that we had died in the land of Egypt! Or would that we had died in this wilderness! ³Why does the Lord bring us into this land, to fall by the sword? Our wives and our little ones will become a prey; would it not be better for us to go back to Egypt?"

⁴And they said to one another, "Let us choose a cap-

tain, and go back to Egypt." ⁵Then Moses and Aaron fell on their faces before all the assembly of the congregation of the people of Israel. ⁶And Joshua the son of Nun and Caleb the son of Jephunneh, who were among those who had spied out the land, rent their clothes, ⁷and said to all the congregation of the people of Israel, "The land, which we passed through to spy it out, is an exceedingly good land. ⁸If the Lord delights in us, he will bring us into this land and give it to us, a land which flows with milk and honey. ⁹Only, do not rebel against the Lord; and do not fear the people of the land, for they are bread for us; their protection is removed from them, and the Lord is with us; do not fear them." ¹⁰But all the congregation said to stone them with stones.

Then the glory of the Lord appeared at the tent of meeting to all the people of Israel. ¹¹And the Lord said to Moses, "How long will this people despise me? And how long will they not believe in me, in spite of all the signs which I have wrought among them? ¹²I will strike them with the pestilence and disinherit them, and I will make of you a nation greater and mightier than they."

¹³But Moses said to the Lord, "Then the Egyptians will hear of it, for thou didst bring up this people in thy might from among them, ¹⁴and they will tell the inhabitants of this land. They have heard that thou, O Lord, art in the midst of this people; for thou, O Lord, art seen face to face, and thy cloud stands over them and thou goest before them, in a pillar of cloud by day and in a pillar of fire by night. ¹⁵Now if thou dost kill this people as one man, then the nations who have heard thy fame will say, ¹⁶'Because the Lord was not able to bring this people into the land which he swore to give to them, therefore he has slain them in the wilderness.' ¹⁷And now, I pray thee, let the power of the Lord be great as thou hast promised, saying, ¹⁸'The Lord is slow to anger, and abounding in steadfast love, forgiving iniquity and transgression, but he will by no means clear the guilty, visiting the iniquity of fathers upon children, upon the third and upon the fourth generation.' ¹⁹Pardon the iniquity of this people, I

pray thee, according to the greatness of thy steadfast love, and according as thou hast forgiven this people, from Egypt even until now."

²⁰Then the Lord said, "I have pardoned, according to your word; ²¹but truly, as I live, and as all the earth shall be filled with the glory of the Lord, ²²none of the men who have seen my glory and my signs which I wrought in Egypt and in the wilderness, and yet have put me to the proof these ten times and have not hearkened to my voice, ²³shall see the land which I swore to give to their fathers; and none of those who despised me shall see it. ²⁴But my servant Caleb, because he has a different spirit and has followed me fully, I will bring into the land into which he went, and his descendants shall possess it. ²⁵Now, since the Amalekites and the Canaanites dwell in the valleys, turn tomorrow and set out for the wilderness by the way to the Red Sea."

²⁶And the Lord said to Moses and to Aaron, ²⁷"How long shall this wicked congregation murmur against me? I have heard the murmurings of the people of Israel, which they murmur against me. ²⁸Say to them, 'As I live, says the Lord, what you have said in my hearing I will do to you; ²⁹your dead bodies shall fall in this wilderness; and of all your numbers, numbered from twenty years old and upward, who have murmured against me, ³⁰not one shall come into the land where I swore that I would make you dwell, except Caleb the son of Jephunneh and Joshua the son of Nun. ³¹But your little ones, who you said would become a prey, I will bring in, and they shall know the land which you have despised. ³²But as for you, your dead bodies shall fall in this wilderness. ³³And your children shall be shepherds in the wilderness forty years, and shall suffer for your faithlessness, until the last of your dead bodies lies in the wilderness. ³⁴According to the number of the days in which you spied out the land, forty days, for every day a year, you shall bear your iniquity, forty years, and you shall know my displeasure.' ³⁵I, the Lord, have spoken; surely this will I do to all this wicked congregation that are gathered together against me: in

this wilderness they shall come to a full end, and there they shall die."

³⁶And the men whom Moses sent to spy out the land, and who returned and made all the congregation to murmur against him by bringing up an evil report against the land, ³⁷the men who brought up an evil report of the land, died by plague before the Lord. ³⁸But Joshua the son of Nun and Caleb the son of Jephunneh remained alive, of those men who went to spy out the land.

³⁹And Moses told these words to all the people of Israel, and the people mourned greatly. ⁴⁰And they rose early in the morning, and went up to the heights of the hill country, saying, "See, we are here, we will go up to the place which the Lord has promised; for we have sinned." ⁴¹But Moses said, "Why now are you transgressing the command of the Lord, for that will not succeed? ⁴²Do not go up lest you be struck down before your enemies, for the Lord is not among you. ⁴³For there the Amalekites and the Canaanites are before you, and you shall fall by the sword; because you have turned back from following the Lord, the Lord will not be with you." ⁴⁴But they presumed to go up to the heights of the hill country, although neither the ark of the covenant of the Lord, nor Moses, departed out of the camp. ⁴⁵Then the Amalekites and the Canaanites who dwelt in that hill country came down, and defeated them and pursued them, even to Hormah.

The "evil report" with which chapter 13 ended forms the context for the series of events which is narrated in Num 14. If our attention was turned away from the wilderness and toward the land in chapter 13, the murmuring in the opening lines of chapter 14 firmly calls us back to what has by now become to the reader a familiar wilderness experience.

The spies' discouraging news about the people of the land led Israel to the same point of despair that other hardships in the wilderness had precipitated. Once again the wanderers opted to rely on the security provided by Egyptian bondage than to trust the precariousness of this freedom journey. Despair approaches full-scale revolt when in v. 4 the people speak of choosing a new leader and returning to Egypt. The community's speech (vv. 2-4) is balanced by Joshua and Caleb's courageous speech (vv. 7-9). Once again, two views, two options are set forth. The courageous speech of Joshua and Caleb is rejected, nearly at the cost of their lives.

As in the case of Miriam and Aaron's murmuring in Num 12, so here the community is summoned to the tent of meeting for Yahweh's judgment. The scene which ensues (vv. 11-19) bears close resemblance to that which took place at Mount Sinai between Moses and Yahweh in the wake of the apostasy at the golden calf. Yahweh laments ("How long. . . ?") Israel's faithless posture. The rhetorical question functions as an accusation against Israel whose response to Yahweh's "signs" was a continuous refusal to "believe in" (i.e., take their stand in, trust in, rely upon) Yahweh. In the face of this the Lord vows to disinherit the Israelites. Then, in words which recall both the first words of invitation to Abraham (Gen 12:1-3) and the invitation to Moses after the sin at the golden calf (Exod 32:10), the Divinity invites Moses to become the beginning of a new people whose history and destiny Yahweh promises to guide.

As in Exod 32, Moses disregards God's invitation and exercises instead his role as intercessor on behalf of the faithless people. In an impassioned speech reminiscent of the style and argumentation of Exod 32:11-14, Moses pleads for the life of Israel just as he had done on the occasion of the golden calf. He reminds God that the act of bringing Israel up out of Egypt had established a reputation for Yahweh among the nations, a reputation for power and love which now must be confirmed.

Moses challenges Yahweh to follow through on the exodus event as Israel was expected to do. He beckons Yahweh to live up to the divine name, "slow to anger and abounding in steadfast love" (vv. 17-18; cf. Exod 34:6-7). Lest the nations conclude that Yahweh is powerless to bring the people into the land, that power which once brought Israel out of Egypt must again be unleashed, this time in forbearance. Yahweh is called to live up to that reputation for forgiveness which Israel had come to know from the time of the exodus: "Pardon the iniquity of this people...according to the greatness of thy steadfast love, and according as thou hast forgiven this people, from Egypt even until now" (v. 19).

Two different versions of Yahweh's decision follow. Verses 20-25 contain the early (Yahwist and/or Elohist) tradition. According to this view, Yahweh pardoned Israel but swore that those who had known the great works in Egypt and in the wilderness but who yet rebelled "these ten times" (i.e., repeatedly) would not inherit the land. Caleb, the courageous spy, was the only exception. The rest were ordered to turn back toward the sea. In this way the Divinity acted upon Israel's recurring wish to turn again toward Egypt.

The Priestly writer's version of Yahweh's response to the people's murmuring appears in vv. 26-35. It omits the word of divine forgiveness but includes the divine vow to punish. According to this version, God's punishment takes its direction from the faithless expectations which Israel had expressed earlier in its fear. The murmurers' dead bodies will fall in the wilderness and only the "little ones" would come into the land. Whereas the only exception to the punishment in the Yahwist's versions was Caleb, the Priestly includes Joshua too. The time for bearing the consequences of their sin will be forty years, corresponding to the number of days which the spies spent in the land. In his emphatic and repeated insistence that God's punishment meant death for the adult sojourners, the Priestly writer hauntingly filled what surely had once been empty words on the lips of the murmurers: "... would that we had died in this wilderness!" (v. 2).

The Priestly writer continues in Num 14:36-38 by including information which the earlier source had not offered. Thus we learn that a plague claimed the lives of the faithless spies though Joshua and Caleb were spared.

The chapter comes to a close with an incident recorded by the early source. As they had refused courage with regard to the land, so now we are told that Israel rebelled against the punishment which Yahweh had assigned to them. They decided that now, rather than to submit to the punishment, they would go up into the land. Moses warned them not to go since it would not be a Holy War and thus would be destined to failure. Yahweh (whose presence was represented in the ark) did not go up with them nor did Moses. Israel, filling its lack of courage with belligerence, advanced and was driven out of the land by a coalition of inhabitants.

LEADERSHIP STRUGGLES
16:1-50

16 Now Korah the son of Izhar, son of Kohath, son of Levi, and Dathan and Abiram the sons of Eliab, and On the son of Peleth, sons of Reuben, ²took men; and they rose up before Moses, with a number of the people of Israel, two hundred and fifty leaders of the congregation, chosen from the assembly, well-known men; ³and they assembled themselves together against Moses and against Aaron, and said to them, "You have gone too far! For all the congregation are holy, every one of them, and the Lord is among them; why then do you exalt yourselves above the assembly of the Lord?" ⁴When Moses heard it, he fell on his face; ⁵and he said to Korah and all his company, "In the morning the Lord will show who is his, and who is holy, and will cause him to come near to him; him whom he will choose he will cause to come near to him. ⁶Do this: take censers, Korah and all his company; ⁷put fire in them and put incense upon them before the Lord tomorrow, and the man whom the Lord chooses shall be the holy one. You have gone too far, sons of Levi!" ⁸And Moses said to Korah, "Hear now, you sons of Levi: ⁹is it too small a thing for you that the God of Israel has separated you from the congregation of Israel, to bring you near to himself, to do service in the tabernacle of the Lord, and to stand before the congregation to minister to them; ¹⁰and that he has brought you near him, and all your brethren the sons of Levi with you? And would you seek the priesthood also? [11]Therefore it is against the Lord that you and all your company have gathered together; what is Aaron that you murmur against him?"

[12]And Moses sent to call Dathan and Abiram the sons of Eliab; and they said, "We will not come up. [13]Is it a small thing that you have brought us up out of a land flowing with milk and honey, to kill us in the wilderness, that you must also make yourself a prince over us? [14]Moreover you have not brought us into a land flowing with milk and honey, nor given us inheritance of fields and vineyards. Will you put out the eyes of these men? We will not come up."

[15]And Moses was very angry, and said to the Lord, "Do not respect their offering. I have not taken one ass from them, and I have not harmed one of them." [16]And Moses said to Korah, "Be present, you and all your company, before the Lord, you and they, and Aaron, tomorrow; [17]and let every one of you take his censer, and put incense upon it, and every one of you bring before the Lord his censer, two hundred and fifty censers; you also, and Aaron, each his censer." [18]So every man took his censer, and they put fire in them and laid incense upon them, and they stood at the entrance of the tent of meeting with Moses and Aaron. [19]Then Korah assembled all the congregation against them at the entrance of the tent of meeting. And the glory of the Lord appeared to all the congregation.

[20]And the Lord said to Moses and to Aaron, [21]"Separate yourselves from among this congregation, that I may consume them in a moment." [22]And they fell on their faces, and said, "O God, the God of the spirits of all flesh, shall one man sin, and wilt thou be angry with all the congregation?" [23]And the Lord said to Moses, [24]"Say to the congregation, Get away from about the dwelling of Korah, Dathan, and Abiram."

[25]Then Moses rose and went to Dathan and Abiram; and the elders of Israel followed him. [26]And he said to the congregation, "Depart, I pray you, from the tents of these

wicked men, and touch nothing of theirs, lest you be swept away with all their sins." ²⁷So they got away from about the dwelling of Korah, Dathan, and Abiram; and Dathan and Abiram came out and stood at the door of their tents, together with their wives, their sons, and their little ones. ²⁸And Moses said, "Hereby you shall know that the Lord has sent me to do all these works, and that it has not been of my own accord. ²⁹If these men die the common death of all men, or if they are visited by the fate of all men, then the Lord has not sent me. ³⁰But if the Lord creates something new, and the ground opens its mouth, and swallows them up, with all that belongs to them, and they go down alive into Sheol, then you shall know that these men have despised the Lord."

³¹And as he finished speaking all these words, the ground under them split asunder; ³²and the earth opened its mouth and swallowed them up, with their households and all the men that belonged to Korah and all their goods. ³³So they and all that belonged to them went down alive into Sheol; and the earth closed over them, and they perished from the midst of the assembly. ³⁴And all Israel that were round about them fled at their cry; for they said, "Lest the earth swallow us up!" ³⁵And fire came forth from the Lord, and consumed the two hundred and fifty men offering the incense.

³⁶Then the Lord said to Moses, ³⁷"Tell Eleazar the son of Aaron the priest to take up the censers out of the blaze; then scatter the fire far and wide. For they are holy, ³⁸the censers of these men who have sinned at the cost of their lives; so let them be made into hammered plates as a covering for the altar, for they offered them before the Lord; therefore they are holy. Thus they shall be a sign to the people of Israel." ³⁹So Eleazar the priest took the bronze censers, which those who burned had offered; and they were hammered out as a covering for the altar, ⁴⁰to be a reminder to the people of Israel, so that no one who is not a priest, who is not of the descendants of Aaron, should draw near to burn incense before the Lord, lest he

become as Korah and as his company — as the Lord said to Eleazar through Moses.

[41]But on the morrow all the congregation of the people of Israel murmured against Moses and against Aaron, saying, "You have killed the people of the Lord." [42]And when the congregation had assembled against Moses and against Aaron, they turned toward the tent of meeting; and behold, the cloud covered it, and the glory of the Lord appeared. [43]And Moses and Aaron came to the front of the tent of meeting, [44]and the Lord said to Moses, [45]"Get away from the midst of this congregation, that I may consume them in a moment." And they fell on their faces. [46]And Moses said to Aaron, "Take your censer, and put fire therein from off the altar, and lay incense on it, and carry it quickly to the congregation, and make atonement for them; for wrath has gone forth from the Lord, the plague has begun." [47]So Aaron took it as Moses said, and ran into the midst of the assembly; and behold, the plague had already begun among the people; and he put on the incense, and made atonement for the people. [48]And he stood between the dead and the living; and the plague was stopped. [49]Now those who died by the plague were fourteen thousand seven hundred, besides those who died in the affair of Korah. [50]And Aaron returned to Moses at the entrance of the tent of meeting, when the plague was stopped.

Several layers of tradition have been joined in this chapter of the Book of Numbers. At least three originally independent strands have been woven together to form a tapestry of concerns about leadership within the community. Simply stated, the resolution of the complex chapter is that Moses' position as leader of the wilderness community is affirmed as is the primacy of Aaron's claim to the priesthood in Israel. But, the authenticity of the privileged positions of these two is clarified only in the context of tensions and struggles initiated by members of the community. The earliest layer of tradition (perhaps from the Yahwist and/or the

Elohist) is the Dathan and Abiram story. To this the Priestly writer added a story about a conflict with Moses enjoined by Korah and two-hundred fifty men. Yet another Priestly hand adapted this already-existing material and shaped it in such a way as to settle a struggle between the Levites and the priestly descendants of Aaron.

The early Dathan and Abiram story which has survived is concentrated in Num 16:1b-2a, 12-15, and 25-34. The initial segment (vv. 1b-2a) identifies Dathan and Abiram as Reubenites. They are said to have been joined by On, the son of Peleth, though the latter is not included in the reference to this incident which appears in Deut 11:6 nor in any other biblical texts. If v. 2a ("took men") belongs to this level of tradition, Dathan and Abiram must be regarded as spokespersons for a group and not just two isolated individuals who raised a controversy with Moses.

The subject of Dathan and Abiram's controversy appears in Num 16:12-15. Moses' grandiose plans for the community had not materialized. His failure to bring them into the Promised Land convinced them that their following him out of Egypt had been a terrible mistake. Astonishingly, for Dathan and Abiram Egypt had now become a land "flowing with milk and honey" (v. 13). For those immersed in wilderness misery, the life of bondage had come to look like a gift. Dathan and Abiram regretted the journey they had made thus far and they refused to go farther. Rejecting both past and future, they would not move. Their rebellion came to concrete expression in their flagrant refusal to obey Moses any longer. In words reminiscent of Exod 2:14, they accused him of making himself a prince over them.

The Dathan and Abiram strand of the complex narrative of Num 16 comes to a conclusion in vv. 25-34. There we are told that Moses approached the two (Korah's name is an addition to v. 27a) and set up a trial in the presence of the elders wherein the truth of the rebels' accusation about Moses' self-exaltation would be judged. The terms of the forthcoming judgment are carefully defined (vv. 28-30). Moses says that while the interpretation of natural death is ambiguous, sudden and disastrous death must be taken as

God's judgment in this matter. The subsequent opening of the earth and the disappearance of the rebels (the reference to Korah and his man in v. 32b is an addition designed to harmonize this story with the Korah traditions) make it clear that Moses' authority in the community was ordained by God. Thus, to rebel against Moses was to rebel against the Divine Self, an act which occasioned the punishment described in vv. 31-34.

In sum, an early level of tradition recorded a controversy in the wilderness initiated by some Reubenites. The issue was Moses' leadership. Because he had led them into a difficult wilderness experience but had not yet succeeded in bringing them through it, they contested his authority over them. But the heart of this issue like so many of the others in the wilderness narratives was regret over having ever left Egypt in the first place, a fundamental rejection of God's movement in Israel's history.

To this early tradition about Dathan and Abiram the Priestly writer added a story about a controversy raised by Korah and two-hundred fifty men over the same issue, authority and community leadership. This story is contained in Num 16:1a, 2b-7b, 18-24, 27a, 35, and 41-50.

Korah, identified in v. 1a as a Levite, heads a rebellion which is directed against both Moses and Aaron. He is joined by two-hundred fifty leaders of the congregation in the conviction that the community is comprised of equals. Their view undermines any justification for an exercise of authority based on the separation of some individuals from the rest of the community for liturgical or other religious functions. Since all are holy, the group complains: "why then do you exalt yourselves above the assembly of the Lord?" (v. 3b). Although the text is ambiguous on the precise matter of dispute, it appears that the controversy involved a question about who could exercise a particular liturgical ministry for when Moses responds to their challenge by setting forth terms for a divine decision on this issue, Korah and his associates are instructed to bring censers to the tent of meeting (vv. 5-7). There, through the divine response to the ritual burning of incense Moses says "the Lord will show who is his, and who is holy, and will cause him to come near to him; him whom he will choose he will cause to come near to him" (v. 5). The narrative about the trial resumes in vv. 18-24 and in v. 35. Divine judgment in the case is clear with the destruction of Korah and the two-hundred fifty (v. 35).

In the late post-exilic work of the Chronicler the descendants of Korah are described as exercising supportive functions in the liturgy although they are not present in the sanctuary. In 2 Chr 20:19 the Korahites are leaders in song, while in 1 Chr 9:19, 31 they are cast in lesser roles as Temple doorkeepers and bakers of cakes. The two cycles of Korah psalms, Pss 42-49 and 84-85 + 87-88, each begins with a melancholy psalm which presupposes separation from the sanctuary.

In one sense, the divine judgment by punishment constitutes the end of Korah's rebellion. However, the appendix which has been added in vv. 41-50 says that the Korah incident was the starting point for another episode wherein all the congregation accused Moses and Aaron saying, "You have killed the people of the Lord" (16:41). The sequence of events which ensues is familiar by now: the Divinity visits the tent of meeting resolving to destroy the community (vv. 42-45). Moses intervenes on behalf of the people, this time by sending Aaron to atone for the community by means of the ritual gesture of moving among them with burning incense. This act was said to appease Yahweh for it stopped a plague which was already in progress.

Thus, two similar but distinct stories are given to us in Num 16. In several instances (in vv. 1, 24, 27 where Korah, Dathan and Abiram are named together) we can find seams where the originally separate pieces have been joined. The combined story, particularly the controversy of Korah, appears to have been used by yet another circle to settle a controversy about the exclusive claim to priesthood made by descendants of Aaron. This rewriting of the Korah story is reflected in vv. 1b, 7c-11, 16-17, and 36-40. In this layer of tradition Aaron alone is the object of controversy.

Verses 7c-11 set the issue in clear relief: the Levites who exercise a special ministry in Israel's cult are rebelling against the Aaronides' exclusive claim to service at the altar in a priestly capacity. At this point the tradition blends with the earlier one about Korah and the two-hundred fifty in setting forth terms whereby the case might be judged, i.e., in the offering of incense. The deaths of Korah and the rest settle the matter in favor of Aaron. The same level of tradition which defended the Aaronides' right over the challenge of the Levites then added an appendix featuring Eleazar, the legitimate heir to the high priestly office of Aaron (vv. 36-40; cf. Num 20:22-29). The censers of the challenging party had become sacred by virtue of their having been used in ritual action of judgment. Having been hallowed in this way, they were set aside for sacred use by being made into a covering for the altar. In saying that this covering was to remind later generations of worshippers of the distinction which was to be maintained between Aaron's priestly ministry and the service of others in the community, verse 40 sets in relief a major thrust in the complex story of Num 16.

ELECTION OF THE LEVITES AND AARON
17:1-11

17 The Lord said to Moses, ²"Speak to the people of Israel, and get from them rods, one for each fathers' house, from all their leaders according to their fathers' houses, twelve rods. Write each man's name upon his rod, ³and write Aaron's name upon the rod of Levi. For there shall be one rod for the head of each fathers' house. ⁴Then you shall deposit them in the tent of meeting before the testimony, where I meet with you. ⁵And the rod of the man whom I choose shall sprout; thus I will make to cease from me the murmurings of the people of Israel, which they murmur against you." ⁶Moses spoke to the people of Israel; and all their leaders gave him rods, one for each leader, according to their fathers' houses, twelve rods; and the rod of Aaron was among their rods. ⁷And Moses deposited the rods before the Lord in the tent of the testimony.

8And on the morrow Moses went into the tent of the testimony; and behold, the rod of Aaron for the house of Levi had sprouted and put forth buds, and produced blossoms, and it bore ripe almonds. 9Then Moses brought out all the rods from before the Lord to all the people of Israel; and they looked, and each man took his rod. 10And the Lord said to Moses, "Put back the rod of Aaron before the testimony, to be kept as a sign for the rebels, that you may make an end of their murmurings against me, lest they die." 11Thus did Moses; as the Lord commanded him, so he did.

The content of Num 17:1-11 bears a general similarity to that of Num 16, i.e., it addresses the legitimacy of a special position within the Israelite community. In this case, the writer's purpose is to demonstrate beyond a doubt God's special election of Aaron and, by extension, the special status of the tribe of Levi. The point is made by a skillful play on one Hebrew word, *matteh*, which means both "rod" (or "staff") and "tribe."

The incident is initiated by God who directs Moses to collect a rod (*matteh*) from a representative of each tribe (*matteh*) of Israel and to deposit the twelve rods in the tent of meeting before the testimony (vv. 2-4). Aaron's rod represented the tribe of Levi. In v. 5 God interprets the event which is about to occur: "The rod of the man whom I choose shall sprout." The purpose of this decisive demonstration of God's election was to bring an end to any further quarrels regarding Aaron's leadership. Verses 6-8 reflect the style of the Priestly writer: Moses carried out the directions God had given.

The rod of Aaron which represented the tribe of Levi not only sprouted but produced blossoms and ripe almonds overnight (v. 8)! Like the jar of manna (Exod 16:32-34), Aaron's rod was to be retained in the sacred spot, "before the testimony," to remind Israel of God's choice. The visible reminder of God's election of Aaron and the tribe of Levi should eliminate any future incidents of murmurings against God's specially chosen leaders.

This story must be viewed as reflecting part of the developments and struggles in ancient Israel's priesthood. A treatment of this complex topic would take us far afield from the purpose of this commentary. Suffice it to say that the story of Num 17:1-11 attempts to legitimate the outcome of power struggles between priestly circles in Israel's post-exilic community. The present text no longer reflects a distinction between Aaronides and Levites (cf. especially Exod 32). On the contrary, it shows not only that Aaronide priests had begun to claim Levitical ancestry but also that Aaron had come to be viewed as preeminent among the Levites. While the rest of the members of the tribe of Levi continued in late post-exilic times to be connected with cultic service, the exercise of their ministry in the Temple was subordinate to those who claimed lineage from Aaron (Exod 28-29; Lev 8-10; Num 16-18).

DEMISE OF THE WILDERNESS LEADERS
20:1-13

20 And the people of Israel, the whole congregation, came into the wilderness of Zin in the first month, and the people stayed in Kadesh; and Miriam died there, and was buried there.

2Now there was no water for the congregation; and they assembled themselves together against Moses and against Aaron. 3And the people contended with Moses, and said, "Would that we had died when our brethren died before the Lord! 4Why have you brought the assembly of the Lord into this wilderness, that we should die here, both we and our cattle? 5And why have you made us come up out of Egypt, to bring us to this evil place? It is no place for grain, or figs, or vines, or pomegranates; and there is no water to drink." 6Then Moses and Aaron went from the presence of the assembly to the door of the tent of meeting, and fell on their faces. And the glory of the

Lord appeared to them, [7]and the Lord said to Moses, [8]"Take the rod, and assemble the congregation, you and Aaron your brother, and tell the rock before their eyes to yield its water; so you shall bring water out of the rock for them; so you shall give drink to the congregation and their cattle." [9]And Moses took the rod from before the Lord, as he commanded him.

[10]And Moses and Aaron gathered the assembly together before the rock, and he said to them, "Hear now, you rebels; shall we bring forth water for you out of this rock?" [11]And Moses lifted up his hand and struck the rock with his rod twice; and water came forth abundantly, and the congregation drank, and their cattle. [12]And the Lord said to Moses and Aaron, "Because you did not believe in me, to sanctify me in the eyes of the people of Israel, therefore you shall not bring this assembly into the land which I have given them." [13]These are the waters of Meribah, where the people of Israel contended with the Lord, and he showed himself holy among them.

Following two more or less self-contained chapters of Priestly composition. Num 20:1b, then, most likely represents an early tradition which has been attached to Num am's death and a murmuring story designed to account for the ensuing deaths of Moses and Aaron as well.

The change in subject and predicates from the "people of Israel, the whole congregation came" to "the people stayed" in vv. 1a and 1b respectively reflect the presence of different literary souces. Verse 1a, an itinerary notice, probably represents the Priestly source while v. 1b, the notice of Miriam's death and burial at Kadesh, lacks itinerary information as well as literary and theological characteristics of Priestly composition. Num 20:1b, then, most likely represents an early tradition which has been attached to Num 20:1a by a late editor.

It is unusual that the itinerary neglects to include the year when it provides a context for the events to be narrated by mentioning the "first month." Scholars have presupposed that the first month of the fortieth year is intended since the death of Aaron follows soon after (Num 20:22-29) and elsewhere (Num 33:38) his death is said to have occurred during the fifth month of the fortieth year.

The story of the water from the rock which appears in Num 20:2-13 is, for the most part, the Priestly writer's version of an earlier tradition which is recorded in Exod 17:1-7. Indications that this narrative belongs to the Priestly school include the appearance of Aaron alongside Moses, the designation of the community as the "congregation," and the prominence of the Lord's glory at the tent of meeting. The narrative follows a pattern which otherwise characterizes stories of life in the wilderness between the sea and Mount Sinai (Exod 15-18). That is to say, a notice of legitimate need (v. 2a) is followed by complaint (vv. 3-5), Moses' intercession (v. 6), and God's gracious response to Israel's need (vv. 7-11). In the initial part of the complaint, the people remember with envy those who have already died "before the Lord," presumably a reference to the deaths of Korah, Dathan, Abiram and their associates which is recorded in Num 16. Otherwise the complaint shares features of form and content in common with other instances of murmuring in the wilderness. The community voices its complaint in the form of rhetorical questions which function as accusations against Moses. Once again we see that the real basis for the complaint about the water situation is the regret that they had let Moses lead them out of Egypt in the first place (v. 5). As has happened so often along the journey, the challenges of freedom have given rise to the desire to be slaves once again.

Moses and Aaron go to the tent of meeting and defer to the divine judgment on the matter (v. 6). Yahweh's response is to provide instructions whereby divine aid might be mediated. Moses is told to take the rod (as in the parallel story of Exod 17) but that water would be given when he *spoke* to the rock in the presence of the congregation. According to v. 11, instead of speaking to the rock, Moses struck it twice with the rod "and water came forth abundantly."

Verse 12 offers the key to the Priestly writer's purpose in

retelling this ancient story of God's gift of water from the rock. Here a verdict is rendered against Moses and Aaron. Their own personal failure in faith will prevent their inheritance of the land. Like the rest of the community, they too must die in the wilderness (cf. Num 14).

It is not difficult to see that the Priestly writer intended to provide a closure to the wilderness experience in Num 20:1-13 by focusing on the deaths of the three wilderness leaders. However, the precise nature of Moses and Aaron's failure in this incident is less than clear. One way to understand it is this: Moses and Aaron had assembled the community before the rock as God had commanded (v. 8). Presumably the purpose of this gathering was for all to witness God's gracious aid. But then instead of speaking to the rock, as Yahweh had commanded, Moses *struck* the rock with his rod (v. 11; cf. v. 8) but only after he had spoken harshly to the assembly. In these words of reproach Moses and Aaron had not only departed from what God had instructed them to do (cf. Num 20:24; 27:14), but they also twisted what was intended as an opportunity for the community to witness a creative word-event of God's power and love into a word-event of doubt and hostility. God's gift was accompanied by resentful, spiteful words instead of by power-filled, gift-bearing words. Both Num 20:12 and Deut 32:51 view this as a failure in faith on Moses' part, although another view retained by the tradition (Ps 106:32-33; Deut 1:37; 3:26; 4:21-22) tends to minimize Moses' actual guilt in the matter by saying that Moses was driven to rash words by the people themselves and so it was on their account that he was punished with death prior to the inheritance of the land.

Two popular etymologies for place names round off the story of Num 20:1-13. Like the parallel story in Exod 17:1-7, the need for water and the gift from the rock was localized at Meribah ("contention") where the community "contended" (from the Hebrew root *rib*) with Yahweh (cf. v. 3, "the people contended with Moses"). Moreover, in saying that this was the place where Yahweh "showed himself holy" (from the Hebrew root *kadash*), the writer undoubtedly intended to offer an explanation of how the Kadesh area with which Meribah was associated (cf. Num 27:14; Deut 32:51; Ezek 47:19; 48:28) received its name.

The attention given to the deaths of the three leaders in Num 20:1-13 provides for the reader a clue that the time of the wilderness wandering was drawing to a conclusion. Indeed, following this story in Num 20:1-13 the texts focus on the journey into the region east of the Jordan River, away from the desert and toward the Promised Land.

APPROACHING THE LAND
20:14—24:25

The final section of the Book of Numbers consists of an almost unwieldy collection of disparate materials. On the one hand, the narrative about Aaron's death and the appointment of his priestly successor in addition to the story of the bronze serpent lead us to think that we have not yet moved beyond the wilderness traditions. On the other hand, the accounts of victory over the Canaanites at Hormah and over the Amorites at Heshbon lead us to think we have already begun the conquest traditions which are featured in the Books of Joshua and Judges. In fact, these closing chapters of the Book of Numbers span two complexes of tradition or perhaps it is more accurate to say that they stand between them. In spiral fashion, they move ahead toward the inheritance of the land even as they double back to a few final scenes in the wilderness. The chapters represent the ambiguous threshold stage from one great phase to another.

The literary character of this section of Numbers is as varied as its content. There are songs and blessings, laws and itineraries, stories and genealogies. The origins of the material range from being very ancient to very late. Relatively short literary pieces of varied sources and purpose are only loosely drawn together, primarily by virtue of a connection with Israel's preparation for coming into the land of Canaan. Although some wilderness traditions are included, the attention of these chapters is clearly turned toward the last of the great themes of the Pentateuch, the inheritance of the Land of Promise. By the end of the Book of Numbers, Israel has come into the region east of the Jordan River. This is the land where some of the tribes ultimately settle (see Num 32) and the region from which all Israel will undertake its definitive passage into Canaan.

We conclude our commentary on the text of the Book of Numbers with an exposition of chapters 22-24, the collection of power-filled words of blessing pronounced over Israel by the professional diviner, Balaam. These chapters in the Book of Numbers comprise a relatively long unit. The starting point for the unit is probably to be found in the four poetic oracles which both describe and set in motion Israel's destiny of well-being interpreted theologically as the result of divine blessing. Some scholars regard the oracles attributed to Balaam as some of the Bible's most ancient poetry. The biblical writers constructed a profound and humorous story to serve as a narrative context within which the four oracles were set. Accordingly the sequence of events surrounding the blessings pronounced over Israel is said to have begun with the desire of the Moabite king, Balak, to have Israel cursed. For this purpose Balak sought the service of a professional speaker of power-filled words, Balaam. At the same time, there is little doubt in the mind of the reader that Balaam serves Yahweh who is directing Israel's destiny toward blessing. Balaam thus stands between the authority and designs of God and of Balak. The story presupposes a common ancient Near Eastern view of the effective power of words of blessing and cursing, i.e., the belief that the word once spoken cannot but come to be. It creates what it speaks. What Balaam speaks, whether blessing or curse, will become reality for Israel.

Chapters 22-24 begin with a narrative which recounts four incidents: two instances of Balak sending messengers to request Balaam's services (Num 22:1-14, 15-20), a folktale involving Balaam's ass (Num 22:21-35), and a brief account of the meeting of Balak and Balaam (Num 22:36-40). There follows a section featuring Balaam's four oracles (Num 22:41—23:12; 23:13-26; 23:27—24:9; 24:10-19). At the end of the unit there appears an appendix consisting mainly of short sayings (Num 24:20-25). With the possible exception of the itinerary notice in Num 22:1b, chapters 22-24 represent a conflation of the early literary traditions of the Yahwist and the Elohist. Traces of originally separate strands may still be seen in the vacillation which occurs in the references to the Divinity ("God" and "Lord") and in contradictions and tensions within the text (compare 22:22 with 22:20 and 23:25 with 23:27; also, compare the description of Balak's messengers as "the princes of Moab" in 22:8, 13, 14 and as "the elders of Moab and the elders of Midian" in 22:7). The literary style of the whole is marked by repetition and subtle humor.

The reader should note that, in reality, the Book of Numbers extends through thirty-six chapters. We have omitted comment on the census and genealogies of Num 26, the civil, religious and cultic laws of Num 27-30, the apportionment of some of the Transjordan region to Reuben, Gad and half the tribe of Manasseh (Num 32), and other instructions and preparations for life in the land. We have included what we judged to adequately represent the composite collection of materials in all of Num 20:14—36:13. With the pronouncement of blessing in chapters 22-24 we have come full circle to the beginning of Israel's unique story with Yahweh as begun in the call of Abraham. Balaam's powerfilled words of blessing in some way speak the fullness of Israel's entire story.

SEEKING PASSAGE THROUGH EDOM
20:14-21

14Moses sent messengers from Kadesh to the king of Edom, "Thus says your brother Israel: You know all the adversity that has befallen us: 15how our fathers went down to Egypt, and we dwelt in Egypt a long time; and the Egyptians dealt harshly with us and our fathers; [16]and when we cried to the Lord, he heard our voice, and sent an angel and brought us forth out of Egypt; and here we are in Kadesh, a city on the edge of your territory. [17]Now let us pass through your land. We will not pass through field or vineyard, neither will we drink water from a well; we will go along the King's Highway, we will not turn aside to the right hand or to the left, until we have passed through your territory." [18]But Edom said to him, "You shall not pass through, lest I come out with the sword against you." [19]And the people of Israel said to him, "We will go up by the highway; and if we drink of your water, I and my cattle, then I will pay for it; let me only pass through on foot, nothing more." [20]But he said, "You shall not pass through." And Edom came out against them with many men, and with a strong force. [21]Thus Edom refused to give Israel passage through his territory; so Israel turned away from him.

Although some material similar to the wilderness traditions appears sporadically in Num 20:14—24:25, for the most part attention in the final chapters of the Book of Numbers is turned toward the inheritance of the land. Such is the case with the present story.

Since hopes of entering Canaan by a southern route were not fulfilled (cf. Num 13-14), the wanderers planned entry into the Promised Land from its eastern border, the Jordan River. The most direct route from their encampment at Kadesh (cf. Num 20:1) to the Transjordan area was what the text refers to as the "King's Highway," a major thoroughfare used by armies and merchants to travel from Ezion-geber on the Gulf of Aqaba through Edom and Moab to Syria. According to Israel's old epic tradition (the Yahwist and/or Elohist), Moses sent messengers to the king of Edom to secure safe passage along this route. Moses' words are introduced with the common messenger formula ("Thus says...") which appears frequently in Israel's prophetic corpus. The identification of Israel as "brother" to Edom accords with the witness of the Book of Genesis (Gen 25:19-

34; cf. Deut 2:4; 23:7; Amos 1:11) wherein it is recorded that Isaac and Rebekah parented two sons: Jacob (i.e., Israel) and Esau (i.e., Edom). Moses' message to Edom begins with a recital which would acquaint Edom with Israel's recent history (vv. 14-16). His request for safe passage through Edom is accompanied by profuse promises that they would pass through at no harm or expense to Edom (v. 17). His request is flatly denied under threat of war (v. 18). Verses 19-20 represent a variant account of the exchange recorded in vv. 17-18.

The function of this little story in the overall narrative is to provide an explanation for the tradition that on its way to the Transjordan area Israel detoured around Edom instead of passing through it on a direct route. This is in contrast to the tradition of Deut 2:1-8 which says that Israel was indeed permitted to pass through Edom on its journey out of the wilderness. The animosity reflected in Num 20:14-21 is consistent with the larger biblical witness which describes a long history of tension between the southern kingdom of Judah and its Edomite neighbors (2 Sam 8:14; 1 Kgs 11:14-15; 2 Kgs 8:20-22; 14:7; Amos 1:11-12; Isa 11:14; Jer 9:25-26; 25:21; 27:3; Obad).

DEATH OF AARON
20:22-29

22And they journeyed from Kadesh, and the people of Israel, the whole congregation, came to Mount Hor. 23And the Lord said to Moses and Aaron at Mount Hor, on the border of the land of Edom, 24"Aaron shall be gathered to his people; for he shall not enter the land which I have given to the people of Israel, because you rebelled against my command at the waters of Meribah. 25Take Aaron and Eleazar his son, and bring them up to Mount Hor; 26and strip Aaron of his garments, and put them upon Eleazar his son; and Aaron shall be gathered to his people, and shall die there." 27Moses did as the Lord commanded; and they went up Mount Hor in the

sight of all the congregation. [28]And Moses stripped
Aaron of his garments, and put them upon Eleazar his
son; and Aaron died there on the top of the mountain.
Then Moses and Eleazar came down from the mountain.
[29]And when all the congregation saw that Aaron was
dead, all the house of Israel wept for Aaron thirty days.

This story includes both closure to the past and provision
for the future. Aaron's death, like Miriam's (Num 20:1),
suggests the completion of the time in the wilderness, the
passage of the generation which witnessed God's signs and
wonders in Egypt and in the desert. His death is also an
occasion for looking to the future, a time to appoint a
legitimate heir to bear Aaron's priesthood into the next
stage of Israel's faith. Hence, on the one hand, we note that
this brief story reminds us of what we have already seen in
the wilderness narratives. For example, the reason for
Aaron's death calls us back to the failure of faith narrated in
Num 20:1-13 just as the appointment of Eleazar reminds us
of Israel's continuing concern for legitimate leadership (cf.
Exod 18; Num 11, 12, 16). On the other hand, it is clear in
this story that Aaron's death is but a necessary closure
which must precede the fulfillment of God's promise regarding the inheritance of the land. The mourning of Aaron,
then, is not without anticipation of what is yet to be, as the
investiture of Eleazar signals.

The vocabulary ("congregation") and style (detailed
divine instructions followed by a notice that they were
obeyed with precision) suggest that this narrative comes
from the Priestly writer. Likewise, the Priestly writer's theological interest can be seen in the explicit interpretation of
Aaron's death as a punishment for sin (v. 24; cf. Num
20:1-13) and in the interest shown for the proper transfer of
his priestly office.

The garments which signify Aaron's priestly office (cf.
Exod 28; Lev 8:7-9) are given to Eleazar at Yahweh's command. According to tradition Aaron had four sons. The two
eldest, Nadab and Abihu, died "before the Lord" (Num
3:2-4; Lev 10; Num 26:60-61) and henceforth Israel's priestly

line was traced through Aaron's son, Eleazar (Exod 6:25), and subsequently through Eleazar's son, Phinehas (cf. Num 25:6-13).

A TASTE OF THE FUTURE:
THE VICTORY AT HORMAH
21:1-3

> **21** When the Canaanite, the king of Arad, who dwelt in the Negeb, heard that Israel was coming by the way of Atharim, he fought against Israel, and took some of them captive. [2]And Israel vowed a vow to the Lord, and said, "If thou wilt indeed give this people into my hand, then I will utterly destroy their cities." [3]And the Lord hearkened to the voice of Israel, and gave over the Canaanites; and they utterly destroyed them and their cities; so the name of the place was called Hormah.

In the present text Israel's notion of Holy War governs an attempt to explain how the place Hormah received its name.

Early Israel ascribed to a theology of Holy War, i.e., the belief that Yahweh was present with Israel securing its life on the battlefield. The presence of the Divine Warrior made war a sacral event calling for certain prescribed practices. One of these was the enforcement of the ban (*herem*) according to which all the spoils and captives of war were dedicated or wholly given over to the Divine Warrior in the form of destruction. The narrator of Num 21:1-3 presents the event at Hormah ("destruction") as the result of the enforcement of the ban (*herem*). In destroying the cities Israel dedicated the spoils of battle to the Divine Warrior who had secured the victory. Judg 1:16-17 offers an alternate version of how Hormah got its name. Although its details differ from those of Num 21:1-3, both accounts trace the name to destruction connected with battle.

Scholars believe Arad to have been located in the northern part of the Negeb, along the access to the central part of Canaan. Less agreement exists on the route indicated by the description in Num 21:1 that Israel approached the land by way of the "Atharim." The RSV translation follows the Greek Septuagint in regarding Atharim as a place name. Other versions propose an alternate understanding based on the Hebrew *tarim* ("spies") and thus see this story as a parallel to the account of Num 14:39-45, i.e., that Israel approached Canaan by a route resembling that taken by the spies forty years earlier. If this understanding is correct, Num 21:1-3 would be a second tradition of Israel's attempt to enter Canaan from the south. The attempt in the present narrative is successful whereas the tradition of Num 14 reflects an attempt which had no positive results.

Num 21:1-3 recounts Israel's first victory in the land of Canaan. As such, it anticipates the theme of the inheritance of the land. The short presentation introduces the standard theological interpretation that Israel's settlement in the land was the fulfillment of Yahweh's saving promise and plan.

SERPENTS IN THE DESERT
21:4-9

4From Mount Hor they set out by the way to the Red Sea, to go around the land of Edom; and the people became impatient on the way. 5And the people spoke against God and against Moses, "Why have you brought us up out of Egypt to die in the wilderness? For there is no food and no water, and we loathe this worthless food." 6Then the Lord sent fiery serpents among the people, and they bit the people, so that many people of Israel died. 7And the people came to Moses, and said, "We have sinned, for we have spoken against the Lord and against you; pray to the Lord, that he take away the serpents from us." So Moses prayed for the people. 8And the Lord said to Moses, "Make a fiery serpent, and set it on a pole; and every one who is bitten, when he sees it, shall live." 9So Moses made a bronze serpent, and set it on a pole; and if a serpent bit a man, he would look at the bronze serpent and live.

Motifs about Israel's life in the wilderness had more or
less come to a close in those parts of Num 20 which centered
on the deaths of the three wilderness leaders. At the same
time, the narratives about seeking passage through Edom
(Num 20:14-21) and the battle at Hormah (Num 20:1-3)
turned our attention to a journey forward which will ultimately result in the full inheritance of the land. At this
juncture the biblical writers offer one final wilderness story
from the old epic (Yahwist and/or Elohist) tradition. The
narrative about the fiery serpents thus lays on the fringes of
the wilderness traditions. The itinerary notice in Num 21:4a
takes us back to the last wilderness stop, Mount Hor.
Because of the need to bypass Edomite territory, Israel had
to turn again toward the desert region. This detour is the
setting for a final story of Israel's murmuring against Moses
and against God along the way.

As in Num 11:1-3 and 16:41-50, the starting point for
Israel's murmuring in the present case is not real need but
simple complaint: "the people became impatient on the
way" (v. 4b). They were dissatisfied with their gifted situation: ". . . we loathe this worthless food" (v. 5). Like so many
other cases of their murmuring in the wilderness, the bottom
line of the complaint was Israel's regret at ever having
allowed God and Moses to bring them out of the conven-
ience of slavery in the first place (v. 5).

The structure of this story has appeared in other murmuring stories in the wilderness between Sinai and the land:
dissatisfaction, not need, gives rise to the murmuring. God's
response is to punish, in this case by sending serpents whose
bite brought death to many in the community. The serpents
are described as fiery (in Hebrew, *seraphim*; cf. the "burning" creatures in Isaiah 6:2, 6). At the people's request,
Moses intercedes with God who then graciously instructs
him regarding the bronze serpent which yields life in the face
of death.

The origin of this story is uncertain. It appears that Israel
joined some of its ancient Near Eastern neighbors in asso-
ciating the serpent symbol with healing. It might be that
later generations of pious Israelites who borrowed some

kind of serpent cult sought to legitimate their practice by telling this story of Moses' establishment of the cult of the bronze serpent at God's command.

The narrative of Num 21:4-9 describes and endorses a practice which comes dangerously close to magic. The Deuteronomic tradition of 2 Kgs 18:4 judged piety centering on the serpent to be apostate. King Hezekiah was credited with having destroyed the bronze serpent (Nehushtan; from the Hebrew *nahash*, "serpent") along with the other objects of idolatrous worship. Subsequently, the writer of the Wisdom of Solomon sought to correct any hint of magical piety by clarifying that one stricken by the serpents' bite was saved "not by what he saw, but by thee, Savior of all" (Wisdom 16:7).

AN OVERVIEW OF THINGS TO COME
21:10-20

10And the people of Israel set out, and encamped in Oboth. 11And they set out from Oboth, and encamped at Iyeabarim, in the wilderness which is opposite Moab, toward the sunrise. 12From there they set out, and encamped in the Valley of Zered. 13From there they set out, and encamped on the other side of the Arnon, which is in the wilderness that extends from the boundary of the Amorites; for the Arnon is the boundary of Moab, between Moab and the Amorites. 14Wherefore it is said in the Book of the Wars of the Lord,

"Waheb in Suphah,
and the valleys of the Arnon,
15and the slope of the valleys
that extends to the seat of Ar,
and leans to the border of Moab."

16And from there they continued to Beer; that is the well of which the Lord said to Moses, "Gather the people together, and I will give them water." 17Then Israel sang this song:

"Spring up, O well! — Sing to it! —

[18]the well which the princes dug,
which the nobles of the people delved,
with the scepter and with their staves."

And from the wilderness they went on to Mattanah, [19]and from Mattanah to Nahaliel, and from Nahaliel to Bamoth, [20]and from Bamoth to the valley lying in the region of Moab by the top of Pisgah which looks down upon the desert.

These few verses contain a swift record of Israel's movement out of the wilderness and into the fertile area on the eastern shore of the Dead Sea which is Moabite territory. In the middle of the itinerary the writer includes selections from two songs, both of which are about water. Just as Israel sang on the occasion of its deliverance from the Egyptians at the sea (Exod 15), so the arrival on rich land after forty years of wandering in the desert occasioned songs celebrating the pledge of sustenance and life which the river and the well symbolized for Israel. Scholars agree that it was the Priestly tradition which recorded the names of Israel's last few campsites in the wilderness (vv. 10-11). The rest of the passage probably comes from an earlier source.

The Arnon, a river which flows into the Dead Sea from the east and which forms the boundary of Moab, is the point of reference in v. 13. Mention of the Arnon reminded the biblical writer of an old song about the same area, so part of the song was attached in vv. 14-15. It is said to be an excerpt from a work which is no longer extant and which is mentioned only here in the Bible. No doubt "The Book of the Wars of the Lord" was a collection of ancient materials featuring the saving acts of Yahweh, the Divine Warrior, on Israel's battlefields. As such, it may have been similar to the Book of Jashar, another ancient work which is referred to in Josh 10:13 and 2 Sam 1:18.

Just as the mention of the Arnon River in v. 13 occasioned the addition of the song in vv. 14-15, so mention of the site named Beer ("well") in v. 16a led the writer to recall Yahweh's gracious gift of water in the wilderness (v. 16b).

The name, Beer, called to mind another work, a "song to the well" now recorded in vv. 17-18.

The section ends, as it begins, with itinerary information although the exact route whereby Israel travelled this territory is not known since scholars are unable to pinpoint the locations of a number of sites mentioned in this text. By the end of this section Israel is situated in Moabite territory, near Pisgah, a mountain in Transjordan territory opposite Jericho.

Subsequent parts of the Book of Numbers will narrate in greater detail how Israel came into Moabite territory. Viewed within this framework, then, Num 21:10-20 functions as a summarizing overview of events which are yet to take place.

MORE VICTORIES IN THE TRANSJORDAN
21:21-35

> [21]Then Israel sent messengers to Sihon king of the Amorites, saying, [22]"Let me pass through your land; we will not turn aside into field or vineyard; we will not drink the water of a well; we will go by the King's Highway, until we have passed through your territory." [23]But Sihon would not allow Israel to pass through his territory. He gathered all his men together, and went out against Israel to the wilderness, and came to Jahaz, and fought against Israel. [24]And Israel slew him with the edge of the sword, and took possession of his land from the Arnon to Jabbok, as far as to the Ammonites; for Jazer was the boundary of the Ammonites. [25]And Israel took all these cities, and Israel settled in all the cities of the Amorites, in Heshbon, and in all its villages. [26]For Heshbon was the city of Sihon the king of the Amorites, who had fought against the former king of Moab and taken all his land out of his hand, as far as the Arnon. [27]Therefore the ballad singers say,
> "Come to Heshbon, let it be built,

let the city of Sihon be established.
28 For fire went forth from Heshbon,
    flame from the city of Sihon.
It devoured Ar of Moab,
    the lords of the heights of the Arnon.
29 Woe to you, O Moab!
    You are undone, O people of Chemosh!
He has made his sons fugitives,
    and his daughters captives,
    to an Amorite king, Sihon.
30 So their posterity perished from Heshbon,
        as far as Dibon,
    and we laid waste until fire spread to Medeba."

31 Thus Israel dwelt in the land of the Amorites. 32 And Moses sent to spy out Jazer; and they took its villages, and dispossessed the Amorites that were there. 33 Then they turned and went up by the way to Bashan; and Og the king of Bashan came out against them, he and all his people, to battle at Edrei. 34 But the Lord said to Moses, "Do not fear him; for I have given him into your hand, and all his people, and his land; and you shall do to him as you did to Sihon king of the Amorites, who dwelt at Heshbon." 35 So they slew him, and his sons, and all his people, until there was not one survivor left to him; and they possessed his land.

This passage recounts how Israel made its way into Transjordanian territories north of Moab. Verses 21-32 describe the conquest of the Amorite country directly north of Moab while vv. 33-35 tell how Israel secured land even farther north in the region of Bashan.

At the time of Israel's arrival, Amorite territory east of the Jordan River was ruled by King Sihon. Israel's meeting with him is initiated in much the same way as the encounter with the king of Edom recorded in Num 20:14-21, i.e., with the sending of messengers to request safe passage through his territory. As in the earlier situation, Israel promises not to deplete the inhabitants' resources of food and water while passing through their territory. The request is simply for safe passage (v. 22). Like the king of Edom before him, the Amorite King Sihon refused Israel's request. In this case, however, battle ensued and Israel emerged victorious (vv. 23-24). Verse 25 describes Israel's settlement in the conquered territory and features especially the settlement of Sihon's capitol, the city of Heshbon. At this point the narrative is interrupted by the inclusion of further traditions about Heshbon. Sihon had come into this city by means of victory over its previous ruler, a Moabite king. The Hebrew writer was familiar with the ballad which celebrated Sihon's victory. The writer cleverly taunts Sihon by citing the very song which the now-defeated Amorite king had once used against his Moabite enemies (vv. 26-30). The completion of the taking of Amorite territory is narrated in summary fashion in vv. 31-32.

The account of the conquest of Bashan which appears in Num 21:33-35 is almost identical to an account of the same event recorded in Deut 3:1-3. This victory is more explicitly interpreted as Yahweh's work than was the previous event. Some of the features in the brief narrative are standard in texts reflecting a Holy War theology. These include assurance of Yahweh's aid which precedes the battle and thus determines beforehand its outcome (v. 34) and the execution of the ban (*herem*) whereby the victory was acknowledged as belonging to the Divine Warrior (v. 35).

Themes belonging to the traditions about Israel's life in the wilderness clearly have been left behind in this account of the conquest of the Transjordanian lands of the Amorites and of Bashan. According to Num 32:33-38 these lands ultimately were inherited and inhabited by the Israelite tribes of Reuben and Gad and the half-tribe of Manasseh, Joseph's son. Thus, by the end of the twenty-first chapter of the Book of Numbers, attention focuses exclusively on the final theme of the great Pentateuchal story, the inheritance of the land promised to the ancestors in the Book of Genesis.

BALAK'S REQUEST
22:1-14

22 Then the people of Israel set out, and encamped in the plains of Moab beyond the Jordan at Jericho. [2]And Balak the son of Zippor saw all that Israel had done to the Amorites. [3]And Moab was in great dread of the people, because they were many; Moab was overcome with fear of the people of Israel. [4]And Moab said to the elders of Midian, "This horde will now lick up all that is round about us, as the ox licks up the grass of the field." So Balak the son of Zippor, who was king of Moab at that time, [5]sent messengers to Balaam the son of Beor at Pethor, which is near the River, in the land of Amaw to call him, saying, "Behold, a people has come out of Egypt; they cover the face of the earth, and they are dwelling opposite me. [6]Come now, curse this people for me, since they are too mighty for me; perhaps I shall be able to defeat them and drive them from the land; for I know that he whom you bless is blessed, and he whom you curse is cursed."

[7]So the elders of Moab and the elders of Midian departed with the fees for divination in their hand; and they came to Balaam, and gave him Balak's message. [8]And he said to them, "Lodge here this night, and I will bring back word to you, as the Lord speaks to me"; so the princes of Moab stayed with Balaam. [9]And God came to Balaam and said, "Who are these men with you?" [10]And Balaam said to God, "Balak the son of Zippor, king of Moab, has sent to me, saying, [11]'Behold, a people has come out of Egypt, and it covers the face of the earth; now come, curse them for me; perhaps I shall be able to fight against them and drive them out.'" [12]God said to Balaam, "You shall not go with them; you shall not curse the people, for they are blessed." [13]So Balaam rose in the morning, and said to the princes of Balak, "Go to your own land; for the Lord has refused to let me go with you." [14]So the princes of Moab rose and went to Balak, and said, "Balaam refuses to come with us."

An itinerary notice prefaces this opening section which introduces the story's chief concern and characters. For readers who are familiar with the conquest tradition, to see Israel encamped east of the Jordan River opposite Jericho (v. 1) is to know that they are poised on the verge of fulfillment; God's promise of the inheritance of the land is about to come true (cf. Josh 1-6). Nevertheless, they are still in Moabite territory.

Verse 2 introduces Balak, the Moabite king, and refers back to the Israelites' conquest of the Amorites (cf. Num 21:21-30) thus providing a reason for the collective fear which the Israelite presence struck in the hearts of the Moabite population (v. 3). This fear, which in some ways recalls that felt by Pharaoh prior to Israel's coming out of Egypt (Exod 1:9-10), prompted Moab to try to muster human resources against Israelite strength by alerting the neighboring Midianites to the threat and by inviting them to form a coalition against Israel (vv. 4, 7). More importantly for the biblical writers, however, Moab's fear prompted Balak to try to muster divine help through the assistance of Balaam.

Balaam was a renowned professional diviner. Contemporary archaeologists have discovered an extra-biblical witness to him at Deir 'Alla, a site in modern Jordan. On a stele found at what appears to have been a shrine Balaam, son of Beor, is described as "a seer of the gods" who received messages from the gods regarding the fate of an enemy nation. The text is thought to date from about 700 B.C. and suggests that Balaam was a figure whose reputation as a seer was shared and utilized in the traditions of various groups over a long period of time in the ancient Near Eastern world.

Many interpreters have understood the biblical traditions to mean that Balaam was from Mesopotamia for Num 22:5 describes him as coming from Pethor "which is near the River." The expression, "the River," is typically used by the writers of the Hebrew Bible to refer to the River Euphrates and the city of Pethor has been identified by some scholars as the ancient city of Petru, thought to lie on one of the northern tributaries emptying into the Euphrates. Other

scholars, however, have viewed the further description of
Pethor, "in the land of Amaw" (v. 5) as a reference to a site in
the land of Ammon, a region just north of Moab. One
recommendation for this latter view is that it is easier to
imagine the diviner traveling on an ass from a nearby country
than across the four-hundred mile stretch from Mesopotamia. Whatever Balaam's origin, he had a widespread reputation as an effective word-bearer and Balak sent from a
distance to secure his services saying, "I know that he whom
you bless is blessed, and he whom you curse is cursed" (v. 6).
The reference to the "fees for divination" in v. 7 suggests that
Balaam was a professional. Such persons were not uncom-
mon in the ancient Near East. They sought access to the
divine will through dreams, visions, and the interpretation
of omens. A power-filled word of curse from Balaam was
expected to break Israel's strength thus complementing Balak's military efforts to get rid of Israel.

Upon hearing Balak's request as delivered by the messengers, Balaam awaited divine guidance. This is the first of
many indications in the text that Balaam will not or can not
put his gift for words at Balak's service independently of
Yahweh's direction. His actions and words in the story
consistently witness to his fundamental allegiance to the
divine. This is clear in Balaam's announcement to the messengers which follows his nocturnal conversation with God:
"the Lord has refused to let me go with you" (v. 13). Likewise, v. 14 offers the first indication that Balaam's fundamental allegiance is not fully comprehended by the
Moabites for when the messengers return to Balak, they
report, "Balaam refuses to come with us." This is a subtle
but significant distortion of Balaam's own assertion that the
real decision was God's.

REQUEST REPEATED
22:15-20

[15]Once again Balak sent princes, more in number and
more honorable than they. [16]And they came to Balaam

and said to him, "Thus says Balak the son of Zippor: 'Let nothing hinder you from coming to me; [17]for I will surely do you great honor, and whatever you say to me I will do; come, curse this people for me.'" [18]But Balaam answered and said to the servants of Balak, "Though Balak were to give me his house full of silver and gold, I could not go beyond the command of the Lord my God, to do less or more. [19]Pray, now, tarry here this night also, that I may know what more the Lord will say to me." [20]And God came to Balaam at night and said to him, "If the men have come to call you, rise, go with them; but only what I bid you, that shall you do."

Verses 15-20 relate a second attempt on Balak's part to solicit the aid of the seer Balaam. This time Balak hoped to coerce Balaam through the enticing power of prestige represented by messengers who were "more in number and more honorable" than the first (v. 15). Balaam again sought God's direction in the matter. This time the Lord commanded that Balaam go in accord with Balak's wish. Balaam is now to join Balak but in order to go God's work.

BALAAM'S ASS
22:21-35

[21]So Balaam rose in the morning, and saddled his ass, and went with the princes of Moab. [22]But God's anger was kindled because he went; and the angel of the Lord took his stand in the way as his adversary. Now he was riding on the ass, and his two servants were with him. [23]And the ass saw the angel of the Lord standing in the road, with a drawn sword in his hand; and the ass turned aside out of the road, and went into the field; and Balaam struck the ass, to turn her into the road. [24]Then the angel of the Lord stood in a narrow path between the vineyards, with a wall on either side. [25]And when the ass saw the angel of the Lord, she pushed against the wall, and pressed Balaam's foot against the wall; so he struck her

again. 26Then the angel of the Lord went ahead, and stood in a narrow place, where there was no way to turn either to the right or to the left. 27When the ass saw the angel of the Lord, she lay down under Balaam; and Balaam's anger was kindled, and he struck the ass with his staff. 28Then the Lord opened the mouth of the ass, and she said to Balaam, "What have I done to you, that you have struck me these three times?" 29And Balaam said to the ass, "Because you have made sport of me. I wish I had a sword in my hand, for then I would kill you." 30And the ass said to Balaam, "Am I not your ass, upon which you have ridden all your life long to this day? Was I ever accustomed to do so to you?" And he said, "No."

31Then the Lord opened the eyes of Balaam, and he saw the angel of the Lord standing in the way, with his drawn sword in his hand; and he bowed his head, and fell on his face. 32And the angel of the Lord said to him, "Why have you struck your ass these three times? Behold, I have come forth to withstand you, because your way is perverse before me; 33and the ass saw me, and turned aside before me these three times. If she had not turned aside from me, surely just now I would have slain you and let her live." 34Then Balaam said to the angel of the Lord, "I have sinned, for I did not know that thou didst stand in the road against me. Now therefore, if it is evil in thy sight, I will go back again." 35And the angel of the Lord said to Balaam, "Go with the men; but only the word which I bid you, that shall you speak." So Balaam went on with the princes of Balak.

The biblical tradition combines theology with humor in the folktale which tells of the incident involving the ass which Balaam rode on his journey to Moabite territory. The bulk of this narrative is thought to derive from the Yahwist although the final text may contain touches added by the Elohist.

Early in the story it becomes clear to the reader that, in traveling to Moabite territory, Balaam is acceding to Balak's request without God's approval (22:22) and it is this action on Balaam's part which precipitates the incident featuring the ass. This textual witness is puzzling in light of the tradition of 22:20 wherein God told Balaam to go with Balak's messengers. One can only posit that the 22:21-35 comes from a different literary strand than the preceding material and that editors failed to harmonize completely the different traditions.

The story featuring Balaam's ass abounds in irony: the renowned seer is blind to the divinely placed adversary (in Hebrew, *satan*) while the animal sees. Likewise, the bearer of power-laden words not only finds himself in dialogue with his ass but is virtually brought to silence by the truth as argued by the animal (vv. 28-30). The ass took action to preserve the life of his master and Balaam's response was to threaten to kill the animal for what it was doing (22:29, 33).

Once Balaam's eyes were opened, he professed to act in accord with God's wishes, not Balak's. The incident concludes in much the same way as 22:20: Balaam is to go to Balak but in doing so he is in the service of God, not Balak (22:35).

BALAAM MEETS BALAK
22:36-40

> 36When Balak heard that Balaam had come, he went out to meet him at the city of Moab, on the boundary formed by the Arnon, at the extremity of the boundary. 37And Balak said to Balaam, "Did I not send to you to call you? Why did you not come to me? Am I not able to honor you?" 38Balaam said to Balak, "Lo, I have come to you! Have I now any power at all to speak anything? The word that God puts in my mouth, that must I speak." 39Then Balaam went with Balak, and they came to Kiriathhuzoth. 40And Balak sacrificed oxen and sheep, and sent to Balaam and to the princes who were with him.

Numbers 22 comes to a close with this brief account of the meeting between Balaam and Balak. Balak's questions (v.

37) reflect the mentality of one accustomed to being in control ("Did I not send to you to call you?. . . Am I not able to honor you?"). Balaam replies by warning Balak that the power behind his words is not his own, for he is coerced by God's designs. It is not in his control to do or to speak what Balak might pay him to do or to speak.

THE FIRST ORACLE
22:41—23:12

41And on the morrow Balak took Balaam and brought him up to Bamothbaal; and from there he saw the nearest of the people.   23 And Balaam said to Balak, "Build for me here seven altars, and provide for me here seven bulls and seven rams." 2Balak did as Balaam had said; and Balak and Balaam offered on each altar a bull and a ram. 3And Balaam said to Balak, "Stand beside your burnt offering, and I will go; perhaps the Lord will come to meet me; and whatever he shows me I will tell you." And he went to a bare height. 4And God met Balaam; and Balaam said to him, "I have prepared the seven altars, and I have offered upon each altar a bull and a ram." 5And the Lord put a word in Balaam's mouth, and said, "Return to Balak, and thus you shall speak." 6And he returned to him, and lo, he and all the princes of Moab were standing beside his burnt offering. 7And Balaam took up his discourse, and said,
"From Aram Balak has brought me,
     the king of Moab from the eastern mountains;
'Come, curse Jacob for me,
     and come, denounce Israel!'
8How can I curse whom God has not cursed?
     How can I denounce whom the
          Lord has not denounced?
9For from the top of the mountains I see him,
     from the hills I behold him;
   lo, a people dwelling alone,
     and not reckoning itself among the nations!
10Who can count the dust of Jacob,

or number the fourth part of Israel?
Let me die the death of the righteous,
  and let my end be like his!"
[11]And Balak said to Balaam, "What have you done to
me? I took you to curse my enemies, and behold, you
have done nothing but bless them." [12]And he answered,
"Must I not take heed to speak what the Lord puts in my
mouth?"

This is the first of four sections wherein Balaam pronounces a word of blessing over Israel. This discourse is delivered
only after careful preparations are made for the presence
and activity of the sacred: animal offerings are sacrificed on
altars according to a sacred number. While Balak attended
his offering, Balaam sought God.

The solemn discourse, recorded in 23:7-10, is carefully
articulated in Hebrew poetic style typically characterized by
the use of two-line parallelism. A succinct summary of
events narrated in chapter 22 appears in poetic form in v. 7.
This is followed (v. 8) by Balaam's rationale for the fact that
what he is about to say goes contrary to the purpose for
which he was hired. Verses 9-10a describe Balaam's vision of
Israel: a people set apart whose strength is measured by its
countless numbers. The description of Israel as "the dust of
Jacob" may be intended as an assertion that the innumera-
ble people now encamped on the borders of the land
embody the fulfillment of God's promise to Abraham that
his descendants would one day be countless like the dust of
the earth (Gen 13:16; cf. Gen 28:14). Balaam finishes his first
discourse with what appears to be a petition that his own life
be blessed with fullness as Israel's is (v. 10b).

Understandably Balak rebukes the diviner for having
blessed instead of cursed (v. 11). Balaam responds with an
assertion he has made several times before: he is bound to
speak in harmony with the One who directs the destiny of
Israel.

THE SECOND ORACLE
23:13-26

¹³And Balak said to him, "Come with me to another place, from which you may see them; you shall see only the nearest of them, and shall not see them all; then curse them for me from there." ¹⁴And he took him to the field of Zophim, to the top of Pisgah, and built seven altars, and offered a bull and a ram on each altar. ¹⁵Balaam said to Balak, "Stand here beside your burnt offering, while I meet the Lord yonder." ¹⁶And the Lord met Balaam, and put a word in his mouth, and said, "Return to Balak, and thus shall you speak." ¹⁷And he came to him, and lo, he was standing beside his burnt offering, and the princes of Moab with him. And Balak said to him, "What has the Lord spoken?" ¹⁸And Balaam took up his discourse, and said,

"Rise, Balak, and hear;
hearken to me, O son of Zippor:
¹⁹God is not man, that he should lie,
or a son of man, that he should repent.
Has he said, and will he not do it?
Or has he spoken, and will he not fulfil it?
²⁰Behold, I received a command to bless:
he has blessed, and I cannot revoke it.
²¹He has not beheld misfortune in Jacob;
nor has he seen trouble in Israel.
The Lord their God is with them.
and the shout of a king is among them.
²²God brings them out of Egypt;
they have as it were the horns of the wild ox.
²³For there is no enchantment against Jacob,
no divination against Israel;
now it shall be said of Jacob and Israel,
'What has God wrought!'
²⁴Behold, a people! As a lioness it rises up
and as a lion it lifts itself;
it does not lie down till it devours the prey,
and drinks the blood of the slain."

²⁵And Balak said to Balaam, "Neither curse them at all, nor bless them at all." ²⁶But Balaam answered Balak, "Did I not tell you, 'All that the Lord says, that I must do'?"

Balak initiates his second attempt to bring a curse on Israel by bringing Balaam to another vantage point, one which prohibits a full view of Israel (v. 13). The exact intent of this is uncertain; perhaps Balak surmised that the first effort to curse had backfired because in ancient Near Eastern mentality the view of a people strong in number would naturally have sparked thoughts of blessing. View of a small population might not bear such an association. Whatever the case, apart from the different vantage point preparations for the pronouncement by the diviner are much the same in this case as in the preceding account (cf. 23:1-3).

Balaam's second discourse follows his second encounter with the Divinity in Moabite territory. This discourse is specifically addressed to Balak (v. 18b). He is rebuked for trying to manipulate the divine plan. God's will to bless cannot be revoked (v. 20). Verses 21-22 describe Israel's state of blessing: God is with them; they bear no misfortune. The exodus is recalled and their strength is likened to "the horns of the wild ox." God's blessing of Israel cannot be checked by human efforts. The discourse ends with an ominous parallel drawn between Israel and a devouring lioness (v. 24).

Following the second discourse, Balak commands Balaam to speak no more (v. 25). It may be that at one time this was the end of one literary tradition about Balaam and Balak and that the remaining discourses represent an originally indepedent version. Balaam responds to Balak's command by attempting to justify his actions with a repetition of the position he has stated consistently (v. 26).

THE THIRD ORACLE
23:27—24:9

²⁷And Balak said to Balaam, "Come now, I will take you to another place; perhaps it will please God that you may curse them for me from there." ²⁸So Balak took Balaam to the top of Peor, that overlooks the desert. ²⁹And Balaam said to Balak, "Build for me here seven altars, and provide for me seven bulls and seven rams." ³⁰And Balak did as Balaam had said, and offered a bull and a ram on each altar.

24 When Balaam saw that it pleased the Lord to bless Israel, he did not go, as at other times, to look for omens, but set his face toward the wilderness. ²And Balaam lifted up his eyes, and saw Israel encamping tribe by tribe. And the Spirit of God came upon him, ³and he took up his discourse, and said,

"The oracle of Balaam the son of Beor,
the oracle of the man whose eye is opened,
⁴the oracle of him who hears the words of God,
who sees the vision of the Almighty,
falling down, but having his eyes uncovered:
⁵How fair are your tents, O Jacob,
your encampments, O Israel!
⁶Like valleys that stretch afar,
like gardens beside a river,
like aloes that the Lord has planted,
like cedar trees beside the waters.
⁷Water shall flow from his buckets,
and his seed shall be in many waters,
his king shall be higher than Agag,
and his kingdom shall be exalted.
⁸God brings him out of Egypt;
he has as it were the horns of the wild ox,
he shall eat up the nations his adversaries,
and shall break their bones in pieces,
and pierce them through with his arrows.
⁹He couched, he lay down like a lion,
and like a lioness; who will rouse him up?

Blessed be every one who blesses you,
and cursed be every one who curses you."

The disjunction between Balak's command that Balaam not speak (23:25) and his ensuing invitation to curse (23:27) might indicate a change in literary sources. Support for this view can be found in the departure from the pattern of the two previous incidents recorded in 24:1-2. Num 23:3-5 and 15-16 portray Balaam as leaving Balak standing beside his burnt offering while the diviner went off to meet God and thus come to know the divine will for Israel. Num 24:1 apparently refers to this in saying that this time Balaam "did not go, as at other times, to look for omens." Instead, upon seeing Israel's encampment, Balaam is ecstatically empowered by the Spirit of God to speak his third discourse. Alongside this uniqueness in the third discourse story, however, one must also acknowledge the likeness of some of its details to what has gone before. For example, just as Balak brought Balaam to a different vantage point after his first effort to curse Israel failed, so here after the second failure the king takes the diviner to another place hoping thereby to bring about a change in Balaam's compulsion to bless. Also, as in the previous cases, careful cultic arrangements are made in preparation for the activity of the sacred, i.e., the altars and their sacrifices are readied.

The third oracle begins with an extended introduction of the oracle giver (24:3-4). In v. 5 the oracle is addressed to Israel in the second person although by v. 7 the reference to Israel changes to third person. Verses 6-7a use natural, oasis-like imagery to describe Israel's blessedness. The tone becomes more explicitly political in v. 7b with its reference to Israel's king and Agag, king of the Amalekites (1 Sam 15:8). In referring to Israel's blessedness as it is expressed in its prowess in the face of enemy nations vv. 8-9 return to the use of imagery drawn from nature, this time from the animal world (cf. Num 23:22, 24).

Balaam's third discourse ends (24:9b) with what appears to be a restatement of Yahwist's account of God's blessing of Abraham as recorded in Gen 12:3. This connection with

Abraham, drawn as Israel is encamped on the border of the land of promise, serves as a poignant though subtle reminder that Israel's present state of blessedness is to be traced to the promise-making One who is faithful.

THE FOURTH ORACLE
24:10-19

¹⁰And Balak's anger was kindled against Balaam, and he struck his hands together; and Balak said to Balaam, "I called you to curse my enemies, and behold, you have blessed them these three times. ¹¹Therefore now flee to your place; I said, 'I will certainly honor you,' but the Lord has held you back from honor." ¹²And Balaam said to Balak, "Did I not tell your messengers whom you sent to me, ¹³'If Balak should give me his house full of silver and gold, I would not be able to go beyond the word of the Lord, to do either good or bad of my own will; what the Lord speaks, that will I speak.'? ¹⁴And now, behold, I am going to my people; come, I will let you know what this people will do to your people in the latter days." ¹⁵And he took up his discourse, and said,

"The oracle of Balaam the son of Beor,
  the oracle of the man whose eye is opened,
¹⁶the oracle of him who hears the words of God,
  and knows the knowledge of the Most High,
who sees the vision of the Almighty,
  falling down, but having his eyes uncovered:
¹⁷I see him, but not now;
  I behold him, but not nigh:
a star shall come forth out of Jacob,
  and a scepter shall rise out of Israel;
it shall crush the forehead of Moab,
  and break down all the sons of Sheth.
¹⁸Edom shall be dispossessed,
  Seir also, his enemies, shall be dispossessed,
  while Israel does valiantly.
¹⁹By Jacob shall dominion be exercised,
  and the survivors of cities be destroyed!"

The narrative setting for Balaam's final discourse is strikingly different from what has gone before. After the three previous attempts to curse resulted in repeated blessing for Israel, Balak angrily dismissed Balaam from his service (vv. 10-11; cf. the clapping of hands here with the witness of Lam 2:15 and Job 27:23). Balaam's final defense is to assert that the Moabite king had known all along that the diviner was compelled to speak only as directed by the God of Israel.

Although he was not invited to do so, Balaam now offers a final discourse on the destinies which Israel and Moab can expect. The self-identification of the oracle-giver is again lengthy and bears similarity to what has gone before (24:15-16; cf. 24:3-4). This is followed by the seer's vision of Israel's blessedness in the future. He speaks of Israel's defeat of Moab (v. 17) and Edom (v. 18), victories which in actuality occurred while Israel was under King David's leadership (2 Sam 8:2, 13-14). This has led scholars to interpret the royal symbols of the star and sceptre envisioned in v. 17 as references to David's rise to power. Balaam's fourth vision of Israel's blessedness thus encompasses the victories which later secured the Davidic empire. As such the discourse speaks of the era of the full fruition of the word of promise which initiated God's story with Israel.

BALAAM'S CONCLUDING WORDS
24:20-25

> ²⁰Then he looked on Amalek, and took up his discourse, and said,
> "Amalek was the first of the nations,
> but in the end he shall come to destruction."
> ²¹And he looked on the Kenite, and took up his discourse, and said,
> "Enduring is your dwelling place,
> and your nest is set in the rock;
> ²²nevertheless Kain shall be wasted.
> How long shall Asshur take you away captive?"
> ²³And he took up his discourse, and said,
> "Alas, who shall live when God does this?

> [24] But ships shall come from Kittim
> and shall afflict Asshur and Eber;
> and he also shall come to destruction."
> [25]Then Balaam rose, and went back to his place; and
> Balak also went his way.

Three brief sayings attributed to Balaam are appended to the biblical record of his four major discourses. The first (24:20) concerns the Amalekites, a nomadic group of desert wanderers who periodically posed a threat to Israel's well-being (see Exod 17:14-16; Judg 6:33; Deut 25:17-19; cf. 1 Sam 15; 1 Sam 30). While the exact intent of the first line of the oracle ("Amalek was the first of nations") remains unclear, the second half of the saying is unmistakably a foretelling of the demise of these longstanding enemies of Israel.

The second short saying (24:21-22) deals with another group whose traditions are connected with the wilderness area, namely the Kenites. According to Judg 4:11 this group bore relationship to Israel through Moses' marriage. However, their name occurs more frequently in texts dealing with the time of Israel's settlement in the land of Judah (see 1 Sam 15:6; 1 Sam 30:29). The writer plays on similar sounding Hebrew words in bringing into close proximity the words for Kenite (*keyni*) and nest (*ken*). The tradition of 24:22a may regard the biblical Kain (see especially Gen 4:2-15) as the ancestor of the Kenite people. Whatever the case, Balaam's vision included the notion that the Kenites, like other enemies of Israel, would be destroyed. The final line of this saying (24:22b) is obscure and its intent uncertain.

Likewise the meaning of Balaam's final saying (24:23-24) is unknown. It appears to foretell the destruction of other peoples (Asshur and Eber) but scholars do not know which peoples are intended. Some have suggested that the lines contain an illusion to the invasion of the Palestinian coastal land by the Sea Peoples during the thirteenth century B.C. The word "Kittim" bears similarity to a word the Greeks used for Cyprus. The name "Eber" bears similarity to the word "Hebrew" and thus some have understood Eber as a fictitious chief and ancestor of the Hebrew people. However, if that is the case, it is difficult to understand its inclusion here as an afflicted people alongside Asshur (probably Assyria). All in all, the intent of these final lines attributed to Balaam is difficult to interpret.

The narrative of Numbers 22-24 closes with the simple notice that Balaam and Balak went their separate ways (24:25). On the surface of things these two were the main characters in this story. Balak sought to use Balaam's gift for words to curse Israel. Instead, Yahweh used Balaam to convert Balak's design for cursing into an occasion for blessing Israel. As it turned out, then, the real story is between Yahweh and Israel. In the overall Pentateuchal story, what began as a tradition of God's promise to Abraham is now on the brink of fulfillment as countless Israelites encamp on the plains of Moab across from Jericho. Balaam's words name and call into being Israel's destiny. The journey is now complete: from the blessing of Abraham (Gen 12:3) to the blessing of Israel (Num 22-24).

EXCURSUS ON TYPOLOGY

In the pages of this commentary on Exodus, Leviticus and Numbers we have traced ancient Israel's exodus from Egypt, its life in the wilderness, its encounter with God at Mount Sinai, and its journey to the borders of the Promised Land. The story has historical roots in a journey undertaken by a group of Hebrews who later formed the nucleus of the nation Israel. But, the biblical account indicates that Israel understood these events in history as inseparable from its experience of the Sacred.

Many of Israel's ancient Near Eastern neighbors told stories about how their gods acted in nature and in the cosmos. In contrast, Israel's experience of God was rooted in history. Israel believed history to be unfolding according to a divine plan — sometimes ambiguous but never arbitrary or chaotic. It was meaningful and purposeful. Because the God who was there was One, there was a constancy in history's unfolding movements. But alongside this constancy and consistency was the anticipation of newness. History never simply repeated itself because of the presence of the One who was not only constant but also dynamic. Such is history when it is bound with the One whose name is Yahweh — "I shall be there, as who I am, I shall be there." The name suggests constant and gracious presence but also divine freedom to be present in ways ever new.

This experience of salvation history as consistent yet ever new is the foundation for typology, i.e., the view that historical events of the past can serve as types or models for subsequent events which unfold in ways akin to older events yet surpassing them in power and meaning. A typological perspective anticipates that the One God molds ongoing history in ways similar to key events from the past. The old event is seen as not having exhausted all the gracious possibilities of a particular situation. The saving potential of an event is not sealed in the past like an ancient (albeit precious) museum piece but can be unleashed anew in another situation which has some new features but which at its center bears similarity to the past. The new event captures a fuller unfolding or outpouring of the past event. Believers can use a typological perspective in trying to interpret ways the Mystery is dynamically present as history presses forward. In doing so they take guidance in awaiting and anticipating new acts of God by remembering the things God has done in the past.

Typology and Hebrew Tradition

Although any saving event might potentially be a type or model for God's future presence-in-power, the types which Israel utilized seem to have been relatively few. They centered on a limited number of key events. One was God's election of David as Israel's Anointed. This event served as a model for Israel's expectation of one like David who would fulfill in a manner not yet experienced Israel's longing for the ideal mediator through whom God's kingship would be exercised in a full and complete way (see Isa 11:1; Jer 23:5; Ezek 37:24-25). Likewise, memory of the election of Zion as the special place of divine presence served as a model or type for expectations of a new center from which the fullness of life would flow (see Isa 1:21-26; Ezek chaps. 40-48).

More pertinent to our work are those instances in which later generations of Israelite believers turned back to the exodus-Sinai-wilderness experiences as models or types for what God was yet to do in its history. During the eighth century, the prophet Hosea reflected upon the turbulence and instability which marked both his homeland of the northern kingdom of Israel and the international situation. He saw on the historical horizon a new act of God in which Israel would be stripped of the bountiful life the Promised Land offered. Hosea interpreted the meaning of this new act of God typologically. He likened it to the trying but intimate experience in the wilderness during the time of Moses:

> Therefore, behold, I will allure her,
> and bring her back into the wilderness,
> and speak tenderly to her.
> . . .
> And there she shall answer as in the days of her youth,
> as at the time when she came out of the land of Egypt.
>
> (see Hos 2:14-20)

In a later era in the southern kingdom, the prophet Jeremiah addressed a community facing displacement from the land in the form of the Babylonian Exile. In this case the prophet recalled a saving event from the past, the exodus, but he did so not so much to stress its likeness to what was to come. Instead he used the comparison to highlight the contrast between what had once been and what was yet to be for God's people:

> [7]"Therefore, behold, the days are coming, says the Lord, when men shall no longer say, 'As the Lord lives who brought up the people out of the land of Egypt,'[8]but 'As the Lord lives who brought up and led the descendants of the house of Israel out of the north country and out of all the countries where he had driven them.' Then they shall dwell in their own land"
>
> (Jer 23:7-8; cf. 16:14-15).

Jeremiah also used the Mosaic covenantal tradition as a point of comparison and contrast when he envisioned the relationship of Yahweh and Israel in the future:

[31]"Behold, the days are coming, says the Lord, when I will make a new covenant with the house of Israel and the house of Judah, [32]not like the covenant which I made with their fathers when I took them by the hand to bring them out of the land of Egypt, my covenant which they broke, though I was their husband, says the Lord. [33]But this is the covenant which I will make with the house of Israel after those days, says the Lord: I will put my law within them, and I will write it upon their hearts; and I will be their God, and they shall be my people. [34]And no longer shall each man teach his neighbor and each his brother, saying, 'Know the Lord,' for they shall all know me, from the least of them to the greatest, says the Lord; for I will forgive their iniquity, and I will remember their sin no more."

(Jer 31:31-34).

It was the great poet of the Exile, the prophet whom we know only as Second Isaiah, whose vision of God's future act was most prominently modeled on the exodus-wilderness traditions of days long past. Of all the ages of Hebrew experience and faith, perhaps it was the exiles who could best understand and relate to the experience of those once rescued from a foreign land and nurtured and guided through the arduous journey home to the Promised Land. Thus, eagerly anticipating God's new act in releasing Judah from its captivity in Babylon, Second Isaiah spoke of the imminent future by remembering the past:

[20]Go forth from Babylon, flee from Chaldea,
  declare this with a shout of joy, proclaim it,
 send it forth to the end of the earth;
  say, "The Lord has redeemed his servant Jacob!"
[21]They thirsted not when he led them through the deserts;
 he made water flow for them from the rock;
 he cleft the rock and the water gushed out.

(Isa 48:20-21)

Again, the poet's words to the exilic situation are modeled on a likeness to the past event of exodus-wilderness:

> 8Thus says the Lord:
> "In a time of favor I have answered you,
>   in a day of salvation I have helped you;
> I have kept you and given you as a covenant to
>   the people,
>   to establish the land,
>   to apportion the desolate heritages;
> 9saying to the prisoners, 'Come forth,'
>   to those who are in darkness 'Appear.'
> They shall feed along the ways,
>   on all bare heights shall be their pasture;
> 10they shall not hunger or thirst,
>   neither scorching wind nor sun shall smite them,
>   for he who has pity on them will lead them,
>   and by springs of water will guide them.
> 11And I will make all my mountains a way,
>   and my highways shall be raised up.

(Isa 49:8-11)

Just as the poet stressed the likeness of God's new act to saving events from the past, he also used models from the past in order to stress that the new events would surpass earlier events in wonder and power:

> 16Thus says the Lord,
>   who makes a way in the sea,
>   a path in the mighty waters,
> 17who brings forth chariot and horse,
>   army and warrior;
>   they lie down, they cannot rise,
>   they are extinguished, quenched like a wick:
> 18"Remember not the former things,
>   nor consider the things of old.
> 19Behold, I am doing a new thing;
>   now it springs forth, do you not perceive it?
> I will make a way in the wilderness
>   and rivers in the desert.

20The wild beasts will honor me,
the jackals and the ostriches;
for I give water in the wilderness,
rivers in the desert,
to give drink to my chosen people,
21 the people whom I formed for myself
that they might declare my praise.

(Isa 43:16-21)

In these texts it is possible to see how the Hebrew tradition used typological interpretation. We see that central events from Israel's historical and religious traditions, and the exodus-Sinai-wilderness events in particular, became types or models to which later generations of believers turned in imagining and interpreting Yahweh's mysterious presence in their own times.

Typology and Early Christian Tradition

Early Christian writers also used typology either to stress the likeness of unfolding events to God's saving work in the past or to highlight the contrast between past saving events and the salvation offered in Christ.

The tradition represented by the gospel of Matthew used Israel's exodus as a type according to which Jesus' flight into Egypt was interpreted. In Matthew 2:15 the evangelist writes that this event happened in Jesus' life as a fuller expression of the prophetic witness of Hosea 11:1: "Out of Egypt have I called my son." Likewise, the synoptic tradition about Jesus' forty-day sojourn in the wilderness (Mark 1:13; Matthew 4:2; Luke 4:2) was probably modeled on the tradition of Israel's forty years of trial in the desert and/or the tradition of Moses' forty days and forty nights with Yahweh at the mountain of God (Exod 24:18).

One of the most profound examples of biblical typology can be seen in the way early Christian writers used ancient Israel's foundational religious experience of exodus as a type according to which the foundational event for Christian believers (i.e., Jesus' passage through death to life) might be understood. The gospel accounts of Mark, Matthew and Luke all represent Jesus' Last Supper as a passover meal (Mark 14:12-25; Matthew 26:17-29; Luke 22:7-23). In the course of the meal Jesus is said to have identified himself with the unleavened bread being broken and with the wine being poured. As they commemorated Israel's passage from Egypt Jesus is said to have told his friends: This is my story. The ancient movement from bondage to freedom thus gave Christians a way to interpret the meaning of Jesus' passage.

The Gospel of John also used the passover tradition but in a different way. In the fourth gospel Jesus' death is presented as coinciding with the time when the passover lambs were being sacrificed in the Temple. Theologically, the evangelist is suggesting that *Jesus* is the passover lamb. This is reiterated in a detail John included about Jesus' death which the other gospel traditions do not mention, i.e., that although the legs of those crucified with him were broken, Jesus' legs were not broken (John 19:31-36). In this detail John wishes readers to recall that Exod 12:46 prescribes that the legs of the passover lamb were not to be broken. John is the only gospel writer to refer to Jesus with the title "Lamb of God" (John 1:29).

John's view on the relationship between the exodus tradition and Jesus' passage is similar to that of Paul. Paul used the ancient passover as a model when he encouraged Christians in the city of Corinth to let go of sin in their lives:

> [6]Your boasting is not good. Do you not know that a little leaven leavens the whole lump? [7]Cleanse out the old leaven that you may be a new lump, as you really are unleavened. For Christ, our paschal lamb, has been sacrificed. [8]Let us, therefore, celebrate the festival, not with the old leaven, the leaven of malice and evil, but with the unleavened bread of sincerity and truth.
>
> (1 Cor 5:6-8; cf. Exod 12:14-20)

Apparently there were some in the community at Corinth who thought that a share in the Christian life of grace was guaranteed by participation in the church's sacramental life (especially baptism and eucharist) and apart from ethical responsibility in other aspects of life. Paul seeks to correct this perspective by drawing an analogy between the contemporary situation in the Corinthian community and that of the ancient exodus-wilderness community:

> I want you to know, brethren, that our fathers were all under the cloud, and all passed through the sea, [2]and all were baptized into Moses in the cloud and in the sea, [3]and all ate the same supernatural food [4]and all drank the same supernatural drink. For they drank from the supernatural Rock which followed them, and the Rock was Christ. [4]Nevertheless with most of them God was not pleased; for they were overthrown in the wilderness.
> [6]Now these things are warnings for us, not to desire evil as they did. [7]Do not be idolators as some of them were; as it is written, "The people sat down to eat and drink and rose up to dance." [8]We must not indulge in immorality as some of them did, and twenty-three thousand fell in a single day. [9]We must not put the Lord to the test, as some of them did and were destroyed by serpents; [10]nor grumble, as some of them did and were destroyed by the Destroyer. [11]Now these things happened to them as a warning, but they were written down for our instruction, upon whom the end of the ages has come. [12]Therefore let any one who thinks that he stands take heed lest he fall. [13]No temptation has overtaken you that is not common to man. God is faithful, and he will not let you be tempted beyond your strength, but with the temptation will also provide the way of escape, that you may be able to endure it.

(1 Cor 10:1-13)

While referring to the gifts which accompanied God's saving presence in the past, Paul points out that just as in the past the supernatural food did not save believers from sin and God's judgment, so in the present situation believers must not delude themselves in thinking that sacramental life (especially the food and drink of the eucharist) insured against the encroachment of sin and God's resulting judgment in the lives of believers. In saying this Paul not only points to the theme of God's gracious gift which is so pronounced in the wilderness narratives but he also refers to the prominent witness to Israel's sin in the wilderness, a rebelliousness which brought God's judgment. For example, in verse 7 he refers back to the apostasy around the golden calf (Exod 32). In verse 8 the twenty-three thousand who fell in one day seem to refer to the twenty-four thousand who died after the apostasy in Moab (Num 25). When Paul cites the destruction by serpents, he refers to the fiery serpents of Num 21:5-6.

These are but a few examples of the way typological interpretation was used by early Christians.

Typology and Ongoing Tradition

The biblical tradition of typology offer contemporary believers examples for approaching ancient traditions. We remember the saving events God has wrought in the past and seek to find there guidance for perceiving and interpreting the ongoing movements of the Sacred in our own ambiguous experience. God's saving presence in the past becomes both a model and a pledge of corresponding signs and wonders in our own day. Accounts of ancient events of exodus-Sinai-wilderness bear the power to reach out and interpret us even as we seek to interpret them. Thus, as we today await deliverance from our bondages, we remember relationships truly bound in trust and the refreshment of wilderness springs. Israel's story becomes our own.

SUGGESTIONS FOR FURTHER READING

Childs, Brevard S., *The Book of Exodus: A Critical Theological Commentary*. The Old Testament Library. Philadelphia: Westminster, 1974.

Gray, George B., *A Critical and Exegetical Commentary on Numbers*. The International Critical Commentary. New York: Charles Scribner's Sons, 1906.

Huesman, S.J., John E., "Exodus," *Jerome Biblical Commentary*. pp. 47-66. Ed. R. E. Brown, J. A. Fitzmyer, R. E. Murphy. Englewood Cliffs, NJ: Prentice-Hall, 1968.

Hyatt, J. Philip, *Exodus*. The Century Bible. London: Oliphants, 1971.

Mays, James L., *The Book of Leviticus. The Book of Numbers*. The Layman's Bible Commentary. Richmond, Va.: John Knox, 1963.

Moriarty, S.J., F. L., "Numbers," *Jerome Biblical Commentary*. pp. 86-100.

Noth, Martin, *Exodus: A Commentary*. Trans. J. S. Bowden. The Old Testament Library. Philadelphia: Westminster, 1962.

_____, *Leviticus: A Commentary*. Trans. J. E. Anderson. The Old Testament Library. Philadelphia: Westminster, 1965.

_____, *Numbers: A Commentary*. Trans. J. D. Martin. The Old Testament Library. Philadelphia: Westminster, 1968.

Plastaras, James, *The God of Exodus: The Theology of the Exodus Narratives*. Milwaukee: Bruce, 1966.

Rylaarsdam, J. Coert, "The Book of Exodus," *The Interpreter's Bible*, vol. I, pp. 833-1099. Ed. G. A. Buttrick, *et al*. New York: Abingdon Press, 1952.

Snaith, N. H., *Leviticus and Numbers.* The Century Bible. London: Thomas Nelson and Sons, 1967.

Wenham, Gordon J., *The Book of Leviticus.* The New International Critical Commentary on the Old Testament. Ed. R. K. Harrison. Grand Rapids: William B. Eerdmans, 1979.

Zerafa, P., "Exodus," *A New Catholic Commentary on Holy Scripture.* pp. 206-227. Ed. R. C. Fuller, L. Johnston, C. Kearns. New York: Nelson, 1969.